2008 U.S. INDUSTRY & MARKET OUTLOOK

NATIONAL EDITION

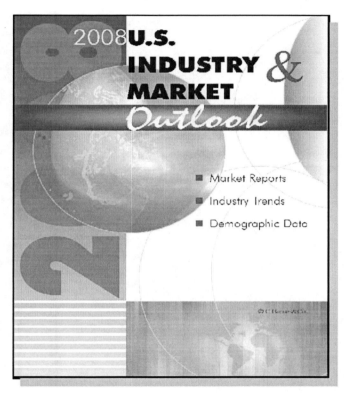

The *2008 U.S. Industry & Market Outlook* report is the leading annual publication that describes over 100 major U.S. industries and 500+ minor industries. Published each year in October, the Outlook report provides the most current and accurate estimates of the size of the largest manufacutring, retail, wholesale and services industries in the United States.

With over 250 pages, the National edition of the 2008 U.S. Industry & Market Outlook features:

2008 establishments, employment and sales totals for each industry

2009 forecast establishments, employment and sales totals

5-year trend establishments and sales totals

Industry financial ratios such as sales per employees, sales per establishment and employees per establishment

2007 establishments and sales totals for 500+ minor industries

Industry definitions and descriptions

The 2008 U.S. Industry & Market Outlook report is available in a National/U.S. States edition (400+ pgs.).

The Outlook report is available for purchase in either PDF, spreadsheet (Excel) or print format edition.

The 2008 U.S. Industry & Market Outlook report is an essential reference tool for industry researchers, market analysts, CEOs and leading industry executives.

Copyright © 2007 By C. Barnes & Co.

Printed in USA
ISBN - 0-9776720-5-0

D1418464

2008 U.S. INDUSTRY & MARKET OUTLOOK
(NATIONAL EDITION)

TABLE OF CONTENTS

TABLE OF CONTENTS

TABLE OF CONTENTS

TABLE OF CONTENTS

INDUSTRY	PAGE NUMBER

SINGLE-FAMILY HOUSING CONSTRUCTION INDUSTRY (NAICS 236115)

INDUSTRY DEFINITION

NAICS 236115: Single-Family Housing Construction. This industry comprises establishments primarily responsible for the entire construction (i.e., new work, additions, alterations, and repairs) of single family residential housing units (e.g., single family detached houses, town houses, or row houses where each housing unit is separated by a ground-to-roof wall and where no housing units are constructed above or below). This industry includes establishments responsible for additions and alterations to mobile homes and on-site assembly of modular and prefabricated houses. Establishments identified as single family construction management firms are also included in this industry. Establishments in this industry may perform work for others or on their own account for sale as speculative or operative builders. Kinds of establishments include single family housing custom builders, general contractors, design builders, engineer-constructors, joint-venture contractors, and turnkey contractors.

INDUSTRY ESTABLISHMENTS, SALES & EMPLOYMENT TRENDS

	Year					Percent Change Year-to-Year			
	2005	2006	2007	2008	2009	05-06	06-07	07-08	08-09
Establishments	112,491	104,586	96,681	90,636	84,969	-7.0%	-7.6%	-6.3%	-6.3%
Sales ($Millions)	139,043	129,441	128,736	128,633	128,050	-6.9%	-0.5%	-0.1%	-0.5%
Employment	627,262	560,794	518,320	485,945	455,657	-10.6%	-7.6%	-6.2%	-6.2%

INDUSTRY RATIOS

(Industry Averages)	Year					Percent Change Year-to-Year			
	2005	2006	2007	2008	2009	05-06	06-07	07-08	08-09
Sales ($M)/Estab.	1.24	1.24	1.33	1.42	1.51	0.1%	7.6%	6.6%	6.2%
Sales ($) per Emp.	221,667	230,816	248,372	264,708	281,022	4.1%	7.6%	6.6%	6.2%
Emps. per Estab.	5.6	5.4	5.4	5.4	5.4	-3.8%	0.0%	0.0%	0.0%

Single-Family Housing Construction Industry (NAICS 236115)

Size of Firm Industry Estimates

Year	Establishments by Size of Firm									Total
	1-4 Emps.	5-9 Emps.	10-19 Emps.	20-49 Emps.	50-99 Emps.	100-249 Emps.	250-499 Emps.	500+ Emps.	Unknown Emps.	Total
2006	73,973	14,641	5,388	1,713	300	122	12	8	522	96,681
2008	69,348	13,726	5,051	1,606	282	114	11	7	490	90,636
2009	65,012	12,867	4,735	1,506	264	107	10	7	459	84,969
Sales ($Millions) by Size of Firm										**Total**
2006	42,699	20,283	21,771	17,008	7,838	9,764	2,320	3,452	3,602	128,736
2008	42,664	20,266	21,753	16,993	7,832	9,756	2,318	3,449	3,603	128,633
2009	42,466	20,172	21,652	16,915	7,795	9,711	2,307	3,434	3,598	128,050
Employment by Size of Firm										**Total**
2006	221,919	87,846	75,433	54,817	18,325	16,162	3,603	6,935	33,280	518,320
2008	208,043	82,353	70,716	51,390	17,180	15,151	3,378	6,501	31,232	485,945
2009	195,035	77,204	66,295	48,177	16,105	14,204	3,167	6,095	29,376	455,657

Sub-Industries – 2007 Industry Estimates

Sub-Industries	Total Establishments	Total Employment	Total Sales ($M)
Single-family housing construction	45,727	227,819	45,738
Single-family home remodeling,	6,147	29,897	4,924
General remodeling, single-family	20,291	93,082	15,129
Mobile home repair, on site	321	1,537	206
Patio and deck construction and repair	891	4,412	571
Repairing fire damage, single-family	337	6,662	979
New construction, single-family houses	22,754	151,929	60,466
Prefabricated single-family house	129	1,886	260
Townhouse construction	85	1,097	462

PLUMBING & HEATING & A/C CONTRACTORS (NAICS 23822)

INDUSTRY DEFINITION

NAICS 23822: Plumbing & Heating & A/C Contractors. This industry comprises establishments primarily engaged in one or more of the following: (1) installing plumbing, heating, and air-conditioning equipment; (2) servicing plumbing, heating, and air-conditioning equipment; and (3) the combined activity of selling and installing plumbing, heating, and air-conditioning equipment. The plumbing, heating, and air-conditioning work performed includes new work, additions, alterations, and maintenance and repairs. The activities performed by these establishments range from duct fabrication and installation at the site to installation of refrigeration equipment, installation of sprinkler systems, and installation of environmental controls.

INDUSTRY ESTABLISHMENTS, SALES & EMPLOYMENT TRENDS

	Year					Percent Change Year-to-Year			
	2005	2006	2007	2008	2009	05-06	06-07	07-08	08-09
Establishments	95,943	96,144	96,345	97,296	98,257	0.2%	0.2%	1.0%	1.0%
Sales ($Millions)	106,997	116,999	124,268	131,978	139,830	9.3%	6.2%	6.2%	5.9%
Employment	970,946	998,759	1,000,911	1,010,809	1,020,802	2.9%	0.2%	1.0%	1.0%

INDUSTRY RATIOS

(Industry Averages)	Year					Percent Change Year-to-Year			
	2005	2006	2007	2008	2009	05-06	06-07	07-08	08-09
Sales ($M)/Estab.	1.12	1.22	1.29	1.36	1.42	9.1%	6.0%	5.2%	4.9%
Sales ($) per Emp.	110,198	117,144	124,155	130,567	136,980	6.3%	6.0%	5.2%	4.9%
Emps. per Estab.	10.1	10.4	10.4	10.4	10.4	2.6%	0.0%	0.0%	0.0%

PLUMBING & HEATING & A/C CONTRACTORS (NAICS 23822)

SIZE OF FIRM INDUSTRY ESTIMATES

Year	Establishments by Size of Firm									Total
	1-4 Emps.	5-9 Emps.	10-19 Emps.	20-49 Emps.	50-99 Emps.	100-249 Emps.	250-499 Emps.	500+ Emps.	Unknown Emps.	
2006	54,616	18,508	12,021	7,616	2,060	835	147	61	481	96,345
2008	55,155	18,691	12,139	7,691	2,080	843	148	61	486	97,296
2009	55,700	18,876	12,259	7,767	2,101	851	149	62	490	98,257
	Sales ($Millions) by Size of Firm									Total
2006	9,788	10,366	18,851	29,003	17,303	17,767	7,025	10,946	3,219	124,268
2008	10,395	11,009	20,020	30,802	18,377	18,869	7,461	11,625	3,421	131,978
2009	11,014	11,664	21,211	32,634	19,470	19,991	7,904	12,316	3,626	139,830
	Employment by Size of Firm									Total
2006	109,233	111,051	168,291	243,698	131,821	115,205	46,158	44,799	30,656	1,000,911
2008	110,311	112,147	169,953	246,103	133,123	116,343	46,613	45,241	30,976	1,010,809
2009	111,400	113,254	171,630	248,533	134,437	117,491	47,073	45,687	31,296	1,020,802

SUB-INDUSTRIES — 2007 INDUSTRY ESTIMATES

Sub-Industries	Total Establishments	Total Employment	Total Sales ($M)
Plumbing, heating, air-conditioning	13,638	126,824	16,250
Boiler and furnace contractors	325	4,058	864
Boiler maintenance contractor	117	1,754	295
Boiler setting contractor	34	624	103
Heating systems repair and	786	5,532	543
Hydronics heating contractor	44	530	74
Plumbing contractors	31,481	286,570	31,199
Septic system construction	1,818	9,987	850
Sprinkler contractors	923	9,178	2,717
Fire sprinkler system installation	1,401	36,464	4,638
Irrigation sprinkler system installation	1,197	12,577	1,093
Heating and air conditioning contractors	18,749	149,336	14,839
Mechanical contractor	5,903	128,904	22,353
Process piping contractor	97	3,172	437
Solar energy contractor	287	2,179	281
Ventilation and duct work contractor	494	10,313	1,412
Warm air heating and air conditioning	17,781	198,635	24,493
Refrigeration contractor	1,272	14,275	1,825

ELECTRICAL CONTRACTORS INDUSTRY (NAICS 23821)

INDUSTRY DEFINITION

NAICS 23821: Electrical Contractors . This industry comprises establishments primarily engaged in one or more of the following: (1) performing electrical work at the site (e.g., installing wiring); (2) servicing electrical equipment at the site; and (3) the combined activity of selling and installing electrical equipment. The electrical work performed includes new work, additions, alterations, and maintenance and repairs.

INDUSTRY ESTABLISHMENTS, SALES & EMPLOYMENT TRENDS

	Year					Percent Change Year-to-Year			
	2005	2006	2007	2008	2009	05-06	06-07	07-08	08-09
Establishments	75,954	76,452	76,949	78,585	80,254	0.7%	0.7%	2.1%	2.1%
Sales ($Millions)	88,135	94,179	99,255	105,437	111,849	6.9%	5.4%	6.2%	6.1%
Employment	836,283	854,013	859,427	877,625	896,320	2.1%	0.6%	2.1%	2.1%

INDUSTRY RATIOS

(Industry Averages)	Year					Percent Change Year-to-Year			
	2005	2006	2007	2008	2009	05-06	06-07	07-08	08-09
Sales ($M)/Estab.	1.16	1.23	1.29	1.34	1.39	6.2%	4.7%	4.0%	3.9%
Sales ($) per Emp.	105,389	110,278	115,489	120,139	124,787	4.6%	4.7%	4.0%	3.9%
Emps. per Estab.	11.0	11.2	11.2	11.2	11.2	1.5%	0.0%	0.0%	0.0%

ELECTRICAL CONTRACTORS INDUSTRY
(NAICS 23821)

SIZE OF FIRM INDUSTRY ESTIMATES

Year	Establishments by Size of Firm									Total
	1-4 Emps.	5-9 Emps.	10-19 Emps.	20-49 Emps.	50-99 Emps.	100-249 Emps.	250-499 Emps.	500+ Emps.	Unknown Emps.	Total
2006	44,738	14,373	8,884	5,654	1,621	801	166	50	660	76,949
2008	45,689	14,678	9,073	5,774	1,655	818	169	51	674	78,585
2009	46,660	14,990	9,266	5,897	1,690	836	173	52	688	80,254
	Sales ($Millions) by Size of Firm									Total
2006	7,339	7,859	14,573	21,641	15,951	14,549	7,711	5,307	4,324	99,255
2008	7,796	8,349	15,482	22,991	16,946	15,456	8,192	5,638	4,587	105,437
2009	8,270	8,856	16,423	24,388	17,976	16,396	8,690	5,980	4,871	111,849
	Employment by Size of Firm									Total
2006	134,214	86,237	124,378	180,935	98,864	106,594	50,487	35,542	42,176	859,427
2008	137,066	88,069	127,021	184,780	100,965	108,859	51,559	36,297	43,008	877,625
2009	139,979	89,941	129,720	188,706	103,111	111,172	52,655	37,068	43,968	896,320

SUB-INDUSTRIES – 2007 INDUSTRY ESTIMATES

Sub-Industries	Total Establishments	Total Employment	Total Sales ($M)
Electrical work	42,241	320,748	32,805
Electric power systems contractors	625	11,000	1,947
Electronic controls installation	558	7,527	833
Computerized controls installation	111	2,066	296
Energy management controls	230	2,717	309
Environmental system control	136	2,167	238
Communications specialization	1,635	28,701	4,114
Cable television installation	658	11,419	1,594
Fiber optic cable installation	590	13,879	1,936
Sound equipment specialization	687	6,482	641
Telephone and telephone equipment	1,889	27,253	2,739
Voice, data, and video wiring contractor	437	6,206	591
Safety and security specialization	3,870	50,424	4,073
Banking machine installation and	89	1,901	114
Computer installation	692	6,232	534
General electrical contractor	22,031	355,677	45,965
Lighting contractor	471	5,028	526

CARPENTRY CONTRACTORS INDUSTRY (NAICS 23835)

INDUSTRY DEFINITION

NAICS 23835: Carpentry Contractors. This industry comprises establishments primarily engaged in framing, carpentry, and finishing work. The carpentry work performed includes new work, additions, alterations, and maintenance and repairs. Activities performed by establishments in this industry range from the installation of doors and windows to paneling, steel framing work, and ship joinery.

INDUSTRY ESTABLISHMENTS, SALES & EMPLOYMENT TRENDS

	Year					Percent Change Year-to-Year			
	2005	2006	2007	2008	2009	05-06	06-07	07-08	08-09
Establishments	33,048	31,154	29,260	27,470	25,788	-5.7%	-6.1%	-6.1%	-6.1%
Sales ($Millions)	18,059	17,527	16,928	16,239	15,576	-2.9%	-3.4%	-4.1%	-4.1%
Employment	201,056	190,305	179,227	167,919	157,636	-5.3%	-5.8%	-6.3%	-6.1%

INDUSTRY RATIOS

(Industry Averages)	Year					Percent Change Year-to-Year			
	2005	2006	2007	2008	2009	05-06	06-07	07-08	08-09
Sales ($M)/Estab.	0.55	0.56	0.58	0.59	0.60	3.0%	2.8%	2.2%	2.2%
Sales ($) per Emp.	89,819	92,100	94,451	96,707	98,809	2.5%	2.6%	2.4%	2.2%
Emps. per Estab.	6.1	6.1	6.1	6.1	6.1	0.4%	0.3%	-0.2%	0.0%

CARPENTRY CONTRACTORS INDUSTRY
(NAICS 23835)

SIZE OF FIRM INDUSTRY ESTIMATES

Year	Establishments by Size of Firm									Total
	1-4 Emps.	5-9 Emps.	10-19 Emps.	20-49 Emps.	50-99 Emps.	100-249 Emps.	250-499 Emps.	500+ Emps.	Unknown Emps.	
2006	22,118	3,947	1,902	910	177	71	14	4	120	29,260
2008	20,764	3,705	1,786	855	166	67	13	4	113	27,470
2009	19,493	3,478	1,676	802	156	63	12	3	106	25,788
	Sales ($Millions) by Size of Firm									Total
2006	4,194	2,079	4,408	3,164	1,117	1,201	439	195	133	16,928
2008	4,024	1,995	4,230	3,037	1,072	1,152	421	187	122	16,239
2009	3,860	1,913	4,057	2,913	1,028	1,105	404	179	117	15,576
	Employment by Size of Firm									Total
2006	66,353	23,679	26,628	28,220	10,602	9,260	4,163	2,257	8,064	179,227
2008	62,292	22,230	24,999	26,492	9,953	8,694	3,908	2,119	7,232	167,919
2009	58,479	20,869	23,469	24,871	9,344	8,162	3,669	1,989	6,784	157,636

SUB-INDUSTRIES – 2007 INDUSTRY ESTIMATES

Sub-Industries	Total Establishments	Total Employment	Total Sales ($M)
Carpentry work	14,109	63,362	5,142
Cabinet and finish carpentry	4,810	21,342	1,534
Cabinet building and installation	2,687	17,762	1,517
Finish and trim carpentry	1,603	8,645	751
Window and door installation and	883	7,035	758
Garage door, installation or erection	1,187	9,514	907
Window and door (prefabricated)	1,568	12,741	1,416
Framing contractor	2,178	34,808	4,581
Lightweight steel framing (metal stud)	111	1,260	122

BREAKFAST CEREAL MANUFACTURING INDUSTRY
(NAICS 31123)

INDUSTRY DEFINITION

NAICS 31123: Breakfast Cereal Manufacturing. This industry comprises establishments primarily responsible for manufacturing cereal breakfast foods and related preparations, except breakfast bars. Establishments primarily engaged in manufacturing granola bars and other types of breakfast bars are classified in 2064.

INDUSTRY ESTABLISHMENTS, SALES & EMPLOYMENT TRENDS

	Year					Percent Change Year-to-Year			
	2005	2006	2007	2008	2009	05-06	06-07	07-08	08-09
Establishments	65	63	61	61	60	-2.9%	-3.0%	-0.8%	-0.8%
Sales ($Millions)	21,421	18,746	18,445	18,458	18,623	-12.5%	-1.6%	0.1%	0.9%
Employment	11,447	10,020	9,720	9,641	9,641	-12.5%	-3.0%	-0.8%	0.0%

INDUSTRY RATIOS

(Industry Averages)	Year					Percent Change Year-to-Year			
	2005	2006	2007	2008	2009	05-06	06-07	07-08	08-09
Sales ($M)/Estab.	329.55	297.00	301.24	303.94	309.20	-9.9%	1.4%	0.9%	1.7%
Sales ($) per Emp.	1,871,311	1,870,891	1,897,558	1,914,583	1,931,710	0.0%	1.4%	0.9%	0.9%
Emps. per Estab.	176.1	158.8	158.8	158.8	160.1	-9.9%	0.0%	0.0%	0.8%

BREAKFAST CEREAL MANUFACTURING INDUSTRY
(NAICS 31123)

SIZE OF FIRM INDUSTRY ESTIMATES

Year	Establishments by Size of Firm									Total
	1-4 Emps.	5-9 Emps.	10-19 Emps.	20-49 Emps.	50-99 Emps.	100-249 Emps.	250-499 Emps.	500+ Emps.	Unknown Emps.	
2006	9	4	5	8	6	16	8	7	3	61
2008	9	4	5	8	6	16	8	7	3	61
2009	8	4	5	8	6	16	8	7	3	60
	Sales ($Millions) by Size of Firm									Total
2006	7	4	7	87	229	1,744	2,767	13,601	0	18,445
2008	7	4	7	87	229	1,745	2,768	13,610	0	18,458
2009	7	4	7	88	231	1,760	2,793	13,732	0	18,623
	Employment by Size of Firm									Total
2006	26	23	62	283	362	2,179	2,143	4,642	0	9,720
2008	26	23	62	281	359	2,162	2,126	4,604	0	9,641
2009	26	23	62	281	359	2,162	2,126	4,604	0	9,641

SUB-INDUSTRIES — 2007 INDUSTRY ESTIMATES

Sub-Industries	Total Establishments	Total Employment	Total Sales ($M)
Cereal breakfast foods	46	7,184	9,838
Coffee substitutes, made from grain	1	27	2
Corn flakes: prepared as cereal	1	16	2
Granola and muesli, except bars and	4	191	25
Infants' foods, cereal type	3	24	18
Oatmeal: prepared as cereal breakfast	1	8	0
Oats, rolled: prepared as cereal	1	9	0
Soy: prepared as cereal breakfast food	1	317	23
Wheat flakes: prepared as cereal	4	1,944	8,536

FROZEN FOOD MANUFACTURING INDUSTRY (NAICS 31141)

INDUSTRY DEFINITION

NAICS 31141: Frozen Food Manufacturing. This industry comprises establishments primarily manufacturing frozen bakery products, except bread and bread-type rolls. Establishments primarily engaged in manufacturing frozen bread and bread-type rolls are classified in 2051.

INDUSTRY ESTABLISHMENTS, SALES & EMPLOYMENT TRENDS

	Year					Percent Change Year-to-Year			
	2005	2006	2007	2008	2009	05-06	06-07	07-08	08-09
Establishments	736	744	752	756	761	1.1%	1.0%	0.6%	0.6%
Sales ($Millions)	22,666	23,104	24,000	24,682	25,382	1.9%	3.9%	2.8%	2.8%
Employment	88,865	86,870	87,810	88,344	89,010	-2.2%	1.1%	0.6%	0.8%

INDUSTRY RATIOS

(Industry Averages)	Year					Percent Change Year-to-Year			
	2005	2006	2007	2008	2009	05-06	06-07	07-08	08-09
Sales ($M)/Estab.	30.80	31.06	31.93	32.63	33.35	0.9%	2.8%	2.2%	2.2%
Sales ($) per Emp.	255,062	265,963	273,320	279,388	285,158	4.3%	2.8%	2.2%	2.1%
Emps. per Estab.	120.7	116.8	116.8	116.8	116.9	-3.3%	0.0%	0.0%	0.1%

FROZEN FOOD MANUFACTURING INDUSTRY
(NAICS 31141)

SIZE OF FIRM INDUSTRY ESTIMATES

Year	Establishments by Size of Firm									Total
	1-4 Emps.	5-9 Emps.	10-19 Emps.	20-49 Emps.	50-99 Emps.	100-249 Emps.	250-499 Emps.	500+ Emps.	Unknown Emps.	
2006	127	61	83	130	87	99	60	46	60	752
2008	128	61	83	131	88	100	60	46	60	756
2009	129	61	84	132	89	101	60	46	60	761
	Sales ($Millions) by Size of Firm									Total
2006	54	64	254	955	1,395	3,909	3,721	13,419	228	24,000
2008	56	66	262	982	1,434	4,021	3,827	13,801	233	24,682
2009	57	68	269	1,010	1,475	4,134	3,935	14,188	247	25,382
	Employment by Size of Firm									Total
2006	382	364	1,320	4,689	6,212	16,901	18,313	36,109	3,520	87,810
2008	384	366	1,329	4,718	6,251	17,008	18,429	36,338	3,520	88,344
2009	387	369	1,337	4,748	6,291	17,116	18,546	36,568	3,648	89,010

SUB-INDUSTRIES — 2007 INDUSTRY ESTIMATES

Sub-Industries	Total Establishments	Total Employment	Total Sales ($M)
Frozen bakery products, except bread	432	62,572	18,354
Buns, sweet: frozen	5	8	1
Cakes, bakery: frozen	127	6,875	1,011
Croissants, frozen	5	626	84
Doughnuts, frozen	10	196	22
Pastries, e.g. danish: frozen	41	1,229	538
Pies, bakery; frozen	117	14,752	3,691
Rolls, sweet: frozen	5	1,378	148
Sponge goods, bakery: frozen	10	172	151

COOKIE CRACKER & PASTA MFG. INDUSTRY (NAICS 31182)

INDUSTRY DEFINITION

NAICS 31182: Cookie Cracker & Pasta Mfg. This industry comprises establishments primarily manufacturing fresh cookies, crackers, pretzels, and similar `dry' bakery products. Establishments primarily engaged in producing other fresh bakery products are classified in 2051.

INDUSTRY ESTABLISHMENTS, SALES & EMPLOYMENT TRENDS

	Year					Percent Change Year-to-Year			
	2005	2006	2007	2008	2009	05-06	06-07	07-08	08-09
Establishments	890	880	870	852	834	-1.1%	-1.1%	-2.1%	-2.1%
Sales ($Millions)	12,580	12,077	11,956	11,653	11,350	-4.0%	-1.0%	-2.5%	-2.6%
Employment	55,974	54,288	53,781	52,702	51,580	-3.0%	-0.9%	-2.0%	-2.1%

INDUSTRY RATIOS

(Industry Averages)	Year					Percent Change Year-to-Year			
	2005	2006	2007	2008	2009	05-06	06-07	07-08	08-09
Sales ($M)/Estab.	14.13	13.72	13.74	13.68	13.61	-2.9%	0.1%	-0.4%	-0.5%
Sales ($) per Emp.	224,747	222,458	222,306	221,113	220,052	-1.0%	-0.1%	-0.5%	-0.5%
Emps. per Estab.	62.9	61.7	61.8	61.9	61.8	-1.9%	0.2%	0.1%	0.0%

COOKIE CRACKER & PASTA MFG. INDUSTRY
(NAICS 31182)

SIZE OF FIRM INDUSTRY ESTIMATES

Year	Establishments by Size of Firm									Total
	1-4 Emps.	5-9 Emps.	10-19 Emps.	20-49 Emps.	50-99 Emps.	100-249 Emps.	250-499 Emps.	500+ Emps.	Unknown Emps.	
2006	204	116	109	126	64	61	41	15	133	870
2008	200	114	106	123	63	60	40	15	130	852
2009	195	111	104	121	61	58	39	15	127	834
Sales ($Millions) by Size of Firm										**Total**
2006	185	47	284	595	1,285	1,842	3,023	3,578	1,117	11,956
2008	180	46	277	580	1,252	1,794	2,945	3,485	1,095	11,653
2009	175	44	270	565	1,220	1,748	2,869	3,395	1,065	11,350
Employment by Size of Firm										**Total**
2006	612	698	1,630	4,153	4,216	9,335	12,995	11,375	8,768	53,781
2008	599	683	1,596	4,065	4,127	9,138	12,720	11,135	8,640	52,702
2009	586	669	1,562	3,979	4,039	8,945	12,452	10,900	8,448	51,580

SUB-INDUSTRIES — 2007 INDUSTRY ESTIMATES

Sub-Industries	Total Establishments	Total Employment	Total Sales ($M)
Cookies and crackers	167	12,535	3,626
Bakery products, dry	95	4,383	325
Biscuits, dry	8	4,025	1
Communion wafers	5	102	7
Cones, ice cream	30	1,321	118
Cookies	360	22,668	5,981
Cracker meal and crumbs	2	143	11
Crackers, dry, nec	21	2,436	524
Matzoths	3	105	49
Pretzels	171	5,168	1,232
Rice cakes	5	296	16
Soda crackers	1	193	17
Sugar wafers	2	403	50
Zwieback	1	3	0

SNACK FOOD MANUFACTURING INDUSTRY (NAICS 31191)

INDUSTRY DEFINITION

NAICS 31191: Snack Food Manufacturing. This industry comprises establishments primarily responsible for manufacturing potato chips, corn chips, and similar snacks. Pretzels and crackers are classified in 2052; candy covered popcorn is classified in 2064; salted, roasted, cooked or canned nuts and seeds are classified in 2068; and packaged unpopped popcorn is classified in 2099.

INDUSTRY ESTABLISHMENTS, SALES & EMPLOYMENT TRENDS

	Year					Percent Change Year-to-Year			
	2005	2006	2007	2008	2009	05-06	06-07	07-08	08-09
Establishments	559	551	543	537	531	-1.4%	-1.4%	-1.1%	-1.1%
Sales ($Millions)	24,164	25,503	27,168	28,720	30,238	5.5%	6.5%	5.7%	5.3%
Employment	42,397	41,575	41,007	40,563	40,125	-1.9%	-1.4%	-1.1%	-1.1%

INDUSTRY RATIOS

(Industry Averages)	Year					Percent Change Year-to-Year			
	2005	2006	2007	2008	2009	05-06	06-07	07-08	08-09
Sales ($M)/Estab.	43.23	46.28	50.02	53.50	56.97	7.1%	8.1%	6.9%	6.5%
Sales ($) per Emp.	569,944	613,429	662,514	708,039	753,585	7.6%	8.0%	6.9%	6.4%
Emps. per Estab.	75.8	75.4	75.5	75.6	75.6	-0.5%	0.1%	0.1%	0.1%

SNACK FOOD MANUFACTURING INDUSTRY (NAICS 31191)

SIZE OF FIRM INDUSTRY ESTIMATES

Year	Establishments by Size of Firm									Total
	1-4 Emps.	5-9 Emps.	10-19 Emps.	20-49 Emps.	50-99 Emps.	100-249 Emps.	250-499 Emps.	500+ Emps.	Unknown Emps.	
2006	119	61	65	89	62	68	29	13	38	543
2008	118	60	65	88	62	67	29	13	38	537
2009	116	59	64	87	61	67	28	13	38	531
	Sales ($Millions) by Size of Firm									Total
2006	406	334	644	1,248	1,451	2,002	2,030	17,809	1,244	27,168
2008	428	353	681	1,319	1,534	2,115	2,145	18,817	1,330	28,720
2009	451	371	716	1,388	1,614	2,226	2,257	19,800	1,416	30,238
	Employment by Size of Firm									Total
2006	358	363	1,046	2,861	4,186	10,237	9,891	9,826	2,240	41,007
2008	353	359	1,034	2,828	4,138	10,120	9,778	9,713	2,240	40,563
2009	349	355	1,022	2,796	4,091	10,004	9,666	9,602	2,240	40,125

SUB-INDUSTRIES — 2007 INDUSTRY ESTIMATES

Sub-Industries	Total Establishments	Total Employment	Total Sales ($M)
Potato chips and similar snacks	263	20,993	20,648
Potato sticks	106	9,630	463
Corn chips and other corn-based snacks	1	17	0
Popcorn, already popped (except candy	30	4,182	68
Tortilla chips	29	280	10
Cheese curls and puffs	73	4,174	74
Onion fries	4	637	1
Pork rinds	4	115	5

SOFT-DRINK MANUFACTURING INDUSTRY (NAICS 312111)

INDUSTRY DEFINITION

NAICS 312111: Soft-Drink Manufacturing. This industry comprises establishments primarily engaged in manufacturing soft drinks and carbonated waters. Fruit and vegetable juices are classified in 2032-2038; fruit syrups for flavoring are classified in 2087; and nonalcoholic cider is classified in 2099. Bottling natural spring waters is classified in 5149.

INDUSTRY ESTABLISHMENTS, SALES & EMPLOYMENT TRENDS

	Year					Percent Change Year-to-Year			
	2005	2006	2007	2008	2009	05-06	06-07	07-08	08-09
Establishments	672	660	648	636	624	-1.8%	-1.8%	-1.8%	-1.8%
Sales ($Millions)	35,144	36,655	37,435	38,043	38,605	4.3%	2.1%	1.6%	1.5%
Employment	63,280	62,679	61,327	60,257	59,141	-0.9%	-2.2%	-1.7%	-1.9%

INDUSTRY RATIOS

(Industry Averages)	Year					Percent Change Year-to-Year			
	2005	2006	2007	2008	2009	05-06	06-07	07-08	08-09
Sales ($M)/Estab.	52.30	55.55	57.80	59.83	61.85	6.2%	4.0%	3.5%	3.4%
Sales ($) per Emp.	555,378	584,802	610,423	631,342	652,759	5.3%	4.4%	3.4%	3.4%
Emps. per Estab.	94.2	95.0	94.7	94.8	94.7	0.9%	-0.3%	0.1%	0.0%

SOFT-DRINK MANUFACTURING INDUSTRY
(NAICS 312111)

SIZE OF FIRM INDUSTRY ESTIMATES

Year	Establishments by Size of Firm									Total
	1-4 Emps.	5-9 Emps.	10-19 Emps.	20-49 Emps.	50-99 Emps.	100-249 Emps.	250-499 Emps.	500+ Emps.	Unknown Emps.	Total
2006	69	24	39	70	95	128	57	11	150	648
2008	67	24	38	68	93	126	56	11	148	636
2009	66	24	37	67	92	123	55	11	145	624
	Sales ($Millions) by Size of Firm									Total
2006	52	48	192	918	2,762	10,037	16,314	5,425	1,688	37,435
2008	53	48	195	932	2,806	10,197	16,575	5,512	1,724	38,043
2009	54	49	198	946	2,848	10,349	16,821	5,594	1,746	38,605
	Employment by Size of Firm									Total
2006	206	147	540	2,226	5,791	17,002	17,488	8,135	9,792	61,327
2008	202	144	530	2,185	5,685	16,692	17,169	7,986	9,664	60,257
2009	198	141	520	2,145	5,582	16,387	16,855	7,840	9,472	59,141

SUB-INDUSTRIES — 2007 INDUSTRY ESTIMATES

Sub-Industries	Total Establishments	Total Employment	Total Sales ($M)
Bottled and canned soft drinks	215	15,982	14,996
Iced tea and fruit drinks, bottled and	8	343	151
Fruit drinks (less than 100% juice):	10	612	91
Lemonade: packaged in cans, bottles,	1	6	0
Tea, iced: packaged in cans, bottles,	3	46	25
Pasteurized and mineral waters, bottled	21	877	1,127
Mineral water, carbonated: packaged in	15	356	40
Water, natural: packaged in cans,	55	1,214	206
Carbonated soft drinks, bottled and	16	2,273	741
Carbonated beverages, nonalcoholic:	89	9,276	13,398
Soft drinks: packaged in cans, bottles,	213	30,342	6,661

BREWERIES & BEER-MAKING INDUSTRY
(NAICS 31212)

INDUSTRY DEFINITION

NAICS 31212: Breweries. This industry comprises establishments primarily engaged in brewing beer, ale, malt liquors, and nonalcoholic beer.

INDUSTRY ESTABLISHMENTS, SALES & EMPLOYMENT TRENDS

	Year					Percent Change Year-to-Year			
	2005	2006	2007	2008	2009	05-06	06-07	07-08	08-09
Establishments	485	467	450	428	408	-3.6%	-3.8%	-4.8%	-4.8%
Sales ($Millions)	24,790	22,168	22,847	23,140	23,361	-10.6%	3.1%	1.3%	1.0%
Employment	30,854	29,014	27,271	26,044	24,930	-6.0%	-6.0%	-4.5%	-4.3%

INDUSTRY RATIOS

(Industry Averages)	Year					Percent Change Year-to-Year			
	2005	2006	2007	2008	2009	05-06	06-07	07-08	08-09
Sales ($M)/Estab.	51.11	47.43	50.79	54.02	57.26	-7.2%	7.1%	6.4%	6.0%
Sales ($) per Emp.	803,448	764,034	837,775	888,511	937,073	-4.9%	9.7%	6.1%	5.5%
Emps. per Estab.	63.6	62.1	60.6	60.8	61.1	-2.4%	-2.3%	0.3%	0.5%

BREWERIES & BEER-MAKING INDUSTRY
(NAICS 31212)

SIZE OF FIRM INDUSTRY ESTIMATES

Year	Establishments by Size of Firm									Total
	1-4 Emps.	5-9 Emps.	10-19 Emps.	20-49 Emps.	50-99 Emps.	100-249 Emps.	250-499 Emps.	500+ Emps.	Unknown Emps.	
2006	146	55	38	55	30	8	8	16	93	450
2008	139	53	36	53	29	8	8	15	89	428
2009	132	50	34	50	28	8	8	14	84	408
	Sales ($Millions) by Size of Firm									Total
2006	68	128	131	692	480	399	676	19,768	504	22,847
2008	68	130	133	701	486	404	685	20,016	518	23,140
2009	69	131	134	707	490	408	691	20,196	535	23,361
	Employment by Size of Firm									Total
2006	437	332	567	1,881	1,947	1,128	2,754	12,657	5,568	27,271
2008	416	316	540	1,791	1,854	1,075	2,623	12,053	5,376	26,044
2009	396	301	514	1,705	1,766	1,023	2,498	11,478	5,248	24,930

SUB-INDUSTRIES — 2007 INDUSTRY ESTIMATES

Sub-Industries	Total Establishments	Total Employment	Total Sales ($M)
Malt beverages	264	11,017	4,019
Malt beverage products	3	328	38
Brewers' grain	10	161	18
Extract, malt	1	21	0
Syrups, malt	0	17	1
Ale (alcoholic beverage)	17	512	130
Beer (alcoholic beverage)	151	15,139	18,631
Liquors, malt	4	59	7
Porter (alcoholic beverage)	0	17	2

WINERIES & WINE-MAKING INDUSTRY (NAICS 31213)

INDUSTRY DEFINITION

NAICS 31213: Wineries. This industry comprises establishments primarily engaged in one or more of the following: (1) growing grapes and manufacturing wine and brandies; (2) manufacturing wine and brandies from grapes and other fruits grown elsewhere; and (3) blending wines and brandies.

INDUSTRY ESTABLISHMENTS, SALES & EMPLOYMENT TRENDS

	Year					Percent Change Year-to-Year			
	2005	2006	2007	2008	2009	05-06	06-07	07-08	08-09
Establishments	1,651	1,733	1,815	1,908	2,021	5.0%	4.7%	5.1%	5.9%
Sales ($Millions)	6,905	7,440	7,615	7,786	8,016	7.7%	2.4%	2.2%	3.0%
Employment	28,844	31,755	33,196	34,883	36,928	10.1%	4.5%	5.1%	5.9%

INDUSTRY RATIOS

(Industry Averages)	Year					Percent Change Year-to-Year			
	2005	2006	2007	2008	2009	05-06	06-07	07-08	08-09
Sales ($M)/Estab.	4.18	4.29	4.20	4.08	3.97	2.6%	-2.3%	-2.7%	-2.8%
Sales ($) per Emp.	239,395	234,293	229,402	223,215	217,077	-2.1%	-2.1%	-2.7%	-2.7%
Emps. per Estab.	17.5	18.3	18.3	18.3	18.3	4.9%	-0.2%	0.0%	-0.1%

WINERIES & WINE-MAKING INDUSTRY
(NAICS 31213)

SIZE OF FIRM INDUSTRY ESTIMATES

Year	Establishments by Size of Firm									Total
	1-4 Emps.	5-9 Emps.	10-19 Emps.	20-49 Emps.	50-99 Emps.	100-249 Emps.	250-499 Emps.	500+ Emps.	Unknown Emps.	Total
2006	866	313	249	241	79	34	15	1	25	1,815
2008	910	329	261	253	83	36	16	1	26	1,908
2009	964	348	277	268	88	38	17	2	28	2,021
	Sales ($Millions) by Size of Firm									Total
2006	334	331	598	1,625	1,523	1,469	1,015	544	176	7,615
2008	341	339	612	1,661	1,558	1,502	1,038	556	179	7,786
2009	351	349	630	1,711	1,604	1,547	1,069	573	182	8,016
	Employment by Size of Firm									Total
2006	1,732	1,876	3,480	7,954	5,062	5,186	4,052	2,511	1,344	33,196
2008	1,821	1,971	3,657	8,359	5,320	5,450	4,259	2,639	1,408	34,883
2009	1,928	2,088	3,874	8,854	5,634	5,773	4,511	2,795	1,472	36,928

SUB-INDUSTRIES — 2007 INDUSTRY ESTIMATES

Sub-Industries	Total Establishments	Total Employment	Total Sales ($M)
Wines, brandy, and brandy spirits	278	4,759	3,232
Wines	1,381	26,126	4,109
Wine coolers (beverages)	4	35	3
Brandy and brandy spirits	1	5	2
Brandy	7	88	3
Brandy spirits	1	8	1
Neutral spirits, fruit	3	13	1
Wine cellars, bonded: engaged in	142	2,163	265

DISTILLERIES & ALCOHOL-MAKING INDUSTRY (NAICS 31214)

INDUSTRY DEFINITION

NAICS 31214: Distilleries. This industry comprises establishments primarily engaged in one or more of the following: (1) distilling potable liquors (except brandies); (2) distilling and blending liquors; and (3) blending and mixing liquors and other ingredients.

INDUSTRY ESTABLISHMENTS, SALES & EMPLOYMENT TRENDS

	Year					Percent Change Year-to-Year			
	2005	2006	2007	2008	2009	05-06	06-07	07-08	08-09
Establishments	99	104	110	113	117	5.5%	5.3%	3.2%	3.2%
Sales ($Millions)	3,957	3,956	3,969	3,880	3,786	0.0%	0.3%	-2.3%	-2.4%
Employment	6,297	6,399	6,651	6,812	7,043	1.6%	3.9%	2.4%	3.4%

INDUSTRY RATIOS

(Industry Averages)	Year					Percent Change Year-to-Year			
	2005	2006	2007	2008	2009	05-06	06-07	07-08	08-09
Sales ($M)/Estab.	39.97	37.86	36.09	34.18	32.33	-5.3%	-4.7%	-5.3%	-5.4%
Sales ($) per Emp.	628,442	618,174	596,762	569,501	537,601	-1.6%	-3.5%	-4.6%	-5.6%
Emps. per Estab.	63.6	61.2	60.5	60.0	60.1	-3.7%	-1.2%	-0.7%	0.2%

DISTILLERIES & ALCOHOL-MAKING INDUSTRY (NAICS 31214)

SIZE OF FIRM INDUSTRY ESTIMATES

Year	\multicolumn{10}{c}{Establishments by Size of Firm}									
	1-4 Emps.	5-9 Emps.	10-19 Emps.	20-49 Emps.	50-99 Emps.	100-249 Emps.	250-499 Emps.	500+ Emps.	Unknown Emps.	Total
2006	25	9	9	10	4	18	5	0	31	110
2008	26	9	9	11	4	19	5	0	32	113
2009	27	10	10	11	4	20	5	0	33	117
\multicolumn{9}{c}{Sales ($Millions) by Size of Firm}										Total
2006	23	19	67	203	144	1,743	1,632	0	138	3,969
2008	23	18	66	198	141	1,706	1,597	0	131	3,880
2009	22	18	64	194	137	1,664	1,558	0	128	3,786
\multicolumn{9}{c}{Employment by Size of Firm}										Total
2006	76	64	128	336	240	2,566	1,640	0	1,600	6,651
2008	79	66	132	347	248	2,648	1,692	0	1,600	6,812
2009	81	68	137	358	256	2,733	1,746	0	1,664	7,043

SUB-INDUSTRIES — 2007 INDUSTRY ESTIMATES

Sub-Industries	Total Establishments	Total Employment	Total Sales ($M)
Distilled and blended liquors	64	3,482	2,069
Distiller's dried grains and solubles, and	5	360	130
Grain alcohol for beverage purposes	3	49	20
Cordials and premixed alcoholic	2	15	3
Cocktails, alcoholic	4	14	2
Cordials, alcoholic	2	229	62
Applejack (alcoholic beverage)	1	1	0
Bourbon whiskey	12	1,638	1,434
Corn whiskey	1	1	0
Gin (alcoholic beverage)	2	67	3
Rum (alcoholic beverage)	6	584	188
Rye whiskey	1	102	49
Vodka (alcoholic beverage)	8	110	7

MEN'S & BOYS' APPAREL MFG. INDUSTRY (NAICS 31522)

INDUSTRY DEFINITION

NAICS 31522: Men's & Boys' Apparel Manufacturing. This industry comprises establishments primarily engaged in manufacturing men's and boys' cut and sew apparel from purchased fabric. Men's and boys' clothing jobbers, who perform entrepreneurial functions involved in apparel manufacture, including buying raw materials, designing and preparing samples, arranging for apparel to be made from their materials, and marketing finished apparel, are included.

INDUSTRY ESTABLISHMENTS, SALES & EMPLOYMENT TRENDS

	Year					Percent Change Year-to-Year			
	2005	2006	2007	2008	2009	05-06	06-07	07-08	08-09
Establishments	780	730	680	636	598	-6.4%	-6.8%	-6.5%	-6.0%
Sales ($Millions)	19,911	21,741	20,617	19,511	18,566	9.2%	-5.2%	-5.4%	-4.8%
Employment	35,304	43,092	40,243	37,589	35,410	22.1%	-6.6%	-6.6%	-5.8%

INDUSTRY RATIOS

(Industry Averages)	Year					Percent Change Year-to-Year			
	2005	2006	2007	2008	2009	05-06	06-07	07-08	08-09
Sales ($M)/Estab.	25.53	29.78	30.30	30.67	31.05	16.6%	1.8%	1.2%	1.2%
Sales ($) per Emp.	563,984	504,530	512,307	519,065	524,327	-10.5%	1.5%	1.3%	1.0%
Emps. per Estab.	45.3	59.0	59.2	59.1	59.2	30.4%	0.2%	-0.1%	0.2%

Men's & Boys' Apparel Mfg. Industry
(NAICS 31522)

Size of Firm Industry Estimates

Year	Establishments by Size of Firm									Total
	1-4 Emps.	5-9 Emps.	10-19 Emps.	20-49 Emps.	50-99 Emps.	100-249 Emps.	250-499 Emps.	500+ Emps.	Unknown Emps.	
2006	190	78	86	114	74	80	24	15	25	680
2008	178	73	80	107	69	75	22	14	23	636
2009	167	68	76	100	65	70	21	13	22	598
Sales ($Millions) by Size of Firm										**Total**
2006	297	210	358	535	1,027	5,011	6,242	6,888	48	20,617
2008	281	199	339	506	972	4,743	5,908	6,519	44	19,511
2009	267	189	323	481	925	4,512	5,621	6,203	45	18,566
Employment by Size of Firm										**Total**
2006	570	466	1,376	3,536	4,856	11,868	7,815	8,412	1,344	40,243
2008	533	436	1,286	3,307	4,540	11,097	7,308	7,866	1,216	37,589
2009	501	410	1,209	3,109	4,268	10,432	6,870	7,394	1,216	35,410

Sub-Industries – 2007 Industry Estimates

Sub-Industries	Total Establishments	Total Employment	Total Sales ($M)
Men's and boy's trousers and slacks	93	7,161	2,619
Men's and boys' jeans and dungarees	20	1,139	362
Dungarees: men's, youths', and boys'	8	1,385	38
Jeans: men's, youths', and boys'	74	6,551	5,331
Men's and boys' dress slacks and shorts	3	45	0
Shorts (outerwear): men's, youths', and	8	340	570
Slacks, dress: men's, youths', and boys'	35	2,225	1,350
Trousers, dress (separate): men's,	22	1,276	38
Men's and boy's suits and coats	81	5,162	3,609
Tailored suits and formal jackets	66	6,322	3,717
Coats, overcoats and vests	10	167	59
Coats, tailored: men's and boys': from	6	781	514
Overcoats and topcoats: men's, youths'	3	109	22
Vests: made from purchased materials	9	145	61
Men's and boys' uniforms	28	2,416	687
Firemen's uniforms: made from	5	241	17
Military uniforms, men's and youths':	46	4,608	1,423
Policemen's uniforms: made from	9	172	202

WOMEN'S & GIRLS' APPAREL MFG. INDUSTRY (NAICS 31523)

INDUSTRY DEFINITION

NAICS 31523: Women's & Girls' Apparel Manufacturing Industry. This industry comprises establishments primarily engaged in manufacturing women's and girls' apparel from purchased fabric. Women's and girls' clothing jobbers, who perform entrepreneurial functions involved in apparel manufacture, including buying raw materials, designing and preparing samples, arranging for apparel to be made from their materials, and marketing finished apparel, are included.

INDUSTRY ESTABLISHMENTS, SALES & EMPLOYMENT TRENDS

	Year					Percent Change Year-to-Year			
	2005	2006	2007	2008	2009	05-06	06-07	07-08	08-09
Establishments	1,548	1,425	1,303	1,183	1,067	-7.9%	-8.6%	-9.2%	-9.7%
Sales ($Millions)	15,370	16,646	15,585	14,416	13,254	8.3%	-6.4%	-7.5%	-8.1%
Employment	43,552	51,900	47,417	43,087	38,932	19.2%	-8.6%	-9.1%	-9.6%

INDUSTRY RATIOS

	Year					Percent Change Year-to-Year			
(Industry Averages)	2005	2006	2007	2008	2009	05-06	06-07	07-08	08-09
Sales ($M)/Estab.	9.93	11.68	11.96	12.19	12.42	17.6%	2.4%	1.9%	1.9%
Sales ($) per Emp.	352,904	320,737	328,686	334,584	340,448	-9.1%	2.5%	1.8%	1.8%
Emps. per Estab.	28.1	36.4	36.4	36.4	36.5	29.4%	0.0%	0.1%	0.1%

WOMEN'S & GIRLS' APPAREL MFG. INDUSTRY (NAICS 31523)

SIZE OF FIRM INDUSTRY ESTIMATES

Year	Establishments by Size of Firm									Total
	1-4 Emps.	5-9 Emps.	10-19 Emps.	20-49 Emps.	50-99 Emps.	100-249 Emps.	250-499 Emps.	500+ Emps.	Unknown Emps.	
2006	454	197	209	240	92	62	21	9	23	1,303
2008	412	179	190	218	83	56	19	8	20	1,183
2009	372	162	172	197	75	50	17	7	18	1,067
	Sales ($Millions) by Size of Firm									Total
2006	143	187	616	1,664	1,375	2,682	2,317	6,569	34	15,585
2008	132	173	569	1,539	1,271	2,480	2,143	6,076	33	14,416
2009	121	159	523	1,415	1,169	2,280	1,970	5,586	31	13,254
	Employment by Size of Firm									Total
2006	1,361	1,185	3,142	8,409	5,679	7,819	6,307	12,362	1,152	47,417
2008	1,235	1,076	2,853	7,634	5,156	7,098	5,726	11,222	1,088	43,087
2009	1,115	971	2,575	6,890	4,654	6,407	5,168	10,129	1,024	38,932

SUB-INDUSTRIES – 2007 INDUSTRY ESTIMATES

Sub-Industries	Total Establishments	Total Employment	Total Sales ($M)
Women's and misses' blouses and	277	10,913	3,775
Blouses, women's and juniors': made	102	10,583	3,336
Shirts, women's and juniors': made from	10	774	179
T-shirts and tops, women's: made from	55	1,439	502
Women's, junior's, and misses' dresses	231	17,719	7,035
Bridal and formal gowns	57	1,068	76
Gowns, formal	24	797	86
Wedding gowns and dresses	83	1,607	207
Dresses,paper, cut and sewn	33	1,828	325
Ensemble dresses: women's, misses',	13	631	58
Housedresses	3	59	5

PAPER MILLS INDUSTRY
(NAICS 32212)

INDUSTRY DEFINITION

NAICS 32212: Paper Mills Industry. This industry comprises establishments primarily engaged in manufacturing paper from pulp. These establishments may manufacture or purchase pulp. In addition, the establishments may convert the paper they make. The activity of making paper classifies an establishment into this industry regardless of the output.

INDUSTRY ESTABLISHMENTS, SALES & EMPLOYMENT TRENDS

	Year					Percent Change Year-to-Year			
	2005	2006	2007	2008	2009	05-06	06-07	07-08	08-09
Establishments	392	421	451	471	493	7.5%	7.0%	4.6%	4.6%
Sales ($Millions)	45,170	45,737	48,045	49,138	50,186	1.3%	5.0%	2.3%	2.1%
Employment	85,093	100,630	107,533	112,743	117,916	18.3%	6.9%	4.8%	4.6%

INDUSTRY RATIOS

(Industry Averages)	Year					Percent Change Year-to-Year			
	2005	2006	2007	2008	2009	05-06	06-07	07-08	08-09
Sales ($M)/Estab.	115.23	108.54	106.59	104.27	101.85	-5.8%	-1.8%	-2.2%	-2.3%
Sales ($) per Emp.	530,831	454,504	446,797	435,844	425,611	-14.4%	-1.7%	-2.5%	-2.3%
Emps. per Estab.	217.1	238.8	238.6	239.2	239.3	10.0%	-0.1%	0.3%	0.0%

PAPER MILLS INDUSTRY
(NAICS 32212)

SIZE OF FIRM INDUSTRY ESTIMATES

Year	Establishments by Size of Firm									Total
	1-4 Emps.	5-9 Emps.	10-19 Emps.	20-49 Emps.	50-99 Emps.	100-249 Emps.	250-499 Emps.	500+ Emps.	Unknown Emps.	
2006	65	21	41	40	52	74	54	78	30	451
2008	68	22	43	41	54	77	56	82	31	471
2009	71	23	45	43	57	81	59	86	33	493
	Sales ($Millions) by Size of Firm									Total
2006	95	98	356	770	2,012	5,736	10,487	28,230	262	48,045
2008	97	100	364	787	2,055	5,860	10,715	28,842	318	49,138
2009	99	102	372	804	2,099	5,985	10,942	29,454	330	50,186
	Employment by Size of Firm									Total
2006	130	126	612	1,349	3,626	10,854	18,306	70,930	1,600	107,533
2008	136	131	640	1,410	3,791	11,349	19,140	74,161	1,984	112,743
2009	142	137	669	1,475	3,964	11,866	20,012	77,539	2,112	117,916

SUB-INDUSTRIES — 2007 INDUSTRY ESTIMATES

Sub-Industries	Total Establishments	Total Employment	Total Sales ($M)
Paper mills	163	65,202	39,695
Towels, tissues and napkins; paper and	27	8,526	618
Parchment, securites, and bank note	6	392	18
Specialty or chemically treated papers	29	4,422	614
Book, bond and printing papers	30	6,483	3,142
Poster and art papers	12	417	60
Stationary, envelope and tablet papers	102	4,821	327
Catalog, magazine, and newsprint	28	4,382	2,524
Wrapping and packaging papers	41	7,439	365
Building and roofing paper, felts and	8	675	58
Pressed and molded pulp and fiber	9	1,574	44
Fine paper	3	910	481
Kraft paper	2	1,579	51
Rope or jute paper	0	15	1
Uncoated paper	1	56	0
Wallpaper (hanging paper)	56	641	46

PRINTING INDUSTRY
(NAICS 32311)

INDUSTRY DEFINITION

NAICS 32311: Printing Industry. This industry comprises establishments primarily engaged in printing on apparel and textile products, paper, metal, glass, plastics, and other materials, except fabric (grey goods). The printing processes employed include, but are not limited to, lithographic, gravure, screen, flexographic, digital, and letterpress. Establishments in this industry do not manufacture the stock that they print but may perform postprinting activities, such as bending, cutting, or laminating the materials they print, and mailing.

INDUSTRY ESTABLISHMENTS, SALES & EMPLOYMENT TRENDS

	Year					Percent Change Year-to-Year			
	2005	2006	2007	2008	2009	05-06	06-07	07-08	08-09
Establishments	32,020	31,809	31,598	31,023	30,458	-0.7%	-0.7%	-1.8%	-1.8%
Sales ($Millions)	96,435	98,626	100,465	100,586	100,672	2.3%	1.9%	0.1%	0.1%
Employment	644,083	641,617	637,295	625,694	614,295	-0.4%	-0.7%	-1.8%	-1.8%

INDUSTRY RATIOS

	Year					Percent Change Year-to-Year			
(Industry Averages)	2005	2006	2007	2008	2009	05-06	06-07	07-08	08-09
Sales ($M)/Estab.	3.01	3.10	3.18	3.24	3.31	2.9%	2.5%	2.0%	1.9%
Sales ($) per Emp.	149,725	153,714	157,643	160,758	163,883	2.7%	2.6%	2.0%	1.9%
Emps. per Estab.	20.1	20.2	20.2	20.2	20.2	0.3%	0.0%	0.0%	0.0%

Printing Industry
(NAICS 32311)

Size of Firm Industry Estimates

Year	\multicolumn{10}{c}{Establishments by Size of Firm}
	1-4 Emps.	5-9 Emps.	10-19 Emps.	20-49 Emps.	50-99 Emps.	100-249 Emps.	250-499 Emps.	500+ Emps.	Unknown Emps.	Total
2006	14,367	6,634	4,382	3,241	1,410	818	203	97	443	31,598
2008	14,105	6,513	4,302	3,182	1,385	803	199	95	435	31,023
2009	13,848	6,395	4,224	3,124	1,359	789	196	94	427	30,458
\multicolumn{9}{c}{Sales ($Millions) by Size of Firm}			Total
2006	3,800	6,316	8,345	15,088	14,323	20,776	10,745	17,379	3,694	100,465
2008	3,804	6,324	8,355	15,106	14,340	20,801	10,757	17,399	3,699	100,586
2009	3,807	6,329	8,362	15,119	14,353	20,819	10,767	17,415	3,701	100,672
\multicolumn{9}{c}{Employment by Size of Firm}			Total
2006	43,100	39,804	61,352	106,968	93,084	126,837	67,643	70,219	28,288	637,295
2008	42,315	39,079	60,235	105,020	91,390	124,528	66,411	68,941	27,776	625,694
2009	41,544	38,368	59,138	103,108	89,726	122,260	65,202	67,685	27,264	614,295

Sub-Industries – 2007 Industry Estimates

Sub-Industries	Total Establishments	Total Employment	Total Sales ($M)
Commercial printing, lithographic	14,555	272,902	45,734
Offset and photolithographic printing	574	11,607	1,454
Offset printing	14,024	287,079	39,774
Photo-offset printing	198	3,550	281
Photolithographic printing	48	920	124
Promotional printing, lithographic	237	6,031	4,208
Business form and card printing,	475	11,281	1,968
Calendar and card printing, lithographic	141	5,844	1,180
Atlas and map printing, lithographic	34	585	71
Poster and decal printing, lithographic	165	4,538	705
Tag, ticket, and schedule printing:	50	1,947	291
Wrapper and seal printing, lithographic	22	410	95
Publication printing, lithographic	1,074	30,600	4,580

PETROLEUM REFINERIES INDUSTRY
(NAICS 32411)

INDUSTRY DEFINITION

NAICS 32411: Petroleum Refineries. Establishments primarily engaged in producing gasoline, kerosene, distillate fuel oils, residual fuel oils, and lubricants, through fractionation or straight distillation of crude oil, redistillation of unfinished petroleum derivatives, cracking or other processes. Establishments of this business also produce aliphatic and aromatic chemicals as byproducts. Natural gasoline from natural gas is classified in mining.

INDUSTRY ESTABLISHMENTS, SALES & EMPLOYMENT TRENDS

	Year					Percent Change Year-to-Year			
	2005	2006	2007	2008	2009	05-06	06-07	07-08	08-09
Establishments	367	385	404	409	414	5.0%	4.8%	1.3%	1.3%
Sales ($Millions)	275,019	284,879	328,865	362,588	397,467	3.6%	15.4%	10.3%	9.6%
Employment	63,004	57,835	60,468	61,252	62,108	-8.2%	4.6%	1.3%	1.4%

INDUSTRY RATIOS

	Year					Percent Change Year-to-Year			
(Industry Averages)	2005	2006	2007	2008	2009	05-06	06-07	07-08	08-09
Sales ($M)/Estab.	749.37	739.31	814.69	886.96	960.08	-1.3%	10.2%	8.9%	8.2%
Sales ($) per Emp.	4,365,104	4,925,687	5,438,619	5,919,665	6,399,627	12.8%	10.4%	8.8%	8.1%
Emps. per Estab.	171.7	150.1	149.8	149.8	150.0	-12.6%	-0.2%	0.0%	0.1%

PETROLEUM REFINERIES INDUSTRY
(NAICS 32411)

SIZE OF FIRM INDUSTRY ESTIMATES

Year	Establishments by Size of Firm									Total
	1-4 Emps.	5-9 Emps.	10-19 Emps.	20-49 Emps.	50-99 Emps.	100-249 Emps.	250-499 Emps.	500+ Emps.	Unknown Emps.	
2006	126	25	20	30	19	44	32	43	67	404
2008	128	25	21	30	19	44	32	43	68	409
2009	130	26	21	31	19	45	32	44	69	414
Sales ($Millions) by Size of Firm										**Total**
2006	7,746	1,876	2,556	4,374	5,012	21,417	38,732	230,115	17,034	328,865
2008	8,539	2,068	2,818	4,822	5,525	23,608	42,696	253,665	18,846	362,588
2009	9,351	2,265	3,086	5,281	6,051	25,853	46,756	277,787	21,036	397,467
Employment by Size of Firm										**Total**
2006	379	151	307	982	1,265	6,776	10,214	36,490	3,904	60,468
2008	384	153	311	995	1,281	6,862	10,344	36,954	3,968	61,252
2009	389	155	315	1,007	1,297	6,949	10,476	37,424	4,096	62,108

SUB-INDUSTRIES — 2007 INDUSTRY ESTIMATES

Sub-Industries	Total Establishments	Total Employment	Total Sales ($M)
Petroleum refining	232	51,195	314,188
Gases and liquefied petroleum gases	15	382	159
Gas, refinery	24	3,526	12,145
Liquefied petroleum gases, LPG	2	88	2
Light distillates	20	716	1,198
Intermediate distillates	1	7	2
Acid oil	0	8	0
Diesel fuels	9	69	10
Oils, fuel	27	1,239	116
Oils, illuminating	2	35	3
Oils, partly refined: sold for rerunning	3	269	10
Still oil	0	-	-
Heavy distillates	18	821	357
Residues	20	988	446
Aromatic chemical products	14	690	18
Nonaromatic chemical products	15	402	205
Fractionation products of crude	1	33	6

PETROCHEMICAL MANUFACTURING INDUSTRY (NAICS 32511)

INDUSTRY DEFINITION

NAICS 332511: Petrochemical Manufacturing Industry. This industry comprises establishments primarily engaged in (1) manufacturing acyclic (i.e., aliphatic) hydrocarbons such as ethylene, propylene, and butylene made from refined petroleum or liquid hydrocarbon and/or (2) manufacturing cyclic aromatic hydrocarbons such as benzene, toluene, styrene, xylene, ethyl benzene, and cumene made from refined petroleum or liquid hydrocarbons.

INDUSTRY ESTABLISHMENTS, SALES & EMPLOYMENT TRENDS

	Year					Percent Change Year-to-Year			
	2005	2006	2007	2008	2009	05-06	06-07	07-08	08-09
Establishments	46	48	49	48	47	3.5%	3.4%	-2.0%	-2.0%
Sales ($Millions)	5,666	4,944	5,097	4,958	4,823	-12.7%	3.1%	-2.7%	-2.7%
Employment	6,427	5,639	5,827	5,713	5,601	-12.3%	3.3%	-2.0%	-2.0%

INDUSTRY RATIOS

(Industry Averages)	Year					Percent Change Year-to-Year			
	2005	2006	2007	2008	2009	05-06	06-07	07-08	08-09
Sales ($M)/Estab.	123.17	103.84	103.56	102.77	101.99	-15.7%	-0.3%	-0.8%	-0.8%
Sales ($) per Emp.	881,532	876,707	874,678	867,846	861,077	-0.5%	-0.2%	-0.8%	-0.8%
Emps. per Estab.	139.7	118.4	118.4	118.4	118.4	-15.2%	0.0%	0.0%	0.0%

Petrochemical Manufacturing Industry (NAICS 32511)

Size of Firm Industry Estimates

Year	Establishments by Size of Firm									Total
	1-4 Emps.	5-9 Emps.	10-19 Emps.	20-49 Emps.	50-99 Emps.	100-249 Emps.	250-499 Emps.	500+ Emps.	Unknown Emps.	Total
2006	10	3	8	7	3	8	6	5	2	49
2008	10	3	7	6	3	7	6	5	2	48
2009	10	3	7	6	3	7	5	5	2	47
Sales ($Millions) by Size of Firm										**Total**
2006	17	12	98	244	127	905	1,597	2,091	6	5,097
2008	16	11	95	237	124	880	1,554	2,034	6	4,958
2009	16	11	93	230	121	856	1,511	1,979	6	4,823
Employment by Size of Firm										**Total**
2006	31	17	121	212	193	1,037	1,880	2,272	64	5,827
2008	31	17	119	208	189	1,017	1,843	2,227	64	5,713
2009	30	16	116	204	186	997	1,806	2,183	64	5,601

Sub-Industries – 2007 Industry Estimates

Sub-Industries	Total Establishments	Total Employment	Total Sales ($M)
Cyclic crudes and intermediates	7	871	493
Dyes and pigments	14	1,740	360
Acid dyes, synthetic	0	1	0
Biological stains	0	3	1
Color lakes or toners	1	3	1
Color pigments, organic	10	1,884	672
Drug dyes, synthetic	0	1	-
Dyes, synthetic organic	3	263	167
Food dyes or colors, synthetic	1	68	25
Phenol, alkylated and cumene	1	194	556
Solvent naphtha	0	6	1
Styrene	1	101	678
Toluene	0	3	1
Cyclic organic intermediates	2	378	783
Tar, coal tar, and related chemicals	1	71	12
Coal tar: crudes, intermediates, and	2	182	1,282
Tar	1	14	4
Chemical indicators	3	43	61

PHARMACEUTICAL PREPARATION MFG. INDUSTRY (NAICS 325412)

INDUSTRY DEFINITION

NAICS 325412: Pharmaceutical Preparation Manufacturing . This U.S. industry comprises establishments primarily engaged in manufacturing in-vivo diagnostic substances and pharmaceutical preparations (except biological) intended for internal and external consumption in dose forms, such as ampoules, tablets, capsules, vials, ointments, powders, solutions, and suspensions.

INDUSTRY ESTABLISHMENTS, SALES & EMPLOYMENT TRENDS

	Year					Percent Change Year-to-Year			
	2005	2006	2007	2008	2009	05-06	06-07	07-08	08-09
Establishments	1,164	1,166	1,167	1,170	1,172	0.1%	0.1%	0.2%	0.2%
Sales ($Millions)	162,854	187,691	209,885	231,081	252,365	15.3%	11.8%	10.1%	9.2%
Employment	143,419	144,744	144,937	145,184	145,431	0.9%	0.1%	0.2%	0.2%

INDUSTRY RATIOS

(Industry Averages)	Year					Percent Change Year-to-Year			
	2005	2006	2007	2008	2009	05-06	06-07	07-08	08-09
Sales ($M)/Estab.	139.91	161.01	179.77	197.55	215.34	15.1%	11.7%	9.9%	9.0%
Sales ($) per Emp.	1,135,509	1,296,711	1,448,112	1,591,645	1,735,291	14.2%	11.7%	9.9%	9.0%
Emps. per Estab.	123.2	124.2	124.1	124.1	124.1	0.8%	0.0%	0.0%	0.0%

PHARMACEUTICAL PREPARATION MFG. INDUSTRY
(NAICS 325412)

SIZE OF FIRM INDUSTRY ESTIMATES

Year	Establishments by Size of Firm									Total
	1-4 Emps.	5-9 Emps.	10-19 Emps.	20-49 Emps.	50-99 Emps.	100-249 Emps.	250-499 Emps.	500+ Emps.	Unknown Emps.	Total
2006	216	99	105	143	87	118	75	75	250	1,167
2008	216	99	105	143	87	118	75	75	250	1,170
2009	217	99	105	143	87	118	75	75	251	1,172
	Sales ($Millions) by Size of Firm									Total
2006	1,082	644	1,038	3,938	4,357	18,318	39,341	137,095	4,072	209,885
2008	1,191	710	1,143	4,336	4,797	20,168	43,315	150,945	4,475	231,081
2009	1,301	775	1,249	4,736	5,239	22,027	47,307	164,854	4,878	252,365
	Employment by Size of Firm									Total
2006	647	593	1,573	4,856	5,735	17,677	25,093	72,892	15,872	144,937
2008	648	594	1,576	4,865	5,746	17,711	25,140	73,031	15,872	145,184
2009	650	596	1,579	4,874	5,757	17,745	25,189	73,171	15,872	145,431

SUB-INDUSTRIES – 2007 INDUSTRY ESTIMATES

Sub-Industries	Total Establishments	Total Employment	Total Sales ($M)
Pharmaceutical preparations	752	114,368	189,527
Drugs affecting neoplasms and	3	326	1,148
Drugs acting on the central nervous	3	862	199
Drugs acting on the cardiovascular	5	1,470	1,413
Drugs acting on the respiratory system	4	1,195	272
Cough medicines	3	194	2,438
Dermatologicals	15	550	651
Vitamin, nutrient, and hematinic	104	3,316	2,179
Intravenous solutions	9	894	188
Vitamin preparations	59	3,615	1,111
Antibiotics, packaged	6	429	889
Druggists' preparations	47	2,548	185
Medicines, capsuled or ampuled	17	1,626	3,100
Pills, pharmaceutical	11	595	74
Proprietary drug products	17	4,091	1,837
Solutions, pharmaceutical	17	4,287	2,354
Tablets, pharmaceutical	5	1,248	961
Veterinary pharmaceutical preparations	30	1,096	322

ELECTRONIC COMPUTER MANUFACTURING INDUSTRY (NAICS 334111)

INDUSTRY DEFINITION

NAICS 334111: Electronic Computer Manufacturing . This U.S. industry comprises establishments primarily engaged in manufacturing and/or assembling electronic computers, such as mainframes, personal computers, workstations, laptops, and computer servers. Computers can be analog, digital, or hybrid. Digital computers, the most common type, are devices that do all of the following: (1) store the processing program or programs and the data immediately necessary for the execution of the program; (2) can be freely programmed in accordance with the requirements of the user; (3) perform arithmetical computations specified by the user; and (4) execute, without human intervention, a processing program that requires the computer to modify its execution by logical decision during the processing run. Analog computers are capable of simulating mathematical models and contain at least analog, control, and programming elements.

INDUSTRY ESTABLISHMENTS, SALES & EMPLOYMENT TRENDS

	Year					Percent Change Year-to-Year			
	2005	2006	2007	2008	2009	05-06	06-07	07-08	08-09
Establishments	605	589	574	553	534	-2.6%	-2.7%	-3.5%	-3.5%
Sales ($Millions)	48,253	58,813	55,513	51,614	47,937	21.9%	-5.6%	-7.0%	-7.1%
Employment	31,947	35,465	34,511	33,037	31,850	11.0%	-2.7%	-4.3%	-3.6%

INDUSTRY RATIOS

(Industry Averages)	Year					Percent Change Year-to-Year			
	2005	2006	2007	2008	2009	05-06	06-07	07-08	08-09
Sales ($M)/Estab.	79.76	99.80	96.78	93.27	89.79	25.1%	-3.0%	-3.6%	-3.7%
Sales ($) per Emp.	1,510,414	1,658,326	1,608,557	1,562,296	1,505,066	9.8%	-3.0%	-2.9%	-3.7%
Emps. per Estab.	52.8	60.2	60.2	59.7	59.7	14.0%	0.0%	-0.8%	-0.1%

ELECTRONIC COMPUTER MANUFACTURING INDUSTRY
(NAICS 334111)

SIZE OF FIRM INDUSTRY ESTIMATES

Year	Establishments by Size of Firm									Total
	1-4 Emps.	5-9 Emps.	10-19 Emps.	20-49 Emps.	50-99 Emps.	100-249 Emps.	250-499 Emps.	500+ Emps.	Unknown Emps.	
2006	198	65	48	51	28	27	10	11	138	574
2008	191	62	46	49	27	26	10	11	133	553
2009	185	60	45	47	26	25	10	11	129	534
	Sales ($Millions) by Size of Firm									Total
2006	131	190	314	729	1,168	3,078	3,971	45,372	560	55,513
2008	122	177	292	678	1,086	2,862	3,694	42,197	506	51,614
2009	114	164	271	630	1,009	2,659	3,430	39,192	468	47,937
	Employment by Size of Firm									Total
2006	397	388	721	1,674	1,791	3,985	3,358	13,174	9,024	34,511
2008	383	375	696	1,615	1,728	3,844	3,239	12,710	8,448	33,037
2009	369	361	671	1,558	1,667	3,709	3,125	12,262	8,128	31,850

SUB-INDUSTRIES – 2007 INDUSTRY ESTIMATES

Sub-Industries	Total Establishments	Total Employment	Total Sales ($M)
Electronic computers	357	15,621	22,667
Computers, digital, analog or hybrid	44	3,865	120
Mainframe computers	36	5,736	200
Minicomputers	24	4,645	4,321
Personal computers (microcomputers)	114	4,645	28,205

TELEPHONE EQUIPMENT MFG. INDUSTRY (NAICS 33421)

INDUSTRY DEFINITION

NAICS 33421: Telephone Apparatus Manufacturing This industry comprises establishments primarily engaged in manufacturing wire telephone and data communications equipment. These products may be standalone or board-level components of a larger system. Examples of products made by these establishments are central office switching equipment, cordless telephones (except cellular), PBX equipment, telephones, telephone answering machines, and data communications equipment, such as bridges, routers, and gateways.

INDUSTRY ESTABLISHMENTS, SALES & EMPLOYMENT TRENDS

	Year					Percent Change Year-to-Year			
	2005	2006	2007	2008	2009	05-06	06-07	07-08	08-09
Establishments	525	501	477	453	430	-4.6%	-4.8%	-5.0%	-5.0%
Sales ($Millions)	18,322	19,400	17,890	16,371	14,954	5.9%	-7.8%	-8.5%	-8.7%
Employment	34,595	36,133	34,387	32,720	31,063	4.4%	-4.8%	-4.8%	-5.1%

INDUSTRY RATIOS

(Industry Averages)	Year					Percent Change Year-to-Year			
	2005	2006	2007	2008	2009	05-06	06-07	07-08	08-09
Sales ($M)/Estab.	34.90	38.74	37.54	36.17	34.79	11.0%	-3.1%	-3.6%	-3.8%
Sales ($) per Emp.	529,623	536,893	520,248	500,325	481,400	1.4%	-3.1%	-3.8%	-3.8%
Emps. per Estab.	65.9	72.2	72.2	72.3	72.3	9.5%	0.0%	0.2%	0.0%

Telephone Equipment Mfg. Industry (NAICS 33421)

Size of Firm Industry Estimates

Year	Establishments by Size of Firm									Total
	1-4 Emps.	5-9 Emps.	10-19 Emps.	20-49 Emps.	50-99 Emps.	100-249 Emps.	250-499 Emps.	500+ Emps.	Unknown Emps.	
2006	95	42	53	72	59	49	12	13	84	477
2008	91	40	50	68	56	46	11	13	79	453
2009	86	38	48	65	54	44	11	12	75	430
Sales ($Millions) by Size of Firm										**Total**
2006	81	196	401	856	1,295	4,588	1,657	8,368	448	17,890
2008	74	179	367	783	1,185	4,197	1,515	7,655	415	16,371
2009	68	164	335	716	1,082	3,834	1,384	6,993	378	14,954
Employment by Size of Firm										**Total**
2006	286	296	796	2,374	4,036	6,847	3,600	11,097	5,056	34,387
2008	272	281	756	2,255	3,833	6,502	3,419	10,539	4,864	32,720
2009	258	267	718	2,141	3,640	6,175	3,247	10,009	4,608	31,063

Sub-Industries — 2007 Industry Estimates

Sub-Industries	Total Establishments	Total Employment	Total Sales ($M)
Telephone and telegraph apparatus	199	16,829	11,792
Telephones and telephone apparatus	74	7,039	2,499
Autotransformers for telephone	0	5	-
Communication headgear, telephone	7	506	51
Facsimile equipment	6	507	353
Headsets, telephone	11	224	102
Modems	10	591	159
Switching equipment, telephone	15	1,777	1,092
Telephone answering machines	3	22	6
Telephone central office equipment, dial	5	193	47
Telephone dialing devices, automatic	6	175	34
Telephone sets, all types except cellular	11	955	77
Telephone station equipment and parts,	6	290	128
Telephones, sound powered (no battery)	1	23	3
Toll switching equipment, telephone	1	37	-
Telegraph and related apparatus	10	271	13
Carrier equipment, telephone or	114	4,944	1,536

RADIO/TV BROADCAST EQUIPMENT INDUSTRY (NAICS 33422)

INDUSTRY DEFINITION

NAICS 33422: Radio/TV Broadcast Equipment. Establishments primarily engaged in manufacturing radio and television broadcasting and communications equipment. Includes closed-circuit and cable television equipment; studio equipment; light communications equipment; transmitters, transceivers and receivers (except household and automotive); cellular radio telephones; communication antennas; receivers; RF power amplifiers; and fixed and mobile radio systems.

INDUSTRY ESTABLISHMENTS, SALES & EMPLOYMENT TRENDS

	Year					Percent Change Year-to-Year			
	2005	2006	2007	2008	2009	05-06	06-07	07-08	08-09
Establishments	1,194	1,155	1,115	1,083	1,052	-3.3%	-3.4%	-2.9%	-2.9%
Sales ($Millions)	38,481	37,162	35,625	34,155	32,761	-3.4%	-4.1%	-4.1%	-4.1%
Employment	89,175	86,420	83,439	80,921	78,655	-3.1%	-3.4%	-3.0%	-2.8%

INDUSTRY RATIOS

(Industry Averages)	Year					Percent Change Year-to-Year			
	2005	2006	2007	2008	2009	05-06	06-07	07-08	08-09
Sales ($M)/Estab.	32.23	32.19	31.95	31.54	31.15	-0.1%	-0.7%	-1.3%	-1.2%
Sales ($) per Emp.	431,527	430,020	426,956	422,078	416,518	-0.3%	-0.7%	-1.1%	-1.3%
Emps. per Estab.	74.7	74.9	74.8	74.7	74.8	0.2%	0.0%	-0.1%	0.1%

Radio/TV Broadcast Equipment Industry (NAICS 33422)

Size of Firm Industry Estimates

Year	Establishments by Size of Firm									
	1-4 Emps.	5-9 Emps.	10-19 Emps.	20-49 Emps.	50-99 Emps.	100-249 Emps.	250-499 Emps.	500+ Emps.	Unknown Emps.	Total
2006	224	130	162	160	107	91	28	33	183	1,115
2008	217	126	157	155	104	89	27	32	177	1,083
2009	211	122	152	151	101	86	27	31	172	1,052
	Sales ($Millions) by Size of Firm									Total
2006	222	321	849	1,725	3,768	6,332	4,899	16,226	1,284	35,625
2008	213	308	814	1,655	3,613	6,073	4,698	15,562	1,220	34,155
2009	204	295	780	1,587	3,465	5,824	4,505	14,923	1,178	32,761
	Employment by Size of Firm									Total
2006	671	777	2,423	5,270	7,047	12,137	9,703	33,572	11,840	83,439
2008	651	755	2,353	5,118	6,843	11,786	9,422	32,602	11,392	80,921
2009	632	733	2,285	4,970	6,645	11,445	9,150	31,659	11,136	78,655

Sub-Industries — 2007 Industry Estimates

Sub-Industries	Total Establishments	Total Employment	Total Sales ($M)
Radio and t.v. communications	308	32,771	18,844
Radio broadcasting and	252	19,954	1,598
Television broadcasting and	98	4,695	898
Radio and t.v. communications	16	92	8
Antennas, transmitting and	50	3,343	425
Digital encoders	13	270	20
Encryption devices	6	209	14
Light communications equipment	6	124	12
Microwave communication equipment	39	3,837	3,824
Mobile communication equipment	40	1,805	234
Radio and television switching	2	199	17
Receiver-transmitter units (transceiver)	10	522	70
Satellites, communications	179	5,844	862
Space satellite communications	32	4,213	3,266
Studio equipment, radio and television	16	332	55
Telemetering equipment, electronic	36	3,203	5,430
Transmitting apparatus, radio or	12	2,027	48

AUDIO & VISUAL EQUIPMENT MFG. INDUSTRY (NAICS 33431)

INDUSTRY DEFINITION

NAICS 33431: Audio & Video Equipment Manufacturing Industry.
This industry comprises establishments primarily engaged in manufacturing electronic audio and video equipment for home entertainment, motor vehicle, public address and musical instrument amplifications. Examples of products made by these establishments are video cassette recorders, televisions, stereo equipment, speaker systems, household-type video cameras, jukeboxes, and amplifiers for musical instruments and public address systems.

INDUSTRY ESTABLISHMENTS, SALES & EMPLOYMENT TRENDS

	Year					Percent Change Year-to-Year			
	2005	2006	2007	2008	2009	05-06	06-07	07-08	08-09
Establishments	528	541	554	551	548	2.4%	2.4%	-0.5%	-0.5%
Sales ($Millions)	8,892	9,410	9,684	9,636	9,590	5.8%	2.9%	-0.5%	-0.5%
Employment	21,019	22,352	22,866	22,746	22,627	6.3%	2.3%	-0.5%	-0.5%

INDUSTRY RATIOS

(Industry Averages)	Year					Percent Change Year-to-Year			
	2005	2006	2007	2008	2009	05-06	06-07	07-08	08-09
Sales ($M)/Estab.	16.84	17.40	17.49	17.50	17.51	3.3%	0.5%	0.0%	0.1%
Sales ($) per Emp.	423,032	420,991	423,500	423,647	423,816	-0.5%	0.6%	0.0%	0.0%
Emps. per Estab.	39.8	41.3	41.3	41.3	41.3	3.8%	-0.1%	0.0%	0.0%

Audio & Visual Equipment Mfg. Industry (NAICS 33431)

Size of Firm Industry Estimates

Year	Establishments by Size of Firm									Total
	1-4 Emps.	5-9 Emps.	10-19 Emps.	20-49 Emps.	50-99 Emps.	100-249 Emps.	250-499 Emps.	500+ Emps.	Unknown Emps.	
2006	219	84	77	75	37	30	10	9	16	554
2008	218	84	77	75	37	30	10	9	16	551
2009	217	83	77	75	36	29	10	9	16	548
Sales ($Millions) by Size of Firm										**Total**
2006	67	94	228	1,219	676	1,120	1,402	4,817	60	9,684
2008	67	94	227	1,213	672	1,114	1,396	4,793	60	9,636
2009	66	93	226	1,207	669	1,109	1,389	4,770	60	9,590
Employment by Size of Firm										**Total**
2006	658	506	1,083	2,488	2,349	4,137	3,274	7,796	576	22,866
2008	654	503	1,077	2,475	2,336	4,114	3,256	7,754	576	22,746
2009	651	500	1,072	2,461	2,324	4,092	3,238	7,712	576	22,627

Sub-Industries – 2007 Industry Estimates

Sub-Industries	Total Establishments	Total Employment	Total Sales ($M)
Household audio and video equipment	120	6,236	4,506
Household audio equipment	37	1,163	240
Amplifiers: radio, public address, or	35	1,317	283
Audio electronic systems	128	2,376	746
Loudspeakers, electrodynamic or	16	1,526	1,136
Microphones	11	185	52
Music distribution apparatus	31	484	73
Sound reproducing equipment	76	2,815	723
Household video equipment	8	967	73
Television receiving sets	7	4,436	1,470
Video camera-audio recorders,	9	91	18
Video cassette recorders/players and	10	328	190
Video triggers (remote control TV	3	162	84
Electronic kits for home assembly:	16	395	13
Home entertainment equipment,	45	385	77

SEMI-CONDUCTOR & ELECTRONIC COMPONENTS MFG. (NAICS 33441)

INDUSTRY DEFINITION

NAICS 33441: Semiconductor and Other Electronic Component Manufacturing This industry comprises establishments primarily engaged in manufacturing semiconductors and other components for electronic applications. Examples of products made by these establishments are capacitors, resistors, microprocessors, bare and loaded printed circuit boards, electron tubes, electronic connectors, and computer modems.

INDUSTRY ESTABLISHMENTS, SALES & EMPLOYMENT TRENDS

	Year					Percent Change Year-to-Year			
	2005	2006	2007	2008	2009	05-06	06-07	07-08	08-09
Establishments	5,226	5,001	4,776	4,575	4,382	-4.3%	-4.5%	-4.2%	-4.2%
Sales ($Millions)	139,779	134,811	127,323	119,867	112,825	-3.6%	-5.6%	-5.9%	-5.9%
Employment	353,233	340,206	325,062	311,188	297,915	-3.7%	-4.5%	-4.3%	-4.3%

INDUSTRY RATIOS

(Industry Averages)	Year					Percent Change Year-to-Year			
	2005	2006	2007	2008	2009	05-06	06-07	07-08	08-09
Sales ($M)/Estab.	26.75	26.96	26.66	26.20	25.75	0.8%	-1.1%	-1.7%	-1.7%
Sales ($) per Emp.	395,712	396,264	391,689	385,192	378,716	0.1%	-1.2%	-1.7%	-1.7%
Emps. per Estab.	67.6	68.0	68.1	68.0	68.0	0.6%	0.1%	-0.1%	-0.1%

SEMI-CONDUCTOR & ELECTRONIC COMPONENTS MFG. (NAICS 33441)

SIZE OF FIRM INDUSTRY ESTIMATES

Year	Establishments by Size of Firm									Total
	1-4 Emps.	5-9 Emps.	10-19 Emps.	20-49 Emps.	50-99 Emps.	100-249 Emps.	250-499 Emps.	500+ Emps.	Unknown Emps.	
2006	1,047	577	672	919	549	395	144	116	355	4,776
2008	1,003	552	644	881	526	379	138	111	340	4,575
2009	961	529	617	844	504	363	132	107	326	4,382
Sales ($Millions) by Size of Firm										**Total**
2006	927	737	2,446	8,586	13,491	19,429	19,805	53,129	8,773	127,323
2008	873	694	2,304	8,088	12,709	18,303	18,656	50,048	8,193	119,867
2009	822	654	2,170	7,617	11,969	17,237	17,570	47,135	7,651	112,825
Employment by Size of Firm										**Total**
2006	3,142	3,459	10,087	30,341	36,782	58,901	49,649	109,852	22,848	325,062
2008	3,010	3,314	9,662	29,064	35,234	56,422	47,559	105,228	21,696	311,188
2009	2,883	3,174	9,256	27,841	33,751	54,047	45,557	100,798	20,608	297,915

SUB-INDUSTRIES — 2007 INDUSTRY ESTIMATES

Sub-Industries	Total Establishments	Total Employment	Total Sales ($M)
Semiconductors and related devices	2,445	154,443	34,065
Semiconductor diodes and rectifiers	113	5,132	1,212
Integrated circuits, semiconductor	1,531	131,649	84,143
Light sensitive devices	177	5,101	781
Radiation sensors	38	431	215
Infrared sensors, solid state	79	8,570	238
Ultra-violet sensors, solid state	21	93	20
Fuel cells, solid state	32	1,302	74
Gunn effect devices	2	7	1
Hall effect devices	2	7	0
Magnetohydrodynamic (MHD) devices	4	4	0
Modules, solid state	46	1,274	191
Molecular devices, solid state	14	68	2
Nuclear detectors, solid state	7	80	7
Optical isolators	7	229	8
Silicon wafers, chemically doped	66	7,122	1,575
Solid state electronic devices, nec	214	4,113	302

SOFTWARE REPRODUCING INDUSTRY (NAICS 334611)

INDUSTRY DEFINITION

NAICS 334611 Software Reproducing This U.S. industry comprises establishments primarily engaged in mass reproducing computer software. These establishments do not generally develop any software, they mass reproduce data and programs on magnetic media, such as diskettes, tapes, or cartridges. Establishments in this industry mass reproduce products, such as CD-ROMs and game cartridges.

INDUSTRY ESTABLISHMENTS, SALES & EMPLOYMENT TRENDS

	Year					Percent Change Year-to-Year			
	2005	2006	2007	2008	2009	05-06	06-07	07-08	08-09
Establishments	309	341	373	408	446	10.4%	9.4%	9.4%	9.3%
Sales ($Millions)	1,096	935	878	799	706	-14.6%	-6.1%	-9.0%	-11.7%
Employment	10,020	10,345	11,172	12,021	13,086	3.2%	8.0%	7.6%	8.9%

INDUSTRY RATIOS

(Industry Averages)	Year					Percent Change Year-to-Year			
	2005	2006	2007	2008	2009	05-06	06-07	07-08	08-09
Sales ($M)/Estab.	3.55	2.74	2.35	1.96	1.58	-22.6%	-14.2%	-16.8%	-19.2%
Sales ($) per Emp.	109,341	90,424	78,600	66,443	53,914	-17.3%	-13.1%	-15.5%	-18.9%
Emps. per Estab.	32.4	30.3	29.9	29.5	29.3	-6.5%	-1.3%	-1.6%	-0.4%

SOFTWARE REPRODUCING INDUSTRY
(NAICS 334611)

SIZE OF FIRM INDUSTRY ESTIMATES

Year	Establishments by Size of Firm									
	1-4 Emps.	5-9 Emps.	10-19 Emps.	20-49 Emps.	50-99 Emps.	100-249 Emps.	250-499 Emps.	500+ Emps.	Unknown Emps.	Total
2006	136	45	32	16	4	7	0	0	124	373
2008	149	50	35	17	4	8	0	0	136	408
2009	163	54	39	19	4	9	0	0	149	446
	Sales ($Millions) by Size of Firm									Total
2006	31	51	73	70	32	189	13	0	418	878
2008	28	47	67	65	30	174	12	0	376	799
2009	25	42	59	57	26	154	10	0	331	706
	Employment by Size of Firm									Total
2006	409	273	452	513	226	1,005	38	0	8,256	11,172
2008	447	298	494	561	247	1,099	42	0	8,832	12,021
2009	489	326	541	613	270	1,201	46	0	9,600	13,086

SUB-INDUSTRIES – 2007 INDUSTRY ESTIMATES

Sub-Industries	Total Establishments	Total Employment	Total Sales ($M)
Computer related services, nec	63	785	11
Computer related maintenance services	13	919	30
Disk and diskette conversion service	0	44	2
Disk and diskette recertification service	0	5	0
Tape recertification service	0	1	0
Word processing equipment	0	8	0
Computer data escrow service	1	19	0
Computer related consulting services	252	7,730	800
Computer hardware requirements	1	48	1
Data processing consultant	11	502	11
Online services technology consultants	32	1,111	23

MAJOR APPLIANCE MANUFACTURING INDUSTRY
(NAICS 33522)

INDUSTRY DEFINITION

NAICS 33522: Appliance Manufacturing Industry. This industry comprises establishments primarily engaged in manufacturing household-type cooking appliances, household-type laundry equipment, household-type refrigerators, upright and chest freezers, and other electrical and nonelectrical major household-type appliances, such as dishwashers, water heaters, and garbage disposal units.

INDUSTRY ESTABLISHMENTS, SALES & EMPLOYMENT TRENDS

	Year					Percent Change Year-to-Year			
	2005	2006	2007	2008	2009	05-06	06-07	07-08	08-09
Establishments	240	242	243	248	253	0.7%	0.7%	1.9%	1.9%
Sales ($Millions)	12,116	13,593	13,969	14,424	14,892	12.2%	2.8%	3.3%	3.2%
Employment	57,089	62,894	63,515	64,673	65,852	10.2%	1.0%	1.8%	1.8%

INDUSTRY RATIOS

(Industry Averages)	Year					Percent Change Year-to-Year			
	2005	2006	2007	2008	2009	05-06	06-07	07-08	08-09
Sales ($M)/Estab.	50.48	56.24	57.40	58.17	58.95	11.4%	2.1%	1.4%	1.3%
Sales ($) per Emp.	212,234	216,128	219,939	223,033	226,139	1.8%	1.8%	1.4%	1.4%
Emps. per Estab.	237.9	260.2	261.0	260.8	260.7	9.4%	0.3%	-0.1%	-0.1%

Major Appliance Manufacturing Industry (NAICS 33522)

Size of Firm Industry Estimates

Year	Establishments by Size of Firm									
	1-4 Emps.	5-9 Emps.	10-19 Emps.	20-49 Emps.	50-99 Emps.	100-249 Emps.	250-499 Emps.	500+ Emps.	Unknown Emps.	Total
2006	61	16	19	27	15	21	18	42	27	243
2008	62	17	20	28	15	21	19	43	28	248
2009	63	17	20	28	16	21	19	44	28	253
Sales ($Millions) by Size of Firm										**Total**
2006	63	20	28	1,130	949	1,503	1,960	8,138	176	13,969
2008	65	21	29	1,167	981	1,553	2,024	8,405	178	14,424
2009	68	22	30	1,206	1,013	1,603	2,090	8,680	180	14,892
Employment by Size of Firm										**Total**
2006	121	97	312	919	999	2,980	6,877	49,416	1,792	63,515
2008	123	99	317	937	1,018	3,036	7,006	50,343	1,792	64,673
2009	126	101	323	954	1,037	3,093	7,138	51,288	1,792	65,852

Sub-Industries – 2007 Industry Estimates

Sub-Industries	Total Establishments	Total Employment	Total Sales ($M)
Household cooking equipment	36	22,101	1,734
Indoor cooking equipment	4	541	397
Convection ovens, including portable:	3	2,486	19
Electric ranges, domestic	3	14,300	4,844
Gas ranges, domestic	3	1,649	439
Microwave ovens, including portable:	1	15	1
Stoves, disk	1	20	1
Barbecues, grills, and braziers (outdoor	70	22,402	6,535
Household refrigerators and freezers	48	20,454	6,068
Freezers, home and farm	17	1,249	190
Ice boxes, household: metal or wood	4	45	37
Refrigerator cabinets, household: metal	6	8,764	108
Refrigerators, mechanical and	24	23,397	6,024

AUTOMOBILE & MOTOR VEHICLE MFG. INDUSTRY (NAICS 33611)

INDUSTRY DEFINITION

NAICS 33611: Automobile & Light Motor Vehicle Manufacturing .
This industry comprises establishments primarily engaged in (1)
manufacturing complete automobile and light duty motor vehicles (i.e.,
body and chassis or unibody) or (2) manufacturing chassis only.

INDUSTRY ESTABLISHMENTS, SALES & EMPLOYMENT TRENDS

	Year					Percent Change Year-to-Year			
	2005	2006	2007	2008	2009	05-06	06-07	07-08	08-09
Establishments	292	278	265	256	247	-4.7%	-4.9%	-3.4%	-3.4%
Sales ($Millions)	415,468	394,179	394,109	397,402	399,938	-5.1%	0.0%	0.8%	0.6%
Employment	130,335	115,852	110,223	106,542	102,921	-11.1%	-4.9%	-3.3%	-3.4%

INDUSTRY RATIOS

(Industry Averages)	Year					Percent Change Year-to-Year			
	2005	2006	2007	2008	2009	05-06	06-07	07-08	08-09
Sales ($M)/Estab.	1,422.84	1,415.92	1,488.43	1,553.07	1,617.34	-0.5%	5.1%	4.3%	4.1%
Sales ($) per Emp.	3,187,694	3,402,426	3,575,557	3,729,998	3,885,873	6.7%	5.1%	4.3%	4.2%
Emps. per Estab.	446.4	416.2	416.3	416.4	416.2	-6.8%	0.0%	0.0%	0.0%

Automobile & Motor Vehicle Mfg. Industry (NAICS 33611)

Size of Firm Industry Estimates

Year	Establishments by Size of Firm									Total
	1-4 Emps.	5-9 Emps.	10-19 Emps.	20-49 Emps.	50-99 Emps.	100-249 Emps.	250-499 Emps.	500+ Emps.	Unknown Emps.	
2006	108	26	22	23	8	9	2	55	17	265
2008	104	25	21	22	8	9	2	53	16	256
2009	100	24	21	21	8	9	2	52	15	247
Sales ($Millions) by Size of Firm										**Total**
2006	203	60	292	733	418	745	887	389,620	1,151	394,109
2008	205	61	294	739	422	751	894	392,836	1,201	397,402
2009	206	61	296	744	425	756	900	395,413	1,137	399,938
Employment by Size of Firm										**Total**
2006	323	154	331	781	530	1,306	638	105,456	704	110,223
2008	312	149	320	755	512	1,262	617	101,912	704	106,542
2009	301	144	309	730	495	1,219	596	98,487	640	102,921

Sub-Industries – 2007 Industry Estimates

Sub-Industries	Total Establishments	Total Employment	Total Sales ($M)
Motor vehicles and car bodies	64	38,939	50,806
Automobile assembly, including	92	41,745	318,239
Ambulances (motor vehicles), assembly	5	707	157
Automobile bodies, passenger car, not	13	2,954	735
Cars, armored, assembly of	2	106	107
Cars, electric, assembly of	2	38	7
Chassis, motor vehicle	16	2,164	946
Hearses (motor vehicles), assembly of	1	94	88
Patrol wagons (motor vehicles),	1	30	7
Taxicabs, assembly of	0	2	0
Truck and tractor truck assembly	9	7,968	17,280
Motor trucks, except off-highway,	1	4,522	528
Truck tractors for highway use,	4	999	2,301
Trucks, pickup, assembly of	2	1,067	2
Military motor vehicle assembly	8	1,452	82
Bus and other large specialty vehicle	45	7,435	2,823

AUTOMOBILE GAS ENGINE & ENGINE PARTS MFG. (NAICS 33631)

INDUSTRY DEFINITION

NAICS 33631: Motor Vehicle Gas Engine & Engine Parts Manufacturing Industry. This industry comprises establishments primarily engaged in manufacturing and/or rebuilding motor vehicle gasoline engines, and engine parts, whether or not for vehicular use.

INDUSTRY ESTABLISHMENTS, SALES & EMPLOYMENT TRENDS

	Year					Percent Change Year-to-Year			
	2005	2006	2007	2008	2009	05-06	06-07	07-08	08-09
Establishments	1,106	1,116	1,126	1,131	1,136	0.9%	0.9%	0.5%	0.5%
Sales ($Millions)	31,263	34,642	36,288	37,622	38,969	10.8%	4.8%	3.7%	3.6%
Employment	83,937	89,636	90,369	90,758	91,149	6.8%	0.8%	0.4%	0.4%

INDUSTRY RATIOS

(Industry Averages)	Year					Percent Change Year-to-Year			
	2005	2006	2007	2008	2009	05-06	06-07	07-08	08-09
Sales ($M)/Estab.	28.27	31.05	32.24	33.27	34.30	9.8%	3.8%	3.2%	3.1%
Sales ($) per Emp.	372,454	386,468	401,559	414,536	427,536	3.8%	3.9%	3.2%	3.1%
Emps. per Estab.	75.9	80.3	80.3	80.3	80.2	5.8%	-0.1%	0.0%	0.0%

Automobile Gas Engine & Engine Parts Mfg. (NAICS 33631)

Size of Firm Industry Estimates

Year	Establishments by Size of Firm									Total
	1-4 Emps.	5-9 Emps.	10-19 Emps.	20-49 Emps.	50-99 Emps.	100-249 Emps.	250-499 Emps.	500+ Emps.	Unknown Emps.	
2006	421	173	117	94	56	72	49	44	102	1,126
2008	423	174	117	94	57	73	50	44	102	1,131
2009	425	175	118	94	57	73	50	45	103	1,136
	Sales ($Millions) by Size of Firm									**Total**
2006	915	470	1,267	1,564	2,575	3,593	4,843	19,001	2,061	36,288
2008	949	487	1,314	1,622	2,670	3,726	5,022	19,705	2,128	37,622
2009	983	505	1,361	1,680	2,766	3,861	5,203	20,416	2,194	38,969
	Employment by Size of Firm									**Total**
2006	1,264	1,211	1,750	3,181	3,774	11,009	16,463	45,251	6,464	90,369
2008	1,270	1,217	1,758	3,196	3,792	11,060	16,540	45,461	6,464	90,758
2009	1,276	1,222	1,767	3,210	3,809	11,111	16,616	45,672	6,464	91,149

Sub-Industries – 2007 Industry Estimates

Sub-Industries	Total Establishments	Total Employment	Total Sales ($M)
Motor vehicle parts and accessories	467	44,732	22,575
Motor vehicle engines and parts	249	13,535	5,779
Motor vehicle transmissions, drive	134	11,121	2,067
Motor vehicle body components and	115	10,176	2,332
Motor vehicle brake systems and parts	49	4,628	1,289
Motor vehicle steering systems and	16	1,176	443
Motor vehicle wheels and parts	43	3,111	1,503
Air conditioner parts, motor vehicle	12	1,426	76
Booster (jump-start) cables, automotive	1	37	5
Dump truck lifting mechanism	2	10	2
Fifth wheel, motor vehicle	1	16	2
Ice scrapers and window brushes, motor	1	10	2
PCV valves	1	10	1
Sanders, motor vehicle safety	3	20	2
Third axle attachments or six wheel	1	15	2
Trailer hitches, motor vehicle	9	291	198
Other vehicle parts	22	56	12

Aircraft Manufacturing Industry (NAICS 336411)

Industry Definition

NAICS 336411: Aircraft Manufacturing . This U.S. industry comprises establishments primarily engaged in one or more of the following: (1) manufacturing or assembling complete aircraft; (2) developing and making aircraft prototypes; (3) aircraft conversion (i.e., major modifications to systems); and (4) complete aircraft overhaul and rebuilding (i.e., periodic restoration of aircraft to original design specifications).

Industry Establishments, Sales & Employment Trends

	Year					Percent Change Year-to-Year			
	2005	2006	2007	2008	2009	05-06	06-07	07-08	08-09
Establishments	359	370	382	389	396	3.2%	3.1%	1.8%	1.8%
Sales ($Millions)	84,349	101,892	106,750	109,767	112,913	20.8%	4.8%	2.8%	2.9%
Employment	70,203	80,110	82,659	83,999	85,618	14.1%	3.2%	1.6%	1.9%

Industry Ratios

	Year					Percent Change Year-to-Year			
(Industry Averages)	2005	2006	2007	2008	2009	05-06	06-07	07-08	08-09
Sales ($M)/Estab.	234.96	275.02	279.47	282.41	285.49	17.1%	1.6%	1.1%	1.1%
Sales ($) per Emp.	1,201,500	1,271,904	1,291,451	1,306,776	1,318,801	5.9%	1.5%	1.2%	0.9%
Emps. per Estab.	195.6	216.2	216.4	216.1	216.5	10.6%	0.1%	-0.1%	0.2%

AIRCRAFT MANUFACTURING INDUSTRY
(NAICS 336411)

SIZE OF FIRM INDUSTRY ESTIMATES

Year	Establishments by Size of Firm									Total
	1-4 Emps.	5-9 Emps.	10-19 Emps.	20-49 Emps.	50-99 Emps.	100-249 Emps.	250-499 Emps.	500+ Emps.	Unknown Emps.	
2006	106	31	26	31	17	17	12	42	101	382
2008	108	31	27	31	17	17	12	43	102	389
2009	110	32	27	32	18	18	12	44	104	396
Sales ($Millions) by Size of Firm										Total
2006	55	29	41	159	264	352	3,022	101,624	1,205	106,750
2008	57	29	42	164	271	362	3,108	104,517	1,218	109,767
2009	58	30	44	169	279	372	3,196	107,486	1,280	112,913
Employment by Size of Firm										Total
2006	317	184	370	1,013	1,117	2,590	4,039	66,628	6,400	82,659
2008	323	187	377	1,030	1,137	2,636	4,110	67,799	6,400	83,999
2009	329	191	383	1,048	1,157	2,682	4,182	68,990	6,656	85,618

SUB-INDUSTRIES – 2007 INDUSTRY ESTIMATES

Sub-Industries	Total Establishments	Total Employment	Total Sales ($M)
Aircraft	243	45,136	45,088
Motorized aircraft	6	636	28
Airplanes, fixed or rotary wing	37	19,884	59,578
Helicopters	35	15,638	1,911
Nonmotorized and lighter-than-air	2	22	4
Airships	4	61	10
Balloons, hot air (aircraft)	9	56	8
Blimps	3	79	5
Dirigibles	0	2	0
Gliders (aircraft)	4	13	2
Hang gliders	8	89	12
Autogiros	0	2	0
Research and development on aircraft	31	1,041	104

KITCHEN CABINET & COUNTERTOP MFG. INDUSTRY (NAICS 33711)

INDUSTRY DEFINITION

NAICS 33711: Kitchen Cabinet & Countertop Mfg Industry. This industry comprises establishments primarily engaged in manufacturing wood or plastics laminated on wood kitchen cabinets, bathroom vanities, and countertops (except freestanding). The cabinets and counters may be made on a stock or custom basis.

INDUSTRY ESTABLISHMENTS, SALES & EMPLOYMENT TRENDS

	Year					Percent Change Year-to-Year			
	2005	2006	2007	2008	2009	05-06	06-07	07-08	08-09
Establishments	9,539	9,936	10,332	10,717	11,117	4.2%	4.0%	3.7%	3.7%
Sales ($Millions)	18,689	20,519	22,660	24,744	26,940	9.8%	10.4%	9.2%	8.9%
Employment	141,756	145,961	151,925	157,601	163,290	3.0%	4.1%	3.7%	3.6%

INDUSTRY RATIOS

(Industry Averages)	Year					Percent Change Year-to-Year			
	2005	2006	2007	2008	2009	05-06	06-07	07-08	08-09
Sales ($M)/Estab.	1.96	2.07	2.19	2.31	2.42	5.4%	6.2%	5.3%	5.0%
Sales ($) per Emp.	131,836	140,578	149,151	157,003	164,985	6.6%	6.1%	5.3%	5.1%
Emps. per Estab.	14.9	14.7	14.7	14.7	14.7	-1.1%	0.1%	0.0%	-0.1%

KITCHEN CABINET & COUNTERTOP MFG. INDUSTRY (NAICS 33711)

SIZE OF FIRM INDUSTRY ESTIMATES

Year	Establishments by Size of Firm									Total
	1-4 Emps.	5-9 Emps.	10-19 Emps.	20-49 Emps.	50-99 Emps.	100-249 Emps.	250-499 Emps.	500+ Emps.	Unknown Emps.	
2006	5,444	2,216	1,408	774	210	122	52	31	77	10,332
2008	5,647	2,299	1,460	803	218	126	54	32	80	10,717
2009	5,857	2,385	1,515	833	226	131	56	33	83	11,117
	Sales ($Millions) by Size of Firm									Total
2006	1,234	1,256	2,074	2,369	2,282	3,274	3,802	6,084	284	22,660
2008	1,347	1,371	2,265	2,587	2,492	3,575	4,152	6,643	311	24,744
2009	1,468	1,494	2,467	2,818	2,714	3,894	4,523	7,236	327	26,940
	Employment by Size of Firm									Total
2006	10,888	13,297	19,711	25,550	13,844	18,407	17,240	28,123	4,864	151,925
2008	11,294	13,793	20,446	26,503	14,360	19,094	17,883	29,172	5,056	157,601
2009	11,715	14,308	21,208	27,491	14,896	19,806	18,550	30,260	5,056	163,290

SUB-INDUSTRIES – 2007 INDUSTRY ESTIMATES

Sub-Industries	Total Establishments	Total Employment	Total Sales ($M)
Wood kitchen cabinets	10,195	149,524	22,486
Vanities, bathroom: wood	137	2,401	173

HOUSEHOLD & INSTITUTIONAL FURNITURE MFG. (NAICS 33712)

INDUSTRY DEFINITION

NAICS 33712: Household and Institutional Furniture Manufacturing
This industry comprises establishments primarily engaged in manufacturing household-type and public building furniture (i.e., library, school, theater, and church furniture). The furniture may be made on a stock or custom basis and may be assembled or unassembled (i.e., knockdown).

INDUSTRY ESTABLISHMENTS, SALES & EMPLOYMENT TRENDS

	Year					Percent Change Year-to-Year			
	2005	2006	2007	2008	2009	05-06	06-07	07-08	08-09
Establishments	7,084	7,142	7,200	7,169	7,139	0.8%	0.8%	-0.4%	-0.4%
Sales ($Millions)	33,161	34,773	35,948	36,491	37,034	4.9%	3.4%	1.5%	1.5%
Employment	219,434	222,642	224,541	223,508	222,543	1.5%	0.9%	-0.5%	-0.4%

INDUSTRY RATIOS

(Industry Averages)	Year					Percent Change Year-to-Year			
	2005	2006	2007	2008	2009	05-06	06-07	07-08	08-09
Sales ($M)/Estab.	4.68	4.87	4.99	5.09	5.19	4.0%	2.5%	1.9%	1.9%
Sales ($) per Emp.	151,120	156,183	160,095	163,265	166,413	3.4%	2.5%	2.0%	1.9%
Emps. per Estab.	31.0	31.2	31.2	31.2	31.2	0.6%	0.0%	0.0%	0.0%

HOUSEHOLD & INSTITUTIONAL FURNITURE MFG.
(NAICS 33712)

SIZE OF FIRM INDUSTRY ESTIMATES

Year	Establishments by Size of Firm									Total
	1-4 Emps.	5-9 Emps.	10-19 Emps.	20-49 Emps.	50-99 Emps.	100-249 Emps.	250-499 Emps.	500+ Emps.	Unknown Emps.	
2006	3,244	1,248	946	762	344	272	125	64	197	7,200
2008	3,231	1,243	942	759	343	271	124	64	196	7,169
2009	3,217	1,237	938	756	341	270	124	63	195	7,139
Sales ($Millions) by Size of Firm										**Total**
2006	858	792	2,001	3,546	3,494	6,453	7,925	10,244	636	35,948
2008	871	804	2,031	3,600	3,547	6,551	8,045	10,400	642	36,491
2009	884	816	2,062	3,654	3,600	6,649	8,165	10,554	651	37,034
Employment by Size of Firm										**Total**
2006	9,733	8,736	13,245	25,152	22,718	45,494	41,966	45,081	12,416	224,541
2008	9,692	8,699	13,189	25,045	22,621	45,299	41,787	44,889	12,288	223,508
2009	9,650	8,662	13,132	24,938	22,524	45,106	41,609	44,698	12,224	222,543

SUB-INDUSTRIES — 2007 INDUSTRY ESTIMATES

Sub-Industries	Total Establishments	Total Employment	Total Sales ($M)
Furniture and fixtures, nec	1,158	5,402	159
Factory furniture and fixtures	875	32,180	1,768
Cabinets, factory	2,135	48,717	11,911
Stools, factory	5	340	9
Tool stands, factory	21	428	28
Work benches, factory	117	1,409	107
Bar, restaurant and cafeteria furniture	550	15,536	668
Bar furniture	101	1,632	44
Cafeteria furniture	21	136	4
Carts, restaurant equipment	294	7,831	297
Food wagons, restaurant	165	1,992	61
Restaurant furniture, wood or metal	587	36,455	2,542
Beds, not household use	144	8,230	718
Hospital beds	229	24,174	6,070
Inflatable beds	53	1,078	71
Other furniture, nec.	742	39,001	11,491

OFFICE FURNITURE MANUFACTURING INDUSTRY (NAICS 33721)

INDUSTRY DEFINITION

NAICS 33721: Office Furniture Manufacturing Industry. This industry comprises establishments primarily engaged in manufacturing office furniture and/or office and store fixtures. The furniture may be made on a stock or custom basis and may be assembled or unassembled (i.e., knockdown).

INDUSTRY ESTABLISHMENTS, SALES & EMPLOYMENT TRENDS

	Year					Percent Change Year-to-Year			
	2005	2006	2007	2008	2009	05-06	06-07	07-08	08-09
Establishments	4,282	4,289	4,297	4,294	4,291	0.2%	0.2%	-0.1%	-0.1%
Sales ($Millions)	22,330	22,888	23,294	23,517	23,747	2.5%	1.8%	1.0%	1.0%
Employment	152,563	152,110	152,417	152,263	152,174	-0.3%	0.2%	-0.1%	-0.1%

INDUSTRY RATIOS

	Year					Percent Change Year-to-Year			
(Industry Averages)	2005	2006	2007	2008	2009	05-06	06-07	07-08	08-09
Sales ($M)/Estab.	5.21	5.34	5.42	5.48	5.53	2.3%	1.6%	1.0%	1.0%
Sales ($) per Emp.	146,363	150,471	152,829	154,448	156,051	2.8%	1.6%	1.1%	1.0%
Emps. per Estab.	35.6	35.5	35.5	35.5	35.5	-0.5%	0.0%	0.0%	0.0%

OFFICE FURNITURE MANUFACTURING INDUSTRY
(NAICS 33721)

SIZE OF FIRM INDUSTRY ESTIMATES

Year	Establishments by Size of Firm									Total
	1-4 Emps.	5-9 Emps.	10-19 Emps.	20-49 Emps.	50-99 Emps.	100-249 Emps.	250-499 Emps.	500+ Emps.	Unknown Emps.	
2006	1,182	714	757	797	391	232	58	22	143	4,297
2008	1,181	713	756	797	391	232	58	22	143	4,294
2009	1,180	713	756	796	391	232	58	22	143	4,291
Sales ($Millions) by Size of Firm										**Total**
2006	368	741	2,042	4,966	2,761	4,646	2,397	4,488	884	23,294
2008	372	748	2,062	5,015	2,788	4,692	2,421	4,532	887	23,517
2009	375	755	2,082	5,064	2,816	4,738	2,444	4,577	896	23,747
Employment by Size of Firm										**Total**
2006	3,545	4,283	11,349	25,517	26,212	35,488	19,862	17,073	9,088	152,417
2008	3,543	4,280	11,342	25,501	26,196	35,466	19,850	17,062	9,024	152,263
2009	3,541	4,277	11,335	25,485	26,180	35,444	19,837	17,052	9,024	152,174

SUB-INDUSTRIES — 2007 INDUSTRY ESTIMATES

Sub-Industries	Total Establishments	Total Employment	Total Sales ($M)
Wood office furniture	2,207	102,277	15,901
Wood office chairs, benches and stools	60	2,387	155
Benches, office: wood	32	514	77
Chairs, office: padded, upholstered, or	177	12,046	1,516
Stools, office: wood	7	29	7
Wood office filing cabinets and	160	2,191	256
Bookcases, office: wood	35	334	172
Cabinets, office: wood	1,267	14,951	1,308
Filing cabinets (boxes), office: wood	25	293	17
Wood office desks and tables	46	481	39
Desks, office: wood	106	6,238	305
Tables, office: wood	57	1,003	75
Panel systems and partitions (free-	117	9,671	3,465

MEDICAL EQUIPMENT & SUPPLIES MFG. INDUSTRY (NAICS 33911)

INDUSTRY DEFINITION

NAICS 33911: Medical Equipment and Supplies Manufacturing This industry comprises establishments primarily engaged in manufacturing medical equipment and supplies. Examples of products made by these establishments are laboratory apparatus and furniture, surgical and medical instruments, surgical appliances and supplies, dental equipment and supplies, orthodontic goods, dentures, and orthodontic appliances.

INDUSTRY ESTABLISHMENTS, SALES & EMPLOYMENT TRENDS

	Year					Percent Change Year-to-Year			
	2005	2006	2007	2008	2009	05-06	06-07	07-08	08-09
Establishments	12,335	12,208	12,082	12,056	12,031	-1.0%	-1.0%	-0.2%	-0.2%
Sales ($Millions)	97,621	104,262	110,565	117,109	123,623	6.8%	6.0%	5.9%	5.6%
Employment	319,271	314,155	310,991	310,365	309,677	-1.6%	-1.0%	-0.2%	-0.2%

INDUSTRY RATIOS

(Industry Averages)	Year					Percent Change Year-to-Year			
	2005	2006	2007	2008	2009	05-06	06-07	07-08	08-09
Sales ($M)/Estab.	7.91	8.54	9.15	9.71	10.27	7.9%	7.2%	6.1%	5.8%
Sales ($) per Emp.	305,762	331,880	355,526	377,327	399,200	8.5%	7.1%	6.1%	5.8%
Emps. per Estab.	25.9	25.7	25.7	25.7	25.7	-0.6%	0.0%	0.0%	0.0%

MEDICAL EQUIPMENT & SUPPLIES MFG. INDUSTRY (NAICS 33911)

SIZE OF FIRM INDUSTRY ESTIMATES

Year	Establishments by Size of Firm									Total
	1-4 Emps.	5-9 Emps.	10-19 Emps.	20-49 Emps.	50-99 Emps.	100-249 Emps.	250-499 Emps.	500+ Emps.	Unknown Emps.	
2006	6,306	2,173	1,360	1,069	435	363	138	92	147	12,082
2008	6,293	2,168	1,357	1,067	434	362	137	92	147	12,056
2009	6,280	2,164	1,354	1,064	433	361	137	92	147	12,031
Sales ($Millions) by Size of Firm										**Total**
2006	3,640	3,512	5,494	16,040	13,295	17,592	14,302	35,671	1,018	110,565
2008	3,856	3,720	5,820	16,989	14,082	18,633	15,148	37,781	1,081	117,109
2009	4,070	3,927	6,144	17,935	14,866	19,670	15,992	39,884	1,136	123,623
Employment by Size of Firm										**Total**
2006	18,919	13,037	20,396	35,268	28,682	55,146	47,075	83,059	9,408	310,991
2008	18,879	13,010	20,354	35,195	28,622	55,031	46,978	82,887	9,408	310,365
2009	18,840	12,983	20,312	35,122	28,563	54,917	46,880	82,715	9,344	309,677

SUB-INDUSTRIES – 2007 INDUSTRY ESTIMATES

Sub-Industries	Total Establishments	Total Employment	Total Sales ($M)
Surgical and medical instruments	7,066	166,602	49,386
Ophthalmic instruments and apparatus	260	2,945	211
Diagnostic apparatus, medical	1,472	25,809	5,974
Veterinarians' instruments and	159	657	71
Rifles, for propelling hypodermics into	7	6	0
Surgical instruments and apparatus	1,732	89,208	52,172
Medical instruments and equipment,	1,115	23,908	2,480
Inhalation therapy equipment	72	829	32
Operating tables	18	98	93
Oxygen tents	11	207	37
Physiotherapy equipment, electrical	65	234	45
Skin grafting equipment	36	110	24
Stethoscopes and stethographs	14	24	2
Ultrasonic medical cleaning equipment	54	352	38

SIGN MANUFACTURING
(NAICS 33995)

INDUSTRY DEFINITION

NAICS 33995: Sign Manufacturing Industry. This industry comprises establishments primarily engaged in manufacturing signs and related displays of all materials (except printing paper and paperboard signs, notices, displays).

INDUSTRY ESTABLISHMENTS, SALES & EMPLOYMENT TRENDS

	Year					Percent Change Year-to-Year			
	2005	2006	2007	2008	2009	05-06	06-07	07-08	08-09
Establishments	6,338	6,462	6,524	6,587	6,650	1.9%	1.0%	1.0%	1.0%
Sales ($Millions)	10,619	11,541	11,994	12,393	12,798	8.7%	3.9%	3.3%	3.3%
Employment	86,733	90,217	91,069	91,929	92,798	4.0%	0.9%	0.9%	0.9%

INDUSTRY RATIOS

	Year					Percent Change Year-to-Year			
(Industry Averages)	2005	2006	2007	2008	2009	05-06	06-07	07-08	08-09
Sales ($M)/Estab.	1.68	1.79	1.84	1.88	1.92	6.6%	2.9%	2.3%	2.3%
Sales ($) per Emp.	122,438	127,925	131,706	134,808	137,917	4.5%	3.0%	2.4%	2.3%
Emps. per Estab.	13.7	14.0	14.0	14.0	14.0	2.0%	0.0%	0.0%	0.0%

SIGN MANUFACTURING
(NAICS 33995)

SIZE OF FIRM INDUSTRY ESTIMATES

Year	Establishments by Size of Firm									
	1-4 Emps.	5-9 Emps.	10-19 Emps.	20-49 Emps.	50-99 Emps.	100-249 Emps.	250-499 Emps.	500+ Emps.	Unknown Emps.	Total
2006	3,391	1,205	861	653	235	126	21	1	33	6,524
2008	3,423	1,217	869	659	238	128	22	1	33	6,587
2009	3,457	1,228	877	666	240	129	22	1	33	6,650
	Sales ($Millions) by Size of Firm									Total
2006	723	642	1,285	2,366	1,856	2,962	1,532	449	179	11,994
2008	747	664	1,327	2,445	1,918	3,061	1,583	464	183	12,393
2009	772	686	1,371	2,526	1,981	3,162	1,635	479	188	12,798
	Employment by Size of Firm									Total
2006	6,782	7,230	12,050	21,546	15,294	18,314	6,609	1,326	1,920	91,069
2008	6,847	7,299	12,166	21,753	15,441	18,490	6,673	1,339	1,920	91,929
2009	6,913	7,370	12,283	21,963	15,590	18,669	6,738	1,352	1,920	92,798

SUB-INDUSTRIES — 2007 INDUSTRY ESTIMATES

Sub-Industries	Total Establishments	Total Employment	Total Sales ($M)
Signs and advertising specialties	5,400	54,997	6,291
Electric signs	228	10,568	1,724
Neon signs	223	4,195	450
Scoreboards, electric	14	630	59
Advertising artwork	82	879	107
Advertising novelties	108	4,378	546
Displays and cutouts, window and lobby	110	7,199	1,423
Displays, paint process	15	560	55
Letters for signs, metal	15	268	33
Name plates: except engraved, etched,	18	1,330	630
Signs, not made in custom sign painting	311	6,065	678

AUTOMOBILE & OTHER VEHICLES WHOLESALE (NAICS 42311)

INDUSTRY DEFINITION

NAICS 42311: Automobile & Other Vehicle Wholesale. This industry comprises establishments primarily engaged in wholesaling new and used passenger automobiles, trucks, trailers, and other motor vehicles, such as motorcycles, motor homes, and snowmobiles.

INDUSTRY ESTABLISHMENTS, SALES & EMPLOYMENT TRENDS

	Year					Percent Change Year-to-Year			
	2005	2006	2007	2008	2009	05-06	06-07	07-08	08-09
Establishments	6,579	6,369	6,159	5,949	5,745	-3.2%	-3.3%	-3.4%	-3.4%
Sales ($Millions)	57,277	55,564	56,897	57,659	60,435	-3.0%	2.4%	1.3%	4.8%
Employment	128,062	120,763	116,825	112,624	112,624	-5.7%	-3.3%	-3.6%	0.0%

INDUSTRY RATIOS

(Industry Averages)	Year					Percent Change Year-to-Year			
	2005	2006	2007	2008	2009	05-06	06-07	07-08	08-09
Sales ($M)/Estab.	8.71	8.72	9.24	9.69	10.52	0.2%	5.9%	4.9%	8.5%
Sales ($) per Emp.	447,260	460,107	487,028	511,966	536,612	2.9%	5.9%	5.1%	4.8%
Emps. per Estab.	19.5	19.0	19.0	18.9	19.6	-2.6%	0.0%	-0.2%	3.5%

Automobile & Other Vehicles Wholesale (NAICS 42311)

Size of Firm Industry Estimates

Year	Establishments by Size of Firm									Total
	1-4 Emps.	5-9 Emps.	10-19 Emps.	20-49 Emps.	50-99 Emps.	100-249 Emps.	250-499 Emps.	500+ Emps.	Unknown Emps.	Total
2006	2,835	918	780	944	410	109	22	5	135	6,159
2008	2,738	887	754	912	396	106	21	4	130	5,949
2009	2,644	857	728	881	382	102	21	4	126	5,745
	Sales ($Millions) by Size of Firm									Total
2006	2,534	2,873	4,709	11,604	13,743	9,779	3,427	5,329	2,899	56,897
2008	2,571	2,915	4,778	11,774	13,945	9,922	3,477	5,407	2,869	57,659
2009	2,695	3,056	5,008	12,341	14,616	10,400	3,644	5,667	3,008	60,435
	Employment by Size of Firm									Total
2006	5,669	5,509	11,705	31,150	27,055	14,984	7,522	4,398	8,832	116,825
2008	5,475	5,321	11,305	30,086	26,131	14,472	7,265	4,248	8,320	112,624
2009	5,475	5,321	11,305	30,086	26,131	14,472	7,265	4,248	8,320	112,624

Sub-Industries — 2007 Industry Estimates

Sub-Industries	Total Establishments	Total Employment	Total Sales ($M)
Automobiles and other motor vehicles	1,579	25,572	11,619
Automotive brokers	636	3,992	862
Automobile auction	501	29,316	9,816
Automobiles	1,409	14,171	18,020
Trucks, noncommercial	51	498	632
Vans, noncommercial	6	269	57
Commercial vehicles	1,536	38,709	14,383
Recreational vehicles, motor homes,	174	1,827	207
Motorized cycles	40	258	54
Mopeds	4	9	2
Motor scooters	70	399	91
Motorcycles	153	1,807	1,155

Motor Vehicle Parts & Supplies Wholesales (NAICS 42312)

Industry Definition

NAICS 42312: Motor Vehicle Parts & Supplies Wholesale. Establishments primarily engaged in the wholesale distribution of new and used passenger automobiles, trucks, trailers, and other motor vehicles, including motorcycles, motor homes, and snowmobiles. Automotive distributors primarily engaged in selling at retail to individual consumers for personal use, and also selling a limited amount of new and used passenger automobiles and trucks at wholesale, are classified in SIC 5511.

Industry Establishments, Sales & Employment Trends

	Year					Percent Change Year-to-Year			
	2005	2006	2007	2008	2009	05-06	06-07	07-08	08-09
Establishments	14,110	14,814	15,518	16,012	16,521	5.0%	4.8%	3.2%	3.2%
Sales ($Millions)	96,557	95,763	100,005	102,277	104,590	-0.8%	4.4%	2.3%	2.3%
Employment	220,491	223,186	233,942	241,284	248,842	1.2%	4.8%	3.1%	3.1%

Industry Ratios

	Year					Percent Change Year-to-Year			
(Industry Averages)	2005	2006	2007	2008	2009	05-06	06-07	07-08	08-09
Sales ($M)/Estab.	6.84	6.46	6.44	6.39	6.33	-5.5%	-0.3%	-0.9%	-0.9%
Sales ($) per Emp.	437,919	429,071	427,475	423,886	420,307	-2.0%	-0.4%	-0.8%	-0.8%
Emps. per Estab.	15.6	15.1	15.1	15.1	15.1	-3.6%	0.1%	0.0%	0.0%

MOTOR VEHICLE PARTS & SUPPLIES WHOLESALES (NAICS 42312)

SIZE OF FIRM INDUSTRY ESTIMATES

Year	Establishments by Size of Firm									Total
	1-4 Emps.	5-9 Emps.	10-19 Emps.	20-49 Emps.	50-99 Emps.	100-249 Emps.	250-499 Emps.	500+ Emps.	Unknown Emps.	
2006	6,614	3,589	2,681	1,550	513	204	44	18	303	15,518
2008	6,825	3,703	2,766	1,600	529	211	46	19	313	16,012
2009	7,042	3,821	2,855	1,651	546	218	47	20	323	16,521
	Sales ($Millions) by Size of Firm									Total
2006	5,238	8,883	13,272	18,420	15,638	16,783	7,027	9,105	5,639	100,005
2008	5,359	9,087	13,577	18,844	15,998	17,169	7,189	9,314	5,739	102,277
2009	5,482	9,296	13,889	19,276	16,365	17,564	7,354	9,528	5,836	104,590
	Employment by Size of Firm									Total
2006	13,228	21,534	40,217	51,166	33,849	28,016	13,308	13,233	19,392	233,942
2008	13,649	22,219	41,497	52,794	34,926	28,907	13,732	13,654	19,904	241,284
2009	14,084	22,926	42,818	54,475	36,038	29,828	14,169	14,088	20,416	248,842

SUB-INDUSTRIES — 2007 INDUSTRY ESTIMATES

Sub-Industries	Total Establishments	Total Employment	Total Sales ($M)
Automobiles and other motor vehicles	3,979	51,207	20,422
Automotive brokers	1,602	7,994	1,515
Automobile auction	1,261	58,704	17,253
Automobiles	3,549	28,378	31,672
Trucks, noncommercial	129	997	1,110
Vans, noncommercial	15	538	100
Commercial vehicles	3,871	77,515	25,281
Recreational vehicles, motor homes,	437	3,658	364
Motorized cycles	100	516	95
Mopeds	10	19	3
Motor scooters	176	799	160
Motorcycles	387	3,618	2,030

FURNITURE WHOLESALE INDUSTRY
(NAICS 42321)

INDUSTRY DEFINITION

NAICS 42321: Furniture Wholesale. Establishments primarily engaged in the wholesale distribution of furniture, including bedsprings, mattresses, and other household furniture; office furniture; and furniture for public parks and buildings. Establishments primarily engaged in the wholesale distribution of partitions, shelving, lockers, and store fixtures are classified in SIC 5046.

INDUSTRY ESTABLISHMENTS, SALES & EMPLOYMENT TRENDS

	Year					Percent Change Year-to-Year			
	2005	2006	2007	2008	2009	05-06	06-07	07-08	08-09
Establishments	5,791	5,622	5,454	5,281	5,113	-2.9%	-3.0%	-3.2%	-3.2%
Sales ($Millions)	19,237	17,856	17,255	16,635	15,505	-7.2%	-3.4%	-3.6%	-6.8%
Employment	77,823	75,339	73,128	70,804	68,543	-3.2%	-2.9%	-3.2%	-3.2%

INDUSTRY RATIOS

(Industry Averages)	Year					Percent Change Year-to-Year			
	2005	2006	2007	2008	2009	05-06	06-07	07-08	08-09
Sales ($M)/Estab.	3.32	3.18	3.16	3.15	3.03	-4.4%	-0.4%	-0.4%	-3.7%
Sales ($) per Emp.	247,184	237,011	235,950	234,944	226,204	-4.1%	-0.4%	-0.4%	-3.7%
Emps. per Estab.	13.4	13.4	13.4	13.4	13.4	-0.3%	0.1%	0.0%	0.0%

FURNITURE WHOLESALE INDUSTRY
(NAICS 42321)

SIZE OF FIRM INDUSTRY ESTIMATES

Year	Establishments by Size of Firm									Total
	1-4 Emps.	5-9 Emps.	10-19 Emps.	20-49 Emps.	50-99 Emps.	100-249 Emps.	250-499 Emps.	500+ Emps.	Unknown Emps.	
2006	2,881	974	701	523	151	56	11	0	157	5,454
2008	2,790	943	679	506	147	55	11	0	152	5,281
2009	2,701	913	657	490	142	53	10	0	147	5,113
	Sales ($Millions) by Size of Firm									**Total**
2006	1,381	1,214	2,622	4,462	2,905	2,702	795	0	1,174	17,255
2008	1,332	1,170	2,528	4,302	2,801	2,605	767	0	1,131	16,635
2009	1,241	1,091	2,356	4,010	2,611	2,428	715	0	1,053	15,505
	Employment by Size of Firm									**Total**
2006	8,643	5,842	9,816	17,253	9,847	7,551	4,257	0	9,920	73,128
2008	8,369	5,656	9,504	16,706	9,535	7,311	4,122	0	9,600	70,804
2009	8,104	5,477	9,203	16,176	9,232	7,079	3,991	0	9,280	68,543

SUB-INDUSTRIES – 2007 INDUSTRY ESTIMATES

Sub-Industries	Total Establishments	Total Employment	Total Sales ($M)
Furniture	2,636	26,394	4,723
Office and public building furniture	348	5,254	1,072
Bar furniture	19	142	17
Cafeteria furniture	5	20	7
Church pews	49	191	24
Filing units	100	1,017	142
Lockers	37	345	71
Office furniture, nec	951	21,585	7,979
Public building furniture, nec	38	562	78
Restaurant furniture, nec	17	228	30
School desks	45	450	86
Theater seats	7	65	7
Household furniture	599	10,864	2,048
Beds and bedding	248	2,609	472
Other furniture	355	3,400	501

HOME FURNISHINGS WHOLESALE INDUSTRY (NAICS 42322)

INDUSTRY DEFINITION

NAICS 42322: Home Furnishings Wholesales. Establishments primarily engaged in the wholesale distribution of homefurnishings and housewares, including antiques; china; glassware and earthenware; lamps (including electric); curtains and draperies; linens and towels; and carpets, linoleum, and all other types of hard and soft surface floor coverings. Wholesale distribution of other electrical household goods is classified in SIC 5064; precious metal flatware in SIC 5094.

INDUSTRY ESTABLISHMENTS, SALES & EMPLOYMENT TRENDS

	Year					Percent Change Year-to-Year			
	2005	2006	2007	2008	2009	05-06	06-07	07-08	08-09
Establishments	7,804	7,791	7,779	7,700	7,622	-0.2%	-0.2%	-1.0%	-1.0%
Sales ($Millions)	31,125	30,993	31,360	31,311	31,222	-0.4%	1.2%	-0.2%	-0.3%
Employment	135,296	132,769	132,613	131,394	129,864	-1.9%	-0.1%	-0.9%	-1.2%

INDUSTRY RATIOS

	Year					Percent Change Year-to-Year			
(Industry Averages)	2005	2006	2007	2008	2009	05-06	06-07	07-08	08-09
Sales ($M)/Estab.	3.99	3.98	4.03	4.07	4.10	-0.3%	1.4%	0.9%	0.7%
Sales ($) per Emp.	230,048	233,433	236,479	238,297	240,423	1.5%	1.3%	0.8%	0.9%
Emps. per Estab.	17.3	17.0	17.0	17.1	17.0	-1.7%	0.0%	0.1%	-0.2%

HOME FURNISHINGS WHOLESALE INDUSTRY (NAICS 42322)

SIZE OF FIRM INDUSTRY ESTIMATES

Year	Establishments by Size of Firm									Total
	1-4 Emps.	5-9 Emps.	10-19 Emps.	20-49 Emps.	50-99 Emps.	100-249 Emps.	250-499 Emps.	500+ Emps.	Unknown Emps.	
2006	3,677	1,459	1,028	681	223	99	29	4	580	7,779
2008	3,640	1,444	1,018	674	220	98	29	4	575	7,700
2009	3,604	1,430	1,008	667	218	97	28	4	569	7,622
Sales ($Millions) by Size of Firm										**Total**
2006	1,882	1,942	3,474	6,066	4,533	5,233	3,007	1,007	4,216	31,360
2008	1,879	1,938	3,467	6,054	4,524	5,222	3,001	1,005	4,221	31,311
2009	1,875	1,934	3,460	6,041	4,515	5,212	2,995	1,003	4,188	31,222
Employment by Size of Firm										**Total**
2006	11,032	8,754	14,398	21,795	14,464	13,520	9,201	2,330	37,120	132,613
2008	10,921	8,665	14,253	21,575	14,318	13,383	9,108	2,306	36,864	131,394
2009	10,811	8,578	14,109	21,358	14,173	13,248	9,016	2,283	36,288	129,864

SUB-INDUSTRIES – 2007 INDUSTRY ESTIMATES

Sub-Industries	Total Establishments	Total Employment	Total Sales ($M)
Homefurnishings	1,233	23,254	4,906
Kitchenware	875	14,787	2,946
Linens and towels	452	9,140	2,864
Window furnishings	867	12,546	1,781
Floor coverings	1,287	27,730	10,606
Carpets	682	13,151	2,282
Floor cushion and padding	41	470	105
Resilient floor coverings: tile or sheet	65	1,482	439
Rugs	283	4,063	697
Wood flooring	139	3,041	857
Decorative home furnishings and	813	8,492	1,998
Decorating supplies	107	1,278	132
Frames and framing, picture and mirror	367	5,641	757
Mirrors and pictures, framed and	75	1,334	171
Pottery	279	2,317	305
Fireplace equipment and accessories	75	1,586	177
Home furnishings, wicker, rattan or reed	37	572	87
Lamps: floor, boudoir, desk	99	1,731	248

OFFICE EQUIPMENT WHOLESALES INDUSTRY (NAICS 42342)

INDUSTRY DEFINITION

NAICS 42342: Office Equipment Wholesales. Establishments primarily engaged in the wholesale distribution of office machines and related equipment, including photocopy and microfilm equipment and safes and vaults. These establishments frequently also sell office supplies, but wholesaling most office supplies is classified in SIC 5111-5113. Wholesaling office furniture is classified in SIC 5021, and wholesaling computers and peripheral equipment is classified in SIC 5045.

INDUSTRY ESTABLISHMENTS, SALES & EMPLOYMENT TRENDS

	Year					Percent Change Year-to-Year			
	2005	2006	2007	2008	2009	05-06	06-07	07-08	08-09
Establishments	7,847	7,637	7,428	7,476	7,524	-2.7%	-2.7%	0.6%	0.6%
Sales ($Millions)	38,131	39,316	39,884	41,600	43,344	3.1%	1.4%	4.3%	4.2%
Employment	172,626	171,494	166,782	167,812	168,912	-0.7%	-2.7%	0.6%	0.7%

INDUSTRY RATIOS

(Industry Averages)	Year					Percent Change Year-to-Year			
	2005	2006	2007	2008	2009	05-06	06-07	07-08	08-09
Sales ($M)/Estab.	4.86	5.15	5.37	5.56	5.76	5.9%	4.3%	3.6%	3.5%
Sales ($) per Emp.	220,886	229,259	239,140	247,899	256,607	3.8%	4.3%	3.7%	3.5%
Emps. per Estab.	22.0	22.5	22.5	22.4	22.4	2.1%	0.0%	0.0%	0.0%

OFFICE EQUIPMENT WHOLESALES INDUSTRY (NAICS 42342)

SIZE OF FIRM INDUSTRY ESTIMATES

Year	Establishments by Size of Firm									Total
	1-4 Emps.	5-9 Emps.	10-19 Emps.	20-49 Emps.	50-99 Emps.	100-249 Emps.	250-499 Emps.	500+ Emps.	Unknown Emps.	Total
2006	2,848	1,370	1,184	1,061	410	219	39	14	283	7,428
2008	2,866	1,379	1,192	1,068	412	220	40	14	285	7,476
2009	2,885	1,388	1,200	1,075	415	222	40	14	286	7,524
	Sales ($Millions) by Size of Firm									Total
2006	1,236	1,635	3,341	7,485	5,998	8,547	5,221	4,585	1,836	39,884
2008	1,289	1,706	3,485	7,808	6,257	8,916	5,447	4,783	1,909	41,600
2009	1,343	1,777	3,631	8,135	6,519	9,290	5,675	4,984	1,990	43,344
	Employment by Size of Firm									Total
2006	8,543	8,222	16,581	35,024	26,209	30,857	12,821	10,476	18,048	166,782
2008	8,599	8,276	16,689	35,252	26,379	31,057	12,904	10,544	18,112	167,812
2009	8,655	8,329	16,797	35,481	26,550	31,259	12,988	10,613	18,240	168,912

SUB-INDUSTRIES – 2007 INDUSTRY ESTIMATES

Sub-Industries	Total Establishments	Total Employment	Total Sales ($M)
Office equipment	4,109	96,378	20,034
Calculating machines	813	9,576	2,079
Copying equipment	661	14,635	1,659
Blueprinting equipment	44	316	40
Duplicating machines	180	6,509	343
Microfilm equipment	64	1,341	162
Micrographic equipment	38	731	83
Mimeograph machines	2	106	8
Photocopy machines	657	25,611	14,007
Whiteprinting equipment	4	38	13
Typewriter and dictation equipment	169	2,630	220
Addressing and mailing machines	39	618	55
Addressing machines	12	347	23
Mailing machines	207	3,562	248
Bank automatic teller machines	114	1,523	532
Check writing, signing, and endorsing	69	556	76
Vaults and safes	244	2,305	303

COMPUTER & EQUIPMENT WHOLESALE INDUSTRY (NAICS 42343)

INDUSTRY DEFINITION

NAICS 42343: Computer & Peripheral Equipment and Software Wholesalers. This U.S. industry comprises establishments primarily engaged in wholesaling computers, computer peripheral equipment, loaded computer boards, and/or computer software.

INDUSTRY ESTABLISHMENTS, SALES & EMPLOYMENT TRENDS

	Year					Percent Change Year-to-Year			
	2005	2006	2007	2008	2009	05-06	06-07	07-08	08-09
Establishments	12,409	11,479	10,549	9,811	9,124	-7.5%	-8.1%	-7.0%	-7.0%
Sales ($Millions)	152,663	141,012	139,276	137,881	136,039	-7.6%	-1.2%	-1.0%	-1.3%
Employment	299,837	262,457	241,254	224,238	208,621	-12.5%	-8.1%	-7.1%	-7.0%

INDUSTRY RATIOS

	Year					Percent Change Year-to-Year			
(Industry Averages)	2005	2006	2007	2008	2009	05-06	06-07	07-08	08-09
Sales ($M)/Estab.	12.30	12.28	13.20	14.05	14.91	-0.1%	7.5%	6.5%	6.1%
Sales ($) per Emp.	509,154	537,277	577,301	614,889	652,086	5.5%	7.4%	6.5%	6.0%
Emps. per Estab.	24.2	22.9	22.9	22.9	22.9	-5.4%	0.0%	-0.1%	0.0%

COMPUTER & EQUIPMENT WHOLESALE INDUSTRY (NAICS 42343)

SIZE OF FIRM INDUSTRY ESTIMATES

Year	Establishments by Size of Firm									Total
	1-4 Emps.	5-9 Emps.	10-19 Emps.	20-49 Emps.	50-99 Emps.	100-249 Emps.	250-499 Emps.	500+ Emps.	Unknown Emps.	
2006	5,175	1,884	1,377	1,059	360	216	88	61	327	10,549
2008	4,813	1,752	1,281	985	335	201	82	56	304	9,811
2009	4,476	1,629	1,191	916	311	187	76	52	283	9,124
	Sales ($Millions) by Size of Firm									Total
2006	4,768	4,773	8,407	17,074	14,348	21,149	21,192	43,700	3,865	139,276
2008	4,721	4,726	8,324	16,906	14,207	20,941	20,984	43,270	3,802	137,881
2009	4,658	4,662	8,212	16,678	14,015	20,659	20,701	42,687	3,768	136,039
	Employment by Size of Firm									Total
2006	15,525	11,303	19,282	34,945	23,404	30,246	29,077	56,417	21,056	241,254
2008	14,438	10,512	17,932	32,498	21,766	28,128	27,041	52,467	19,456	224,238
2009	13,428	9,776	16,676	30,223	20,242	26,159	25,148	48,794	18,176	208,621

SUB-INDUSTRIES — 2007 INDUSTRY ESTIMATES

Sub-Industries	Total Establishments	Total Employment	Total Sales ($M)
Computers, peripherals, and software	4,664	110,459	58,490
Computer peripheral equipment	1,089	24,340	15,427
Disk drives	26	705	1,486
Keying equipment	9	66	24
Printers, computer	102	6,686	763
Terminals, computer	35	840	208
Accounting machines using machine	19	448	151
Anti-static equipment and devices	13	201	45
Computer software	2,526	51,066	41,416
Computers and accessories, personal	418	8,046	3,399
Computers, nec	1,590	37,304	15,539
Mainframe computers	46	923	2,282
Word processing equipment	12	170	47

HARDWARE WHOLESALE INDUSTRY
(NAICS 42371)

INDUSTRY DEFINITION

NAICS 42371: Hardware Wholesales. Establishments primarily engaged in the wholesale distribution of cutlery and general hardware, including handsaws; saw blades; brads, staples, and tacks; and bolts, nuts, rivets, and screws. Establishments primarily engaged in the wholesale distribution of nails, noninsulated wire, and screening are classified in SIC 5051.

INDUSTRY ESTABLISHMENTS, SALES & EMPLOYMENT TRENDS

	Year					Percent Change Year-to-Year			
	2005	2006	2007	2008	2009	05-06	06-07	07-08	08-09
Establishments	7,066	6,542	6,019	5,631	5,269	-7.4%	-8.0%	-6.4%	-6.4%
Sales ($Millions)	27,555	22,724	20,914	19,447	18,128	-17.5%	-8.0%	-7.0%	-6.8%
Employment	99,208	87,814	80,798	75,266	70,604	-11.5%	-8.0%	-6.8%	-6.2%

INDUSTRY RATIOS

	Year					Percent Change Year-to-Year			
(Industry Averages)	2005	2006	2007	2008	2009	05-06	06-07	07-08	08-09
Sales ($M)/Estab.	3.90	3.47	3.47	3.45	3.44	-10.9%	0.0%	-0.6%	-0.4%
Sales ($) per Emp.	277,748	258,771	258,840	258,373	256,755	-6.8%	0.0%	-0.2%	-0.6%
Emps. per Estab.	14.0	13.4	13.4	13.4	13.4	-4.4%	0.0%	-0.4%	0.3%

HARDWARE WHOLESALE INDUSTRY
(NAICS 42371)

SIZE OF FIRM INDUSTRY ESTIMATES

Year	Establishments by Size of Firm									Total
	1-4 Emps.	5-9 Emps.	10-19 Emps.	20-49 Emps.	50-99 Emps.	100-249 Emps.	250-499 Emps.	500+ Emps.	Unknown Emps.	
2006	3,022	1,141	894	594	141	60	12	4	153	6,019
2008	2,828	1,067	837	556	132	56	11	4	143	5,631
2009	2,646	999	783	520	123	52	10	4	134	5,269
Sales ($Millions) by Size of Firm										**Total**
2006	1,206	1,252	2,587	4,567	2,378	2,811	2,170	3,033	910	20,914
2008	1,123	1,166	2,410	4,253	2,214	2,618	2,021	2,825	816	19,447
2009	1,046	1,086	2,244	3,961	2,062	2,438	1,882	2,631	777	18,128
Employment by Size of Firm										**Total**
2006	9,066	6,844	12,518	19,022	8,742	8,393	3,842	2,643	9,728	80,798
2008	8,483	6,404	11,713	17,798	8,180	7,853	3,595	2,473	8,768	75,266
2009	7,937	5,992	10,960	16,653	7,654	7,348	3,363	2,314	8,384	70,604

SUB-INDUSTRIES — 2007 INDUSTRY ESTIMATES

Sub-Industries	Total Establishments	Total Employment	Total Sales ($M)
Hardware	2,686	38,937	12,818
Bolts, nuts, and screws	303	2,991	360
Bolts	208	2,642	508
Nuts (hardware)	164	3,116	627
Rivets	8	101	21
Screws	87	1,653	648
Hand tools	483	5,146	927
Cutlery	110	1,434	466
Garden tools, hand	22	167	30
Power tools and accessories	236	2,123	325
Power handtools	71	1,090	459
Saw blades	60	568	89
Miscellaneous fasteners	546	6,642	873
Brads	2	16	1
Staples	27	217	29
Tacks	6	9	1
Builders' hardware, nec	999	13,946	2,733

PRINTING & WRITING PAPER WHOLESALES (NAICS 42411)

INDUSTRY DEFINITION

NAICS 42411: Printing & Writing Paper Wholesales. Establishments primarily engaged in the wholesale distribution of printing and writing paper, including envelope paper; fine paper; and groundwood paper.

INDUSTRY ESTABLISHMENTS, SALES & EMPLOYMENT TRENDS

	Year					Percent Change Year-to-Year			
	2005	2006	2007	2008	2009	05-06	06-07	07-08	08-09
Establishments	1,754	1,660	1,566	1,491	1,419	-5.4%	-5.7%	-4.8%	-4.8%
Sales ($Millions)	12,582	12,052	11,699	11,356	11,041	-4.2%	-2.9%	-2.9%	-2.8%
Employment	34,000	32,115	30,372	28,797	27,407	-5.5%	-5.4%	-5.2%	-4.8%

INDUSTRY RATIOS

(Industry Averages)	Year					Percent Change Year-to-Year			
	2005	2006	2007	2008	2009	05-06	06-07	07-08	08-09
Sales ($M)/Estab.	7.17	7.26	7.47	7.62	7.78	1.2%	2.9%	2.0%	2.1%
Sales ($) per Emp.	370,050	375,256	385,189	394,340	402,847	1.4%	2.6%	2.4%	2.2%
Emps. per Estab.	19.4	19.3	19.4	19.3	19.3	-0.2%	0.2%	-0.4%	0.0%

PRINTING & WRITING PAPER WHOLESALES
(NAICS 42411)

SIZE OF FIRM INDUSTRY ESTIMATES

Year	Establishments by Size of Firm									Total
	1-4 Emps.	5-9 Emps.	10-19 Emps.	20-49 Emps.	50-99 Emps.	100-249 Emps.	250-499 Emps.	500+ Emps.	Unknown Emps.	
2006	741	212	226	192	69	41	2	0	88	1,566
2008	706	201	215	182	66	39	2	0	83	1,491
2009	672	192	205	174	63	37	2	0	79	1,419
	Sales ($Millions) by Size of Firm									**Total**
2006	468	468	1,072	2,119	2,104	3,862	415	0	1,191	11,699
2008	456	455	1,043	2,061	2,047	3,757	404	0	1,133	11,356
2009	443	443	1,014	2,004	1,990	3,654	393	0	1,100	11,041
	Employment by Size of Firm									**Total**
2006	2,224	1,270	3,395	6,325	4,579	6,318	694	0	5,568	30,372
2008	2,118	1,209	3,232	6,021	4,359	6,014	660	0	5,184	28,797
2009	2,016	1,151	3,077	5,732	4,150	5,726	629	0	4,928	27,407

SUB-INDUSTRIES – 2007 INDUSTRY ESTIMATES

Sub-Industries	Total Establishments	Total Employment	Total Sales ($M)
Printing and writing paper	1,009	20,635	3,128
Fine paper	172	3,905	3,514
Printing paper	353	5,562	4,769
Writing paper	33	270	289

MEN'S & BOYS' CLOTHING WHOLESALES INDUSTRY (NAICS 42432)

INDUSTRY DEFINITION

NAICS 42432: Men's & Boys' Clothing Wholesales. Establishments primarily engaged in the wholesale distribution of men's and boys' apparel and furnishings, sportswear, hosiery, underwear, nightwear, and work clothing.

INDUSTRY ESTABLISHMENTS, SALES & EMPLOYMENT TRENDS

	Year					Percent Change Year-to-Year			
	2005	2006	2007	2008	2009	05-06	06-07	07-08	08-09
Establishments	3,936	3,928	3,737	3,614	3,533	-0.2%	-4.9%	-3.3%	-2.2%
Sales ($Millions)	19,001	18,691	18,243	18,002	17,957	-1.6%	-2.4%	-1.3%	-0.2%
Employment	64,240	61,958	58,859	56,851	55,573	-3.6%	-5.0%	-3.4%	-2.2%

INDUSTRY RATIOS

(Industry Averages)	Year					Percent Change Year-to-Year			
	2005	2006	2007	2008	2009	05-06	06-07	07-08	08-09
Sales ($M)/Estab.	4.83	4.76	4.88	4.98	5.08	-1.4%	2.6%	2.0%	2.0%
Sales ($) per Emp.	295,786	301,675	309,946	316,649	323,130	2.0%	2.7%	2.2%	2.0%
Emps. per Estab.	16.3	15.8	15.7	15.7	15.7	-3.4%	-0.1%	-0.1%	0.0%

MEN'S & BOYS' CLOTHING WHOLESALES INDUSTRY (NAICS 42432)

SIZE OF FIRM INDUSTRY ESTIMATES

Year	Establishments by Size of Firm									
	1-4 Emps.	5-9 Emps.	10-19 Emps.	20-49 Emps.	50-99 Emps.	100-249 Emps.	250-499 Emps.	500+ Emps.	Unknown Emps.	Total
2006	2,058	626	451	305	117	65	19	5	92	3,737
2008	1,990	606	436	295	113	63	18	5	89	3,614
2009	1,945	592	426	288	110	62	18	5	87	3,533
	Sales ($Millions) by Size of Firm									Total
2006	1,297	1,382	2,131	3,397	2,638	3,520	2,516	788	574	18,243
2008	1,280	1,364	2,104	3,354	2,604	3,474	2,484	778	560	18,002
2009	1,277	1,361	2,099	3,345	2,597	3,466	2,478	776	558	17,957
	Employment by Size of Firm									Total
2006	6,173	3,759	6,312	9,763	7,591	9,060	6,122	4,255	5,824	58,859
2008	5,969	3,635	6,103	9,440	7,340	8,761	5,920	4,114	5,568	56,851
2009	5,836	3,553	5,966	9,229	7,176	8,565	5,787	4,022	5,440	55,573

SUB-INDUSTRIES – 2007 INDUSTRY ESTIMATES

Sub-Industries	Total Establishments	Total Employment	Total Sales ($M)
Men's and boy's clothing	1,763	27,282	9,371
Men's and boys' hats, scarves, and	243	3,532	849
Men's and boys' robes, nightwear, and	52	1,077	158
Men's and boys' outerwear	122	2,013	639
Men's and boys' furnishings	205	2,361	734
Men's and boys' suits and trousers	21	487	133
Suits, men's and boys'	18	644	90
Trousers, men's and boys'	19	654	492
Men's and boys' sportswear and work	147	1,650	343
Beachwear, men's and boys'	19	251	71
Sportswear, men's and boys'	591	11,121	3,349
Uniforms, men's and boys'	189	3,008	516
Work clothing, men's and boys'	70	569	123
Shirts, men's and boys'	246	3,838	1,126
Sweaters, men's and boys'	32	372	249

WOMEN'S & CHILDREN'S CLOTHING WHOLESALE (NAICS 42433)

INDUSTRY DEFINITION

NAICS 42433: Women's & Children's Clothing Wholesales.
Establishments primarily engaged in the wholesale distribution of women's, children's, and infants' clothing and accessories, including hosiery, lingerie, millinery, and furs.

INDUSTRY ESTABLISHMENTS, SALES & EMPLOYMENT TRENDS

	Year					Percent Change Year-to-Year			
	2005	2006	2007	2008	2009	05-06	06-07	07-08	08-09
Establishments	6,748	6,539	6,329	6,123	5,920	-3.1%	-3.2%	-3.3%	-3.3%
Sales ($Millions)	33,766	31,642	33,006	34,077	35,025	-6.3%	4.3%	3.2%	2.8%
Employment	90,480	81,894	79,366	76,869	74,353	-9.5%	-3.1%	-3.1%	-3.3%

INDUSTRY RATIOS

	Year					Percent Change Year-to-Year			
(Industry Averages)	2005	2006	2007	2008	2009	05-06	06-07	07-08	08-09
Sales ($M)/Estab.	5.00	4.84	5.21	5.57	5.92	-3.3%	7.8%	6.7%	6.3%
Sales ($) per Emp.	373,184	386,381	415,874	443,315	471,060	3.5%	7.6%	6.6%	6.3%
Emps. per Estab.	13.4	12.5	12.5	12.6	12.6	-6.6%	0.1%	0.1%	0.0%

WOMEN'S & CHILDREN'S CLOTHING WHOLESALE (NAICS 42433)

SIZE OF FIRM INDUSTRY ESTIMATES

Year	Establishments by Size of Firm									Total
	1-4 Emps.	5-9 Emps.	10-19 Emps.	20-49 Emps.	50-99 Emps.	100-249 Emps.	250-499 Emps.	500+ Emps.	Unknown Emps.	Total
2006	3,841	951	621	443	196	90	14	7	169	6,329
2008	3,716	920	601	428	190	87	13	6	164	6,123
2009	3,593	889	581	414	183	84	13	6	158	5,920
	Sales ($Millions) by Size of Firm									Total
2006	2,668	1,981	3,021	5,843	6,106	6,496	3,350	2,980	561	33,006
2008	2,754	2,045	3,119	6,032	6,303	6,705	3,459	3,076	584	34,077
2009	2,831	2,102	3,205	6,199	6,478	6,892	3,555	3,162	602	35,025
	Employment by Size of Firm									Total
2006	7,683	5,705	8,699	13,283	12,548	11,727	4,363	4,670	10,688	79,366
2008	7,432	5,519	8,415	12,849	12,139	11,344	4,221	4,518	10,432	76,869
2009	7,186	5,337	8,137	12,425	11,738	10,970	4,081	4,368	10,112	74,353

SUB-INDUSTRIES – 2007 INDUSTRY ESTIMATES

Sub-Industries	Total Establishments	Total Employment	Total Sales ($M)
Women's and children's clothing	3,284	38,002	16,951
Women's and children's outerwear	172	2,286	891
Women's and children's lingerie and	347	7,033	1,842
Women's and children's sportswear and	85	1,563	468
Sportswear, women's and children's	461	8,433	5,067
Swimsuits: women's, children's, and	58	644	206
Women's and children's accessories	990	11,957	4,643
Children's goods	550	4,059	1,457
Women's and children's dresses, suits,	73	742	319
Blouses	31	629	175
Dresses	124	1,899	319
Skirts	7	68	28
Suits: women's, children's, and infants'	6	35	7
Coordinate sets: women's, children's,	13	265	77
Hospital gowns, women's and children's	7	69	31
Rack merchandise jobbers	11	88	21
Sweaters, women's and children's	56	1,023	414
Uniforms, women's and children's	56	572	89

GENERAL-LINE GROCERY WHOLESALE INDUSTRY (NAICS 42441)

INDUSTRY DEFINITION

NAICS 42441: General-Line Grocery Wholesale. Establishments primarily engaged in the wholesale distribution of a general line of groceries. Establishments primarily engaged in roasting coffee, blending tea, or grinding and packaging spices are classified under food processing.

INDUSTRY ESTABLISHMENTS, SALES & EMPLOYMENT TRENDS

	Year					Percent Change Year-to-Year			
	2005	2006	2007	2008	2009	05-06	06-07	07-08	08-09
Establishments	3,667	3,517	3,367	3,250	3,137	-4.1%	-4.3%	-3.5%	-3.5%
Sales ($Millions)	116,954	119,887	114,835	110,366	106,049	2.5%	-4.2%	-3.9%	-3.9%
Employment	135,587	138,310	132,389	127,833	123,357	2.0%	-4.3%	-3.4%	-3.5%

INDUSTRY RATIOS

(Industry Averages)	Year					Percent Change Year-to-Year			
	2005	2006	2007	2008	2009	05-06	06-07	07-08	08-09
Sales ($M)/Estab.	31.89	34.09	34.11	33.96	33.81	6.9%	0.1%	-0.4%	-0.4%
Sales ($) per Emp.	862,578	866,797	867,407	863,362	859,691	0.5%	0.1%	-0.5%	-0.4%
Emps. per Estab.	37.0	39.3	39.3	39.3	39.3	6.4%	0.0%	0.0%	0.0%

GENERAL-LINE GROCERY WHOLESALE INDUSTRY (NAICS 42441)

SIZE OF FIRM INDUSTRY ESTIMATES

Year	Establishments by Size of Firm									Total
	1-4 Emps.	5-9 Emps.	10-19 Emps.	20-49 Emps.	50-99 Emps.	100-249 Emps.	250-499 Emps.	500+ Emps.	Unknown Emps.	
2006	1,659	504	364	278	129	104	76	62	191	3,367
2008	1,601	486	352	269	125	101	73	60	185	3,250
2009	1,545	469	339	259	121	97	71	58	178	3,137
	Sales ($Millions) by Size of Firm									Total
2006	1,656	4,729	4,364	5,334	5,466	11,244	29,088	49,606	3,348	114,835
2008	1,591	4,544	4,194	5,126	5,253	10,805	27,952	47,669	3,231	110,366
2009	1,529	4,367	4,030	4,926	5,048	10,383	26,861	45,808	3,097	106,049
	Employment by Size of Firm									Total
2006	4,977	3,024	5,465	8,907	8,544	15,360	25,477	48,155	12,480	132,389
2008	4,804	2,919	5,275	8,597	8,247	14,826	24,591	46,479	12,096	127,833
2009	4,636	2,817	5,091	8,298	7,960	14,310	23,735	44,862	11,648	123,357

SUB-INDUSTRIES — 2007 INDUSTRY ESTIMATES

Sub-Industries	Total Establishments	Total Employment	Total Sales ($M)
Groceries, general line	1,861	94,933	99,620
Food brokers	1,506	37,457	15,216

BEER & ALE WHOLESALE INDUSTRY
(NAICS 42481)

INDUSTRY DEFINITION

NAICS 42481: Beer & Ale Wholesale. Establishments
primarily engaged in the wholesale distribution of beer, ale, porter, and
other fermented malt beverages.

INDUSTRY ESTABLISHMENTS, SALES & EMPLOYMENT TRENDS

	Year					Percent Change Year-to-Year			
	2005	2006	2007	2008	2009	05-06	06-07	07-08	08-09
Establishments	2,485	2,386	2,286	2,205	2,134	-4.0%	-4.2%	-3.6%	-3.2%
Sales ($Millions)	36,051	37,187	38,976	40,632	42,289	3.1%	4.8%	4.2%	4.1%
Employment	113,464	107,155	102,731	99,153	96,048	-5.6%	-4.1%	-3.5%	-3.1%

INDUSTRY RATIOS

(Industry Averages)	Year					Percent Change Year-to-Year			
	2005	2006	2007	2008	2009	05-06	06-07	07-08	08-09
Sales ($M)/Estab.	14.51	15.59	17.05	18.43	19.81	7.4%	9.4%	8.1%	7.5%
Sales ($) per Emp.	317,734	347,035	379,398	409,789	440,284	9.2%	9.3%	8.0%	7.4%
Emps. per Estab.	45.7	44.9	44.9	45.0	45.0	-1.6%	0.0%	0.1%	0.0%

BEER & ALE WHOLESALE INDUSTRY (NAICS 42481)

SIZE OF FIRM INDUSTRY ESTIMATES

Year	1-4 Emps.	5-9 Emps.	10-19 Emps.	20-49 Emps.	50-99 Emps.	100-249 Emps.	250-499 Emps.	500+ Emps.	Unknown Emps.	Total
Establishments by Size of Firm										
2006	472	215	327	504	339	231	38	2	155	2,286
2008	455	207	316	486	327	222	37	2	149	2,205
2009	441	201	306	471	316	215	35	2	144	2,134
Sales ($Millions) by Size of Firm										Total
2006	957	488	1,795	5,655	10,067	12,866	5,425	611	1,113	38,976
2008	997	508	1,871	5,893	10,491	13,409	5,653	637	1,172	40,632
2009	1,038	529	1,947	6,133	10,918	13,954	5,883	663	1,225	42,289
Employment by Size of Firm										Total
2006	1,416	1,506	5,236	17,151	22,374	32,734	11,618	904	9,792	102,731
2008	1,365	1,452	5,049	16,538	21,574	31,564	11,203	872	9,536	99,153
2009	1,322	1,406	4,888	16,012	20,889	30,561	10,847	844	9,280	96,048

SUB-INDUSTRIES – 2007 INDUSTRY ESTIMATES

Sub-Industries	Total Establishments	Total Employment	Total Sales ($M)
Beer and ale	759	21,889	6,310
Ale	21	921	569
Beer and other fermented malt liquors	1,504	79,904	32,092
Porter	3	16	4

WINE & ALCOHOLIC BEVERAGES WHOLESALES
(NAICS 42482)

INDUSTRY DEFINITION

NAICS 42482: Wine & Alcoholic Beverages Wholesales. Establishments primarily engaged in the wholesale distribution of distilled spirits, including neutral spirits and ethyl alcohol used in blended wines and distilled liquors.

INDUSTRY ESTABLISHMENTS, SALES & EMPLOYMENT TRENDS

	Year					Percent Change Year-to-Year			
	2005	2006	2007	2008	2009	05-06	06-07	07-08	08-09
Establishments	1,937	1,936	1,935	1,940	1,945	0.0%	0.0%	0.2%	0.2%
Sales ($Millions)	37,490	37,576	39,374	41,100	42,847	0.2%	4.8%	4.4%	4.3%
Employment	73,072	71,205	71,171	71,339	71,572	-2.6%	0.0%	0.2%	0.3%

INDUSTRY RATIOS

(Industry Averages)	Year					Percent Change Year-to-Year			
	2005	2006	2007	2008	2009	05-06	06-07	07-08	08-09
Sales ($M)/Estab.	19.35	19.41	20.35	21.19	22.03	0.3%	4.8%	4.1%	4.0%
Sales ($) per Emp.	513,050	527,724	553,234	576,116	598,656	2.9%	4.8%	4.1%	3.9%
Emps. per Estab.	37.7	36.8	36.8	36.8	36.8	-2.5%	0.0%	0.0%	0.1%

WINE & ALCOHOLIC BEVERAGES WHOLESALES (NAICS 42482)

SIZE OF FIRM INDUSTRY ESTIMATES

Year	Establishments by Size of Firm									
	1-4 Emps.	5-9 Emps.	10-19 Emps.	20-49 Emps.	50-99 Emps.	100-249 Emps.	250-499 Emps.	500+ Emps.	Unknown Emps.	Total
2006	797	278	243	262	126	113	44	15	62	1,935
2008	799	278	243	262	126	113	44	15	63	1,940
2009	801	279	244	263	126	113	44	15	63	1,945
	Sales ($Millions) by Size of Firm									**Total**
2006	699	761	2,259	3,641	3,708	9,881	8,720	8,976	730	39,374
2008	729	794	2,358	3,801	3,871	10,314	9,102	9,369	760	41,100
2009	760	828	2,458	3,962	4,034	10,750	9,487	9,765	803	42,847
	Employment by Size of Firm									**Total**
2006	2,391	1,666	3,395	8,634	8,302	15,891	14,877	12,175	3,840	71,171
2008	2,397	1,671	3,404	8,655	8,323	15,931	14,914	12,205	3,840	71,339
2009	2,403	1,675	3,412	8,677	8,343	15,971	14,951	12,236	3,904	71,572

SUB-INDUSTRIES – 2007 INDUSTRY ESTIMATES

Sub-Industries	Total Establishments	Total Employment	Total Sales ($M)
Wine and distilled beverages	417	16,012	8,960
Wine	1,009	28,668	13,051
Brandy and brandy spirits	6	145	1,449
Wine coolers, alcoholic	10	311	125
Liquor	376	21,463	11,182
Cocktails, alcoholic: premixed	11	180	48
Neutral spirits	8	372	32
Bottling wines and liquors	98	4,019	4,527

BOOK/PERIODICAL/NEWSPAPER WHOLESALES (NAICS 42492)

INDUSTRY DEFINITION

NAICS 42492: Book & Periodical & Newspaper Wholesales. Establishments primarily engaged in the wholesale distribution of books, periodicals, and newspapers.

INDUSTRY ESTABLISHMENTS, SALES & EMPLOYMENT TRENDS

	Year					Percent Change Year-to-Year			
	2005	2006	2007	2008	2009	05-06	06-07	07-08	08-09
Establishments	3,172	3,007	2,842	2,695	2,562	-5.2%	-5.5%	-5.2%	-4.9%
Sales ($Millions)	16,542	16,340	15,866	15,352	14,880	-1.2%	-2.9%	-3.2%	-3.1%
Employment	79,606	75,922	71,936	68,181	64,737	-4.6%	-5.3%	-5.2%	-5.1%

INDUSTRY RATIOS

(Industry Averages)	Year					Percent Change Year-to-Year			
	2005	2006	2007	2008	2009	05-06	06-07	07-08	08-09
Sales ($M)/Estab.	5.21	5.43	5.58	5.70	5.81	4.2%	2.7%	2.0%	2.0%
Sales ($) per Emp.	207,793	215,214	220,556	225,170	229,856	3.6%	2.5%	2.1%	2.1%
Emps. per Estab.	25.1	25.3	25.3	25.3	25.3	0.6%	0.3%	-0.1%	-0.1%

Book/Periodical/Newspaper Wholesales (NAICS 42492)

Size of Firm Industry Estimates

Year	Establishments by Size of Firm									Total
	1-4 Emps.	5-9 Emps.	10-19 Emps.	20-49 Emps.	50-99 Emps.	100-249 Emps.	250-499 Emps.	500+ Emps.	Unknown Emps.	
2006	1,388	452	361	286	129	80	23	20	103	2,842
2008	1,316	429	342	271	123	75	22	19	98	2,695
2009	1,251	407	325	258	117	72	20	18	93	2,562
	Sales ($Millions) by Size of Firm									**Total**
2006	437	380	1,933	1,831	1,834	3,032	1,689	4,031	699	15,866
2008	423	367	1,871	1,772	1,775	2,934	1,635	3,902	672	15,352
2009	410	356	1,815	1,718	1,721	2,846	1,586	3,784	644	14,880
	Employment by Size of Firm									**Total**
2006	2,776	2,711	5,415	9,432	8,279	11,454	7,681	17,531	6,656	71,936
2008	2,633	2,571	5,135	8,945	7,852	10,862	7,285	16,625	6,272	68,181
2009	2,503	2,444	4,881	8,503	7,464	10,326	6,925	15,804	5,888	64,737

Sub-Industries — 2007 Industry Estimates

Sub-Industries	Total Establishments	Total Employment	Total Sales ($M)
Books, periodicals, and newspapers	413	14,615	1,937
Books	1,364	31,511	9,029
Magazines	460	15,782	3,467
Newspapers	492	7,884	770
Periodicals	63	1,957	643
Comic books	49	186	19

NEW CAR DEALERS INDUSTRY
(NAICS 44111)

INDUSTRY DEFINITION

NAICS 44111: New Car Dealers. Establishments primarily engaged in the retail sale of new automobiles or new and used automobiles. These establishments frequently maintain repair departments and carry stocks of replacement parts, tires, batteries, and automotive accessories. These establishments also frequently sell pickups and vans at retail.

INDUSTRY ESTABLISHMENTS, SALES & EMPLOYMENT TRENDS

	Year					Percent Change Year-to-Year			
	2005	2006	2007	2008	2009	05-06	06-07	07-08	08-09
Establishments	28,449	28,564	28,679	28,720	28,762	0.4%	0.4%	0.1%	0.1%
Sales ($Millions)	540,143	573,895	602,402	626,351	650,397	6.2%	5.0%	4.0%	3.8%
Employment	1,292,890	1,295,979	1,301,199	1,303,071	1,304,945	0.2%	0.4%	0.1%	0.1%

INDUSTRY RATIOS

	Year					Percent Change Year-to-Year			
(Industry Averages)	2005	2006	2007	2008	2009	05-06	06-07	07-08	08-09
Sales ($M)/Estab.	18.99	20.09	21.01	21.81	22.61	5.8%	4.5%	3.8%	3.7%
Sales ($) per Emp.	417,779	442,828	462,959	480,673	498,410	6.0%	4.5%	3.8%	3.7%
Emps. per Estab.	45.4	45.4	45.4	45.4	45.4	-0.2%	0.0%	0.0%	0.0%

New Car Dealers Industry
(NAICS 44111)

Size of Firm Industry Estimates

Year	Establishments by Size of Firm									Total
	1-4 Emps.	5-9 Emps.	10-19 Emps.	20-49 Emps.	50-99 Emps.	100-249 Emps.	250-499 Emps.	500+ Emps.	Unknown Emps.	
2006	4,547	1,844	3,269	8,243	5,767	2,586	208	8	2,208	28,679
2008	4,554	1,846	3,274	8,255	5,775	2,590	208	8	2,211	28,720
2009	4,560	1,849	3,278	8,267	5,784	2,594	208	8	2,214	28,762
	Sales ($Millions) by Size of Firm									Total
2006	6,998	5,878	18,685	139,552	183,850	163,473	66,264	4,614	13,089	602,402
2008	7,276	6,111	19,428	145,100	191,159	169,972	68,898	4,797	13,608	626,351
2009	7,555	6,346	20,174	150,671	198,498	176,498	71,543	4,981	14,129	650,397
	Employment by Size of Firm									Total
2006	13,641	12,906	52,301	288,520	380,629	343,972	63,605	4,505	141,120	1,301,199
2008	13,661	12,925	52,376	288,938	381,180	344,470	63,697	4,511	141,312	1,303,071
2009	13,680	12,944	52,452	289,356	381,732	344,969	63,789	4,518	141,504	1,304,945

Sub-Industries – 2007 Industry Estimates

Sub-Industries	Total Establishments	Total Employment	Total Sales ($M)
New and used car dealers	8,571	286,141	163,496
Automobiles, new and used	17,809	965,191	420,355
Pickups, new and used	1,054	13,168	3,624
Trucks, tractors, and trailers: new and	1,209	36,229	14,719
Vans, new and used	35	470	209

FURNITURE STORES INDUSTRY
(NAICS 44211)

INDUSTRY DEFINITION

NAICS 44211: Furniture Stores. Establishments primarily engaged in the retail sale of household furniture. These stores may also sell homefurnishings, major appliances, and floor coverings.

INDUSTRY ESTABLISHMENTS, SALES & EMPLOYMENT TRENDS

	Year					Percent Change Year-to-Year			
	2005	2006	2007	2008	2009	05-06	06-07	07-08	08-09
Establishments	30,652	30,377	30,102	30,052	30,003	-0.9%	-0.9%	-0.2%	-0.2%
Sales ($Millions)	48,471	51,065	53,768	56,540	59,290	5.4%	5.3%	5.2%	4.9%
Employment	363,643	363,323	359,981	359,399	358,818	-0.1%	-0.9%	-0.2%	-0.2%

INDUSTRY RATIOS

(Industry Averages)	Year					Percent Change Year-to-Year			
	2005	2006	2007	2008	2009	05-06	06-07	07-08	08-09
Sales ($M)/Estab.	1.58	1.68	1.79	1.88	1.98	6.3%	6.3%	5.3%	5.0%
Sales ($) per Emp.	133,293	140,551	149,364	157,318	165,238	5.4%	6.3%	5.3%	5.0%
Emps. per Estab.	11.9	12.0	12.0	12.0	12.0	0.8%	0.0%	0.0%	0.0%

FURNITURE STORES INDUSTRY
(NAICS 44211)

SIZE OF FIRM INDUSTRY ESTIMATES

Year	Establishments by Size of Firm									Total
	1-4 Emps.	5-9 Emps.	10-19 Emps.	20-49 Emps.	50-99 Emps.	100-249 Emps.	250-499 Emps.	500+ Emps.	Unknown Emps.	
2006	14,108	6,681	4,771	2,616	443	110	37	6	1,332	30,102
2008	14,084	6,670	4,763	2,612	442	110	37	6	1,329	30,052
2009	14,061	6,659	4,755	2,607	442	110	37	6	1,327	30,003
	Sales ($Millions) by Size of Firm									Total
2006	4,512	5,698	9,664	13,666	5,103	4,693	3,946	1,237	5,250	53,768
2008	4,745	5,991	10,162	14,370	5,366	4,935	4,149	1,301	5,522	56,540
2009	4,975	6,283	10,656	15,069	5,627	5,174	4,351	1,364	5,791	59,290
	Employment by Size of Firm									Total
2006	28,215	40,084	66,793	81,098	27,477	14,966	11,697	4,467	85,184	359,981
2008	28,169	40,018	66,683	80,964	27,432	14,941	11,677	4,459	85,056	359,399
2009	28,122	39,952	66,573	80,830	27,386	14,917	11,658	4,452	84,928	358,818

SUB-INDUSTRIES – 2007 INDUSTRY ESTIMATES

Sub-Industries	Total Establishments	Total Employment	Total Sales ($M)
Furniture stores	21,490	272,452	41,964
Beds and accessories	1,190	9,285	1,228
Bedding and bedsprings	467	3,619	1,017
Mattresses	1,355	9,440	1,212
Waterbeds and accessories	219	2,805	462
Customized furniture and cabinets	370	3,591	401
Cabinet work, custom	1,473	14,799	1,378
Custom made furniture, except cabinets	577	4,072	488
Bar fixtures, equipment and supplies	53	435	64
Cabinets, except custom made: kitchen	346	2,732	296
Juvenile furniture	338	4,947	763
Office furniture	1,415	24,456	3,519
Outdoor and garden furniture	560	4,910	669
Unfinished furniture	249	2,438	306

APPLIANCE/TV/ELECTRONICS STORES INDUSTRY
(NAICS 44311)

INDUSTRY DEFINITION

NAICS 44311: Appliance/TV/Electronics Stores. Establishments primarily engaged in the retail sale of electric and gas refrigerators, stoves, and other household appliances, such as electric irons, percolators, hot plates, and vacuum cleaners. Many such stores also sell radio and television sets. Retail stores operated by public utility companies and primarily engaged in the sale of electric and gas appliances for household use are classified in this business.

INDUSTRY ESTABLISHMENTS, SALES & EMPLOYMENT TRENDS

	Year					Percent Change Year-to-Year			
	2005	2006	2007	2008	2009	05-06	06-07	07-08	08-09
Establishments	37,710	39,586	41,461	43,167	44,943	5.0%	4.7%	4.1%	4.1%
Sales ($Millions)	55,570	63,008	69,751	76,134	82,930	13.4%	10.7%	9.2%	8.9%
Employment	460,924	490,668	514,185	535,050	556,860	6.5%	4.8%	4.1%	4.1%

INDUSTRY RATIOS

	Year					Percent Change Year-to-Year			
(Industry Averages)	2005	2006	2007	2008	2009	05-06	06-07	07-08	08-09
Sales ($M)/Estab.	1.47	1.59	1.68	1.76	1.85	8.0%	5.7%	4.8%	4.6%
Sales ($) per Emp.	120,563	128,413	135,654	142,293	148,924	6.5%	5.6%	4.9%	4.7%
Emps. per Estab.	12.2	12.4	12.4	12.4	12.4	1.4%	0.1%	-0.1%	0.0%

APPLIANCE/TV/ELECTRONICS STORES INDUSTRY (NAICS 44311)

SIZE OF FIRM INDUSTRY ESTIMATES

Year	Establishments by Size of Firm									Total
	1-4 Emps.	5-9 Emps.	10-19 Emps.	20-49 Emps.	50-99 Emps.	100-249 Emps.	250-499 Emps.	500+ Emps.	Unknown Emps.	
2006	21,829	11,242	3,874	1,722	858	841	9	11	1,078	41,461
2008	22,728	11,704	4,033	1,793	893	876	9	12	1,122	43,167
2009	23,663	12,186	4,199	1,867	930	912	10	12	1,168	44,943
	Sales ($Millions) by Size of Firm									Total
2006	4,904	8,839	7,832	9,284	8,675	24,467	972	2,954	1,825	69,751
2008	5,353	9,649	8,550	10,134	9,469	26,709	1,061	3,225	1,984	76,134
2009	5,831	10,511	9,314	11,040	10,315	29,095	1,155	3,513	2,155	82,930
	Employment by Size of Firm									Total
2006	65,488	67,451	54,236	55,101	54,919	132,884	2,786	12,007	69,312	514,185
2008	68,183	70,227	56,468	57,368	57,179	138,352	2,901	12,501	71,872	535,050
2009	70,989	73,117	58,791	59,729	59,532	144,045	3,020	13,015	74,624	556,860

SUB-INDUSTRIES – 2007 INDUSTRY ESTIMATES

Sub-Industries	Total Establishments	Total Employment	Total Sales ($M)
Household appliance stores	16,203	227,349	58,638
Gas household appliances	375	5,125	281
Gas ranges	39	224	8
Electric household appliances	3,757	90,349	2,096
Air conditioning room units, self-	865	10,383	403
Electric household appliances, major	3,207	49,834	3,359
Electric household appliances, small	245	2,262	97
Electric ranges	49	324	14
Fans, electric	271	2,338	149
Garbage disposals	155	1,785	80
Microwave ovens	53	434	16
Vacuum cleaners	9,572	72,957	2,297
Appliance parts	918	7,229	243
Kitchens, complete (sinks, cabinets,	992	9,705	584
Sewing machines	4,478	30,624	1,125
Stoves, household, nec	201	1,403	61
Suntanning equipment and supplies	53	1,627	290
Kerosene heaters	30	234	8

COMPUTER & SOFTWARE STORES INDUSTRY (NAICS 44312)

INDUSTRY DEFINITION

NAICS 44312: Computer & Software Stores. Establishments primarily engaged in the retail sale of computers, computer peripheral equipment, and software. Establishments primarily engaged in the sale of computers, computer peripheral equipment and software for business or professional use are classified in SIC 5045.

INDUSTRY ESTABLISHMENTS, SALES & EMPLOYMENT TRENDS

	Year					Percent Change Year-to-Year			
	2005	2006	2007	2008	2009	05-06	06-07	07-08	08-09
Establishments	11,918	11,592	11,266	11,012	10,763	-2.7%	-2.8%	-2.3%	-2.3%
Sales ($Millions)	32,223	28,875	27,133	25,531	24,001	-10.4%	-6.0%	-5.9%	-6.0%
Employment	144,568	136,263	132,185	129,315	126,613	-5.7%	-3.0%	-2.2%	-2.1%

INDUSTRY RATIOS

(Industry Averages)	Year					Percent Change Year-to-Year			
	2005	2006	2007	2008	2009	05-06	06-07	07-08	08-09
Sales ($M)/Estab.	2.70	2.49	2.41	2.32	2.23	-7.9%	-3.3%	-3.7%	-3.8%
Sales ($) per Emp.	222,892	211,909	205,265	197,434	189,563	-4.9%	-3.1%	-3.8%	-4.0%
Emps. per Estab.	12.1	11.8	11.7	11.7	11.8	-3.1%	-0.2%	0.1%	0.2%

COMPUTER & SOFTWARE STORES INDUSTRY
(NAICS 44312)

SIZE OF FIRM INDUSTRY ESTIMATES

Year	Establishments by Size of Firm									Total
	1-4 Emps.	5-9 Emps.	10-19 Emps.	20-49 Emps.	50-99 Emps.	100-249 Emps.	250-499 Emps.	500+ Emps.	Unknown Emps.	Total
2006	5,692	3,277	909	298	206	22	28	1	833	11,266
2008	5,563	3,203	889	291	202	21	28	1	814	11,012
2009	5,438	3,130	869	285	197	21	27	1	796	10,763
Sales ($Millions) by Size of Firm										**Total**
2006	1,610	3,089	2,229	1,965	3,892	1,155	5,331	889	6,973	27,133
2008	1,514	2,905	2,096	1,848	3,660	1,086	5,013	836	6,572	25,531
2009	1,422	2,728	1,969	1,736	3,437	1,020	4,708	785	6,197	24,001
Employment by Size of Firm										**Total**
2006	11,384	19,660	11,822	9,529	13,415	2,774	8,623	1,795	53,184	132,185
2008	11,127	19,216	11,555	9,314	13,112	2,712	8,428	1,755	52,096	129,315
2009	10,876	18,783	11,295	9,104	12,816	2,651	8,238	1,715	51,136	126,613

SUB-INDUSTRIES – 2007 INDUSTRY ESTIMATES

Sub-Industries	Total Establishments	Total Employment	Total Sales ($M)
Computer and software stores	7,911	84,231	17,994
Computer peripheral equipment	566	8,200	2,057
Modems, monitors, terminals, and disk	208	2,244	450
Printers and plotters: computers	95	1,070	396
Computer software and accessories	804	9,377	1,909
Computer tapes	7	76	12
Magnetic disks	21	186	49
Software, business and non-game	496	7,410	1,602
Software, computer games	456	5,837	1,411
Word processing equipment and	15	219	29
Personal computers	687	13,336	1,224

HOME CENTERS INDUSTRY
(NAICS 44411)

INDUSTRY DEFINITION

NAICS 44411: Home Centers. This industry comprises establishments known as home centers primarily engaged in retailing a general line of new home repair and improvement materials and supplies, such as lumber, plumbing goods, electrical goods, tools, housewares, hardware, and lawn and garden supplies, with no one merchandise line predominating. The merchandise lines are normally arranged in separate departments.

INDUSTRY ESTABLISHMENTS, SALES & EMPLOYMENT TRENDS

	Year					Percent Change Year-to-Year			
	2005	2006	2007	2008	2009	05-06	06-07	07-08	08-09
Establishments	6,084	6,346	6,607	6,944	7,298	4.3%	4.1%	5.1%	5.1%
Sales ($Millions)	109,683	113,205	125,882	140,753	151,921	3.2%	11.2%	11.8%	7.9%
Employment	514,731	507,979	528,916	556,024	584,351	-1.3%	4.1%	5.1%	5.1%

INDUSTRY RATIOS

(Industry Averages)	Year					Percent Change Year-to-Year			
	2005	2006	2007	2008	2009	05-06	06-07	07-08	08-09
Sales ($M)/Estab.	18.03	17.84	19.05	20.27	20.82	-1.0%	6.8%	6.4%	2.7%
Sales ($) per Emp.	213,088	222,854	238,001	253,142	259,982	4.6%	6.8%	6.4%	2.7%
Emps. per Estab.	84.6	80.1	80.1	80.1	80.1	-5.4%	0.0%	0.0%	0.0%

HOME CENTERS INDUSTRY
(NAICS 44411)

SIZE OF FIRM INDUSTRY ESTIMATES

Year	Establishments by Size of Firm									Total
	1-4 Emps.	5-9 Emps.	10-19 Emps.	20-49 Emps.	50-99 Emps.	100-249 Emps.	250-499 Emps.	500+ Emps.	Unknown Emps.	
2006	1,104	677	904	755	254	2,595	140	1	177	6,607
2008	1,161	712	950	793	267	2,728	147	1	187	6,944
2009	1,220	748	998	834	281	2,867	155	1	196	7,298
	Sales ($Millions) by Size of Firm									Total
2006	378	657	2,167	4,653	3,337	91,848	19,210	500	3,132	125,882
2008	423	734	2,422	5,202	3,730	102,671	21,474	559	3,538	140,753
2009	456	793	2,614	5,615	4,026	110,826	23,180	604	3,808	151,921
	Employment by Size of Firm									Total
2006	2,209	4,739	12,653	24,154	16,266	415,247	41,507	813	11,328	528,916
2008	2,321	4,981	13,299	25,386	17,096	436,430	43,625	854	12,032	556,024
2009	2,440	5,235	13,977	26,681	17,968	458,693	45,850	898	12,608	584,351

SUB-INDUSTRIES – 2007 INDUSTRY ESTIMATES

Sub-Industries	Total Establishments	Total Employment	Total Sales ($M)
Lumber and other building materials	2,546	324,234	97,445
Lumber products	817	58,311	10,483
Door and window products	640	26,779	2,659
Doors, storm: wood or metal	59	3,150	410
Doors, wood or metal, except storm	37	1,877	239
Garage doors, sale and installation	441	18,957	2,018
Jalousies	2	101	11
Sash, wood or metal	4	194	9
Screens, door and window	87	2,343	249
Windows, storm: wood or metal	93	5,936	841
Insulation and energy conservation	139	5,224	1,493
Prefabricated buildings	210	8,645	1,395
Masonry materials and supplies	643	36,191	4,338
Bathroom fixtures, equipment and	70	3,832	556
Cabinets, kitchen	383	13,973	1,728
Other materials	435	19,168	2,006

HARDWARE STORES INDUSTRY
(NAICS 44413)

INDUSTRY DEFINITION

NAICS 44413: Hardware Stores. Establishments primarily engaged in the retail sale of a number of basic hardware lines, such as tools, builders' hardware, paint and glass, housewares and household appliances, and cutlery.

INDUSTRY ESTABLISHMENTS, SALES & EMPLOYMENT TRENDS

	Year					Percent Change Year-to-Year			
	2005	2006	2007	2008	2009	05-06	06-07	07-08	08-09
Establishments	14,488	14,368	14,248	14,103	13,959	-0.8%	-0.8%	-1.0%	-1.0%
Sales ($Millions)	18,985	20,039	21,148	22,088	23,009	5.6%	5.5%	4.4%	4.2%
Employment	164,902	162,865	161,499	159,938	158,393	-1.2%	-0.8%	-1.0%	-1.0%

INDUSTRY RATIOS

(Industry Averages)	Year					Percent Change Year-to-Year			
	2005	2006	2007	2008	2009	05-06	06-07	07-08	08-09
Sales ($M)/Estab.	1.31	1.39	1.48	1.57	1.65	6.4%	6.4%	5.5%	5.2%
Sales ($) per Emp.	115,127	123,040	130,949	138,106	145,264	6.9%	6.4%	5.5%	5.2%
Emps. per Estab.	11.4	11.3	11.3	11.3	11.3	-0.4%	0.0%	0.1%	0.1%

HARDWARE STORES INDUSTRY
(NAICS 44413)

SIZE OF FIRM INDUSTRY ESTIMATES

Year	Establishments by Size of Firm									Total
	1-4 Emps.	5-9 Emps.	10-19 Emps.	20-49 Emps.	50-99 Emps.	100-249 Emps.	250-499 Emps.	500+ Emps.	Unknown Emps.	
2006	5,788	3,426	3,040	1,497	229	38	3	0	228	14,248
2008	5,729	3,391	3,009	1,482	227	38	3	0	226	14,103
2009	5,670	3,356	2,978	1,467	225	37	3	0	224	13,959
Sales ($Millions) by Size of Firm										**Total**
2006	1,318	2,341	5,886	7,163	2,089	1,517	291	0	543	21,148
2008	1,377	2,445	6,146	7,481	2,181	1,584	304	0	570	22,088
2009	1,434	2,547	6,402	7,791	2,272	1,650	317	0	597	23,009
Employment by Size of Firm										**Total**
2006	17,363	20,555	42,555	46,419	13,984	5,212	884	0	14,528	161,499
2008	17,186	20,346	42,121	45,946	13,841	5,159	875	0	14,464	159,938
2009	17,011	20,139	41,692	45,478	13,700	5,106	866	0	14,400	158,393

SUB-INDUSTRIES – 2007 INDUSTRY ESTIMATES

Sub-Industries	Total Establishments	Total Employment	Total Sales ($M)
Hardware stores	10,804	134,341	16,774
Tools	1,516	7,478	1,194
Chainsaws	301	1,400	194
Snowblowers	34	195	36
Tools, hand	303	1,909	297
Tools, power	259	3,354	694
Builders' hardware	688	9,890	1,518
Door locks and lock sets	94	968	139
Pumps and pumping equipment	250	1,965	302

GROCERY STORES INDUSTRY
(NAICS 44511)

INDUSTRY DEFINITION

NAICS 44511: Grocery Stores Industry. This industry comprises establishments generally known as supermarkets and grocery stores primarily engaged in retailing a general line of food, such as canned and frozen foods; fresh fruits and vegetables; and fresh and prepared meats, fish, and poultry. Included in this industry are delicatessen-type establishments primarily engaged in retailing a general line of food.

INDUSTRY ESTABLISHMENTS, SALES & EMPLOYMENT TRENDS

	Year					Percent Change Year-to-Year			
	2005	2006	2007	2008	2009	05-06	06-07	07-08	08-09
Establishments	68,804	67,925	67,046	66,697	66,351	-1.3%	-1.3%	-0.5%	-0.5%
Sales ($Millions)	571,009	586,044	600,934	617,050	633,017	2.6%	2.5%	2.7%	2.6%
Employment	2,494,326	2,484,370	2,452,211	2,439,391	2,426,698	-0.4%	-1.3%	-0.5%	-0.5%

INDUSTRY RATIOS

(Industry Averages)	Year					Percent Change Year-to-Year			
	2005	2006	2007	2008	2009	05-06	06-07	07-08	08-09
Sales ($M)/Estab.	8.30	8.63	8.96	9.25	9.54	4.0%	3.9%	3.2%	3.1%
Sales ($) per Emp.	228,923	235,892	245,058	252,952	260,855	3.0%	3.9%	3.2%	3.1%
Emps. per Estab.	36.3	36.6	36.6	36.6	36.6	0.9%	0.0%	0.0%	0.0%

GROCERY STORES INDUSTRY
(NAICS 44511)

SIZE OF FIRM INDUSTRY ESTIMATES

Year	Establishments by Size of Firm									Total
	1-4 Emps.	5-9 Emps.	10-19 Emps.	20-49 Emps.	50-99 Emps.	100-249 Emps.	250-499 Emps.	500+ Emps.	Unknown Emps.	
2006	23,984	7,437	6,635	9,397	10,260	7,310	486	21	1,516	67,046
2008	23,859	7,399	6,601	9,348	10,206	7,272	484	21	1,508	66,697
2009	23,735	7,360	6,566	9,299	10,153	7,234	481	21	1,500	66,351
	Sales ($Millions) by Size of Firm									Total
2006	11,715	7,266	16,565	62,220	144,773	245,964	73,767	29,949	8,716	600,934
2008	12,029	7,461	17,009	63,889	148,658	252,563	75,746	30,752	8,943	617,050
2009	12,341	7,654	17,449	65,542	152,505	259,099	77,706	31,548	9,173	633,017
	Employment by Size of Firm									Total
2006	71,953	44,624	92,891	319,496	677,141	986,810	146,427	15,908	96,960	2,452,211
2008	71,578	44,393	92,408	317,835	673,621	981,680	145,666	15,826	96,384	2,439,391
2009	71,206	44,162	91,928	316,183	670,119	976,577	144,909	15,743	95,872	2,426,698

SUB-INDUSTRIES – 2007 INDUSTRY ESTIMATES

Sub-Industries	Total Establishments	Total Employment	Total Sales ($M)
Grocery stores	24,032	609,709	77,303
Supermarkets	1,739	137,141	25,829
Supermarkets, chain	3,935	835,009	363,014
Supermarkets, greater than 100,000	10	2,497	1,560
Supermarkets, independent	912	81,470	15,657
Supermarkets, 55,000 - 65,000 square	16	3,474	142
Supermarkets, 66,000 - 99,000 square	11	1,584	2,661
Convenience stores	13,761	170,405	18,961
Convenience stores, chain	5,093	107,452	34,845
Convenience stores, independent	5,291	66,206	11,291
Cooperative food stores	123	6,428	810
Delicatessen stores	3,616	41,029	3,581
Frozen food and freezer plans, except	48	1,598	1,517
Grocery stores, chain	1,068	158,915	14,464
Grocery stores, independent	7,391	229,294	29,298

BEER & WINE & LIQUOR STORES INDUSTRY (NAICS 44531)

INDUSTRY DEFINITION

NAICS 44531: Beer & Wine & Liquor Stores. Establishments primarily engaged in the retail sale of packaged alcoholic beverages, such as ale, beer, wine, and liquor, for consumption off the premises. Stores selling prepared drinks for consumption on the premises are classified in SIC 5813.

INDUSTRY ESTABLISHMENTS, SALES & EMPLOYMENT TRENDS

	Year					Percent Change Year-to-Year			
	2005	2006	2007	2008	2009	05-06	06-07	07-08	08-09
Establishments	30,280	30,500	30,720	31,003	31,288	0.7%	0.7%	0.9%	0.9%
Sales ($Millions)	16,009	18,089	19,202	20,267	21,353	13.0%	6.2%	5.5%	5.4%
Employment	168,355	176,136	177,356	178,914	180,606	4.6%	0.7%	0.9%	0.9%

INDUSTRY RATIOS

	Year					Percent Change Year-to-Year			
(Industry Averages)	2005	2006	2007	2008	2009	05-06	06-07	07-08	08-09
Sales ($M)/Estab.	0.53	0.59	0.63	0.65	0.68	12.2%	5.4%	4.6%	4.4%
Sales ($) per Emp.	95,089	102,701	108,267	113,276	118,230	8.0%	5.4%	4.6%	4.4%
Emps. per Estab.	5.6	5.8	5.8	5.8	5.8	3.9%	0.0%	0.0%	0.0%

BEER & WINE & LIQUOR STORES INDUSTRY (NAICS 44531)

SIZE OF FIRM INDUSTRY ESTIMATES

Year	Establishments by Size of Firm									
	1-4 Emps.	5-9 Emps.	10-19 Emps.	20-49 Emps.	50-99 Emps.	100-249 Emps.	250-499 Emps.	500+ Emps.	Unknown Emps.	Total
2006	19,397	7,484	2,688	687	69	14	1	0	377	30,720
2008	19,575	7,553	2,713	694	70	15	1	0	381	31,003
2009	19,755	7,623	2,738	700	71	15	1	0	384	31,288
	Sales ($Millions) by Size of Firm									Total
2006	4,984	5,017	4,204	3,301	696	453	89	205	253	19,202
2008	5,261	5,295	4,438	3,485	735	478	94	217	265	20,267
2009	5,542	5,579	4,675	3,671	774	503	99	228	280	21,353
	Employment by Size of Firm									Total
2006	58,190	44,905	34,944	21,305	3,947	1,722	310	723	11,310	177,356
2008	58,726	45,319	35,266	21,501	3,983	1,738	313	730	11,340	178,914
2009	59,266	45,736	35,590	21,698	4,020	1,754	316	737	11,490	180,606

SUB-INDUSTRIES – 2007 INDUSTRY ESTIMATES

Sub-Industries	Total Establishments	Total Employment	Total Sales ($M)
Liquor stores	18,369	103,682	11,141
Wine and beer	457	4,289	295
Beer (packaged)	4,389	29,270	3,636
Wine	2,638	14,251	1,667
Hard liquor	4,867	25,864	2,463

PHARMACIES & DRUG STORES INDUSTRY
(NAICS 44611)

INDUSTRY DEFINITION

NAICS 44611 Pharmacies and Drug Stores – This industry comprises establishments known as pharmacies and drug stores engaged in retailing prescription or nonprescription drugs and medicines.

INDUSTRY ESTABLISHMENTS, SALES & EMPLOYMENT TRENDS

	Year					Percent Change Year-to-Year			
	2005	2006	2007	2008	2009	05-06	06-07	07-08	08-09
Establishments	43,030	42,471	41,912	41,723	41,534	-1.3%	-1.3%	-0.5%	-0.5%
Sales ($Millions)	167,217	192,356	216,917	241,646	266,189	15.0%	12.8%	11.4%	10.2%
Employment	943,151	932,825	920,902	916,492	912,418	-1.1%	-1.3%	-0.5%	-0.4%

INDUSTRY RATIOS

(Industry Averages)	Year					Percent Change Year-to-Year			
	2005	2006	2007	2008	2009	05-06	06-07	07-08	08-09
Sales ($M)/Estab.	3.89	4.53	5.18	5.79	6.41	16.5%	14.3%	11.9%	10.7%
Sales ($) per Emp.	177,296	206,208	235,548	263,664	291,740	16.3%	14.2%	11.9%	10.6%
Emps. per Estab.	21.9	22.0	22.0	22.0	22.0	0.2%	0.0%	0.0%	0.0%

PHARMACIES & DRUG STORES INDUSTRY (NAICS 44611)

SIZE OF FIRM INDUSTRY ESTIMATES

Year	Establishments by Size of Firm									Total
	1-4 Emps.	5-9 Emps.	10-19 Emps.	20-49 Emps.	50-99 Emps.	100-249 Emps.	250-499 Emps.	500+ Emps.	Unknown Emps.	
2006	7,677	7,130	10,155	11,959	2,381	140	16	6	2,446	41,912
2008	7,643	7,098	10,110	11,905	2,370	139	16	6	2,435	41,723
2009	7,608	7,066	10,064	11,851	2,359	138	16	6	2,424	41,534
	Sales ($Millions) by Size of Firm									Total
2006	9,067	14,035	29,318	61,202	39,051	18,552	14,459	15,491	15,741	216,917
2008	10,102	15,637	32,665	68,187	43,508	20,669	16,109	17,260	17,509	241,646
2009	11,128	17,225	35,981	75,111	47,926	22,768	17,745	19,012	19,294	266,189
	Employment by Size of Firm									Total
2006	23,032	49,913	152,332	370,721	140,463	18,999	4,974	3,795	156,672	920,902
2008	22,928	49,687	151,645	369,048	139,829	18,913	4,952	3,778	155,712	916,492
2009	22,825	49,463	150,960	367,382	139,198	18,828	4,929	3,761	155,072	912,418

SUB-INDUSTRIES – 2007 INDUSTRY ESTIMATES

Sub-Industries	Total Establishments	Total Employment	Total Sales ($M)
Drug stores and proprietary stores	9,952	195,753	41,727
Drug stores	30,948	706,596	174,878
Proprietary (non-prescription medicine)	1,012	18,553	312

GAS STATIONS WITH CONVENIENCE STORES (NAICS 44711)

INDUSTRY DEFINITION

NAICS 44711: Gas Stations with Convenience Stores. This industry comprises establishments primarily engaged in selling gasoline and lubricating oils. These establishments frequently sell other merchandise, such as tires, batteries, and other automobile parts, or perform minor repair work. Gasoline stations combined with other activities, such as grocery stores, convenience stores, or carwashes, are classified according to the primary activity.

INDUSTRY ESTABLISHMENTS, SALES & EMPLOYMENT TRENDS

	Year					Percent Change Year-to-Year			
	2005	2006	2007	2008	2009	05-06	06-07	07-08	08-09
Establishments	97,032	101,743	106,455	110,457	114,610	4.9%	4.6%	3.8%	3.8%
Sales ($Millions)	152,630	178,641	198,090	216,044	235,078	17.0%	10.9%	9.1%	8.8%
Employment	1,044,288	1,113,544	1,165,148	1,208,921	1,254,344	6.6%	4.6%	3.8%	3.8%

INDUSTRY RATIOS

(Industry Averages)	Year					Percent Change Year-to-Year			
	2005	2006	2007	2008	2009	05-06	06-07	07-08	08-09
Sales ($M)/Estab.	1.57	1.76	1.86	1.96	2.05	11.6%	6.0%	5.1%	4.9%
Sales ($) per Emp.	146,157	160,426	170,013	178,708	187,411	9.8%	6.0%	5.1%	4.9%
Emps. per Estab.	10.8	10.9	10.9	10.9	10.9	1.7%	0.0%	0.0%	0.0%

Gas Stations with Convenience Stores (NAICS 44711)

Size of Firm Industry Estimates

Year	Establishments by Size of Firm									Total
	1-4 Emps.	5-9 Emps.	10-19 Emps.	20-49 Emps.	50-99 Emps.	100-249 Emps.	250-499 Emps.	500+ Emps.	Unknown Emps.	
2006	32,516	40,510	23,584	4,437	409	57	9	0	4,933	106,455
2008	33,739	42,033	24,471	4,604	424	59	9	0	5,118	110,457
2009	35,007	43,613	25,391	4,777	440	61	9	0	5,311	114,610
	Sales ($Millions) by Size of Firm									**Total**
2006	14,691	41,181	63,932	50,122	13,855	4,192	1,684	629	7,804	198,090
2008	16,022	44,913	69,727	54,665	15,111	4,571	1,837	687	8,510	216,044
2009	17,434	48,870	75,871	59,481	16,443	4,974	1,998	747	9,259	235,078
	Employment by Size of Firm									**Total**
2006	97,548	243,057	330,176	141,999	24,942	7,581	2,675	1,329	315,840	1,165,148
2008	101,216	252,196	342,590	147,339	25,880	7,866	2,775	1,379	327,680	1,208,921
2009	105,021	261,679	355,472	152,879	26,853	8,162	2,880	1,430	339,968	1,254,344

Sub-Industries – 2007 Industry Estimates

Sub-Industries	Total Establishments	Total Employment	Total Sales ($M)
Gasoline service stations	47,727	454,556	14,706
Filling stations, gasoline	56,058	625,947	177,407
Marine service station	402	4,165	94
Truck stops	2,267	80,480	5,884

Men's Clothing Stores Industry (NAICS 44811)

Industry Definition

NAICS 44811: Men's Clothing Stores. This industry comprises establishments primarily engaged in retailing a general line of new men's and boys' clothing. These establishments may provide basic alterations, such as hemming, taking in or letting out seams, or lengthening or shortening sleeves.

Industry Establishments, Sales & Employment Trends

	Year					Percent Change Year-to-Year			
	2005	2006	2007	2008	2009	05-06	06-07	07-08	08-09
Establishments	9,164	8,811	8,458	8,093	7,745	-3.9%	-4.0%	-4.3%	-4.3%
Sales ($Millions)	12,610	12,395	12,017	11,558	11,115	-1.7%	-3.0%	-3.8%	-3.8%
Employment	100,242	96,544	92,636	88,835	85,026	-3.7%	-4.0%	-4.1%	-4.3%

Industry Ratios

(Industry Averages)	Year					Percent Change Year-to-Year			
	2005	2006	2007	2008	2009	05-06	06-07	07-08	08-09
Sales ($M)/Estab.	1.38	1.41	1.42	1.43	1.44	2.2%	1.0%	0.5%	0.5%
Sales ($) per Emp.	125,794	128,382	129,726	130,101	130,720	2.1%	1.0%	0.3%	0.5%
Emps. per Estab.	10.9	11.0	11.0	11.0	11.0	0.2%	0.0%	0.2%	0.0%

MEN'S CLOTHING STORES INDUSTRY (NAICS 44811)

SIZE OF FIRM INDUSTRY ESTIMATES

Year	Establishments by Size of Firm									Total
	1-4 Emps.	5-9 Emps.	10-19 Emps.	20-49 Emps.	50-99 Emps.	100-249 Emps.	250-499 Emps.	500+ Emps.	Unknown Emps.	
2006	3,620	2,343	1,587	419	36	9	2	0	439	8,458
2008	3,465	2,243	1,519	401	34	9	2	0	420	8,093
2009	3,315	2,146	1,454	384	33	8	2	0	402	7,745
	Sales ($Millions) by Size of Firm									Total
2006	1,115	2,165	3,747	3,012	898	658	243	0	181	12,017
2008	1,072	2,082	3,603	2,897	863	632	234	0	175	11,558
2009	1,031	2,002	3,465	2,786	830	608	225	0	168	11,115
	Employment by Size of Firm									Total
2006	10,861	14,061	22,223	13,416	2,142	1,153	619	0	28,160	92,636
2008	10,394	13,455	21,266	12,839	2,050	1,104	592	0	27,136	88,835
2009	9,946	12,876	20,350	12,286	1,962	1,056	567	0	25,984	85,026

SUB-INDUSTRIES — 2007 INDUSTRY ESTIMATES

Sub-Industries	Total Establishments	Total Employment	Total Sales ($M)
Men's and boys' clothing stores	5,940	67,242	7,999
Clothing accessories: men's and boys'	631	5,278	832
Clothing, male: everyday, except suits	394	6,802	707
Clothing, sportswear, men's and boys'	873	7,521	1,187
Haberdashery stores	38	231	24
Hats, men's and boys'	151	602	58
Suits, men's	388	4,793	1,195
Tie shops	42	165	16

WOMEN'S CLOTHING STORES INDUSTRY (NAICS 44812)

INDUSTRY DEFINITION

NAICS 44812: Women's Clothing Stores . This industry comprises establishments primarily engaged in retailing a general line of new women's, misses' and juniors' clothing, including maternity wear. These establishments may provide basic alterations, such as hemming, taking in or letting out seams, or lengthening or shortening sleeves.

INDUSTRY ESTABLISHMENTS, SALES & EMPLOYMENT TRENDS

	Year					Percent Change Year-to-Year			
	2005	2006	2007	2008	2009	05-06	06-07	07-08	08-09
Establishments	34,022	33,233	32,444	31,983	31,529	-2.3%	-2.4%	-1.4%	-1.4%
Sales ($Millions)	47,154	49,424	51,674	54,050	56,354	4.8%	4.6%	4.6%	4.3%
Employment	362,191	346,894	338,334	333,530	328,982	-4.2%	-2.5%	-1.4%	-1.4%

INDUSTRY RATIOS

	Year					Percent Change Year-to-Year			
(Industry Averages)	2005	2006	2007	2008	2009	05-06	06-07	07-08	08-09
Sales ($M)/Estab.	1.39	1.49	1.59	1.69	1.79	7.3%	7.1%	6.1%	5.8%
Sales ($) per Emp.	130,190	142,477	152,732	162,054	171,299	9.4%	7.2%	6.1%	5.7%
Emps. per Estab.	10.6	10.4	10.4	10.4	10.4	-1.9%	-0.1%	0.0%	0.1%

Women's Clothing Stores Industry
(NAICS 44812)

Size of Firm Industry Estimates

Year	Establishments by Size of Firm									Total
	1-4 Emps.	5-9 Emps.	10-19 Emps.	20-49 Emps.	50-99 Emps.	100-249 Emps.	250-499 Emps.	500+ Emps.	Unknown Emps.	
2006	11,681	9,966	7,271	2,784	358	80	13	3	285	32,444
2008	11,515	9,825	7,168	2,744	353	79	13	3	281	31,983
2009	11,352	9,685	7,066	2,705	348	78	13	3	277	31,529
Sales ($Millions) by Size of Firm										**Total**
2006	2,695	5,749	10,906	14,451	6,357	5,533	3,074	2,520	389	51,674
2008	2,819	6,013	11,407	15,115	6,649	5,788	3,215	2,636	407	54,050
2009	2,939	6,269	11,892	15,758	6,932	6,034	3,352	2,748	429	56,354
Employment by Size of Firm										**Total**
2006	23,362	69,765	101,800	86,289	21,469	11,031	4,516	2,118	17,984	338,334
2008	23,031	68,774	100,354	85,064	21,164	10,875	4,452	2,088	17,728	333,530
2009	22,704	67,798	98,929	83,856	20,863	10,720	4,389	2,059	17,664	328,982

Sub-Industries — 2007 Industry Estimates

Sub-Industries	Total Establishments	Total Employment	Total Sales ($M)
Women's clothing stores	16,923	167,153	14,988
Women's specialty clothing stores	659	5,600	1,352
Boutiques	2,238	11,111	725
Bridal shops	3,071	20,384	2,003
Dress shops	449	4,041	227
Women's sportswear	364	3,890	767
Maternity wear	643	4,569	125
Ready-to-wear apparel, women's	7,831	117,373	31,076
Teenage apparel	266	4,215	411

FAMILY CLOTHING STORES INDUSTRY
(NAICS 44814)

INDUSTRY DEFINITION

NAICS 44814: Family Clothing Stores . This industry comprises establishments primarily engaged in retailing a general line of new clothing for men, women, and children, without specializing in sales for an individual gender or age group. These establishments may provide basic alterations, such as hemming, taking in or letting out seams, or lengthening or shortening sleeves.

INDUSTRY ESTABLISHMENTS, SALES & EMPLOYMENT TRENDS

	Year					Percent Change Year-to-Year			
	2005	2006	2007	2008	2009	05-06	06-07	07-08	08-09
Establishments	26,519	28,017	29,516	30,873	32,292	5.7%	5.3%	4.6%	4.6%
Sales ($Millions)	69,648	75,143	82,081	88,439	95,195	7.9%	9.2%	7.7%	7.6%
Employment	716,864	739,813	779,618	815,498	852,931	3.2%	5.4%	4.6%	4.6%

INDUSTRY RATIOS

(Industry Averages)	Year					Percent Change Year-to-Year			
	2005	2006	2007	2008	2009	05-06	06-07	07-08	08-09
Sales ($M)/Estab.	2.63	2.68	2.78	2.86	2.95	2.1%	3.7%	3.0%	2.9%
Sales ($) per Emp.	97,156	101,571	105,284	108,448	111,610	4.5%	3.7%	3.0%	2.9%
Emps. per Estab.	27.0	26.4	26.4	26.4	26.4	-2.3%	0.0%	0.0%	0.0%

FAMILY CLOTHING STORES INDUSTRY (NAICS 44814)

SIZE OF FIRM INDUSTRY ESTIMATES

Year	Establishments by Size of Firm									Total
	1-4 Emps.	5-9 Emps.	10-19 Emps.	20-49 Emps.	50-99 Emps.	100-249 Emps.	250-499 Emps.	500+ Emps.	Unknown Emps.	
2006	6,864	4,925	5,217	6,312	3,567	383	91	41	2,116	29,516
2008	7,180	5,152	5,457	6,602	3,731	400	95	43	2,213	30,873
2009	7,510	5,388	5,707	6,905	3,903	419	100	45	2,315	32,292
	Sales ($Millions) by Size of Firm									Total
2006	1,718	3,081	7,615	20,400	21,571	9,180	7,963	7,134	3,421	82,081
2008	1,851	3,320	8,204	21,980	23,241	9,890	8,580	7,687	3,687	88,439
2009	1,992	3,573	8,831	23,659	25,017	10,646	9,235	8,274	3,968	95,195
	Employment by Size of Firm									Total
2006	13,729	29,551	78,253	201,976	217,597	45,554	32,994	24,476	135,488	779,618
2008	14,360	30,910	81,850	211,260	227,599	47,648	34,511	25,601	141,760	815,498
2009	15,020	32,330	85,612	220,971	238,061	49,838	36,097	26,777	148,224	852,931

SUB-INDUSTRIES – 2007 INDUSTRY ESTIMATES

Sub-Industries	Total Establishments	Total Employment	Total Sales ($M)
Family clothing stores	24,284	718,720	80,428
Jeans stores	627	15,059	269
Unisex clothing stores	4,605	45,839	1,385

BOOK STORES RETAILING INDUSTRY
(NAICS 451211)

INDUSTRY DEFINITION

NAICS 451211: Book Stores. This industry comprises establishments primarily engaged in the retail sale of new books and magazines. Establishments primarily engaged in the retail sale of used books are classified in 5932.

INDUSTRY ESTABLISHMENTS, SALES & EMPLOYMENT TRENDS

	Year					Percent Change Year-to-Year			
	2005	2006	2007	2008	2009	05-06	06-07	07-08	08-09
Establishments	11,302	11,171	11,040	10,905	10,771	-1.2%	-1.2%	-1.2%	-1.2%
Sales ($Millions)	15,728	17,405	18,403	19,268	20,110	10.7%	5.7%	4.7%	4.4%
Employment	151,418	151,915	150,175	148,373	146,592	0.3%	-1.1%	-1.2%	-1.2%

INDUSTRY RATIOS

(Industry Averages)	Year					Percent Change Year-to-Year			
	2005	2006	2007	2008	2009	05-06	06-07	07-08	08-09
Sales ($M)/Estab.	1.39	1.56	1.67	1.77	1.87	12.0%	7.0%	6.0%	5.7%
Sales ($) per Emp.	103,872	114,571	122,546	129,863	137,184	10.3%	7.0%	6.0%	5.6%
Emps. per Estab.	13.4	13.6	13.6	13.6	13.6	1.5%	0.0%	0.0%	0.0%

BOOK STORES RETAILING INDUSTRY
(NAICS 451211)

SIZE OF FIRM INDUSTRY ESTIMATES

Year	Establishments by Size of Firm									Total
	1-4 Emps.	5-9 Emps.	10-19 Emps.	20-49 Emps.	50-99 Emps.	100-249 Emps.	250-499 Emps.	500+ Emps.	Unknown Emps.	
2006	4,438	2,678	1,878	1,297	471	50	8	3	217	11,040
2008	4,384	2,645	1,855	1,281	465	50	8	3	214	10,905
2009	4,330	2,613	1,833	1,265	459	49	8	3	212	10,771
Sales ($Millions) by Size of Firm										**Total**
2006	1,532	2,157	2,810	3,581	3,793	1,386	1,421	711	1,013	18,403
2008	1,604	2,258	2,942	3,749	3,970	1,450	1,488	744	1,063	19,268
2009	1,674	2,357	3,070	3,912	4,143	1,514	1,552	776	1,113	20,110
Employment by Size of Firm										**Total**
2006	13,314	16,070	26,299	41,495	28,721	6,673	2,354	1,169	14,080	150,175
2008	13,151	15,872	25,976	40,984	28,367	6,591	2,325	1,155	13,952	148,373
2009	12,989	15,677	25,656	40,480	28,019	6,510	2,297	1,141	13,824	146,592

SUB-INDUSTRIES – 2007 INDUSTRY ESTIMATES

Sub-Industries	Total Establishments	Total Employment	Total Sales ($M)
Book stores	8,661	121,850	15,871
Books, foreign	52	459	16
Books, religious	1,160	12,867	836
Children's books	173	1,220	66
College book stores	510	11,142	1,496
Comic books	484	2,637	119

RECORD & CD & TAPE STORES INDUSTRY (NAICS 45122)

INDUSTRY DEFINITION

NAICS 45122: Prerecorded Tape, Compact Disc, and Record Stores .
This industry comprises establishments primarily engaged in retailing new prerecorded audio and video tapes, compact discs (CDs), and phonograph records.

INDUSTRY ESTABLISHMENTS, SALES & EMPLOYMENT TRENDS

	Year					Percent Change Year-to-Year			
	2005	2006	2007	2008	2009	05-06	06-07	07-08	08-09
Establishments	5,663	5,419	5,174	4,869	4,582	-4.3%	-4.5%	-5.9%	-5.9%
Sales ($Millions)	8,460	7,585	7,471	7,209	6,949	-10.3%	-1.5%	-3.5%	-3.6%
Employment	68,835	61,060	58,365	55,075	51,705	-11.3%	-4.4%	-5.6%	-6.1%

INDUSTRY RATIOS

(Industry Averages)	Year					Percent Change Year-to-Year			
	2005	2006	2007	2008	2009	05-06	06-07	07-08	08-09
Sales ($M)/Estab.	1.49	1.40	1.44	1.48	1.52	-6.3%	3.1%	2.6%	2.4%
Sales ($) per Emp.	122,895	124,219	128,001	130,894	134,404	1.1%	3.0%	2.3%	2.7%
Emps. per Estab.	12.2	11.3	11.3	11.3	11.3	-7.3%	0.1%	0.3%	-0.2%

RECORD & CD & TAPE STORES INDUSTRY
(NAICS 45122)

SIZE OF FIRM INDUSTRY ESTIMATES

Year	Establishments by Size of Firm									Total
	1-4 Emps.	5-9 Emps.	10-19 Emps.	20-49 Emps.	50-99 Emps.	100-249 Emps.	250-499 Emps.	500+ Emps.	Unknown Emps.	
2006	2,169	1,333	931	491	120	8	1	0	125	5,174
2008	2,041	1,254	876	462	113	7	1	0	118	4,869
2009	1,920	1,180	824	435	106	7	1	0	111	4,582
Sales ($Millions) by Size of Firm										**Total**
2006	232	1,141	1,494	2,626	1,026	457	400	0	94	7,471
2008	224	1,101	1,442	2,533	990	441	386	0	93	7,209
2009	216	1,061	1,390	2,442	955	425	372	0	88	6,949
Employment by Size of Firm										**Total**
2006	4,338	9,330	12,104	16,196	6,955	1,079	299	0	8,064	58,365
2008	4,082	8,779	11,389	15,240	6,545	1,016	281	0	7,744	55,075
2009	3,841	8,261	10,717	14,341	6,158	956	265	0	7,168	51,705

SUB-INDUSTRIES — 2007 INDUSTRY ESTIMATES

Sub-Industries	Total Establishments	Total Employment	Total Sales ($M)
Record and prerecorded tape stores	1,058	16,909	2,318
Video discs and tapes, prerecorded	625	6,015	324
Video discs, prerecorded	35	1,090	188
Video tapes, prerecorded	211	2,430	190
Records, audio discs, and tapes	624	6,274	688
Audio tapes, prerecorded	216	4,406	1,421
Compact discs	637	6,354	1,616
Records	1,770	14,887	727

DEPARTMENT STORES INDUSTRY
(NAICS 45211)

INDUSTRY DEFINITION

NAICS 45211: Department Stores Industry . This industry comprises establishments known as department stores primarily engaged in retailing a wide range of the following new products with no one merchandise line predominating: apparel, furniture, appliances and home furnishings; and selected additional items, such as paint, hardware, toiletries, cosmetics, photographic equipment, jewelry, toys, and sporting goods. Merchandise lines are normally arranged in separate departments.

INDUSTRY ESTABLISHMENTS, SALES & EMPLOYMENT TRENDS

	Year					Percent Change Year-to-Year			
	2005	2006	2007	2008	2009	05-06	06-07	07-08	08-09
Establishments	11,996	11,688	11,379	11,185	10,994	-2.6%	-2.6%	-1.7%	-1.7%
Sales ($Millions)	402,192	401,065	399,151	398,806	398,406	-0.3%	-0.5%	-0.1%	-0.1%
Employment	1,529,779	1,506,434	1,467,078	1,441,599	1,417,402	-1.5%	-2.6%	-1.7%	-1.7%

INDUSTRY RATIOS

	Year					Percent Change Year-to-Year			
(Industry Averages)	2005	2006	2007	2008	2009	05-06	06-07	07-08	08-09
Sales ($M)/Estab.	33.53	34.31	35.08	35.66	36.24	2.3%	2.2%	1.7%	1.6%
Sales ($) per Emp.	262,909	266,235	272,072	276,641	281,082	1.3%	2.2%	1.7%	1.6%
Emps. per Estab.	127.5	128.9	128.9	128.9	128.9	1.1%	0.0%	0.0%	0.0%

DEPARTMENT STORES INDUSTRY
(NAICS 45211)

SIZE OF FIRM INDUSTRY ESTIMATES

Year	Establishments by Size of Firm									Total
	1-4 Emps.	5-9 Emps.	10-19 Emps.	20-49 Emps.	50-99 Emps.	100-249 Emps.	250-499 Emps.	500+ Emps.	Unknown Emps.	
2006	407	85	61	245	2,464	4,371	1,339	82	2,324	11,379
2008	400	84	60	241	2,421	4,296	1,316	81	2,285	11,185
2009	393	82	59	236	2,380	4,223	1,293	79	2,245	10,994
	Sales ($Millions) by Size of Firm									Total
2006	385	215	378	2,572	36,246	183,741	112,546	57,691	5,378	399,151
2008	385	215	378	2,570	36,216	183,589	112,453	57,643	5,359	398,806
2009	384	214	377	2,567	36,178	183,397	112,335	57,583	5,370	398,406
	Employment by Size of Firm									Total
2006	1,222	511	914	8,320	167,521	660,010	431,046	48,671	148,864	1,467,078
2008	1,201	502	898	8,178	164,657	648,727	423,677	47,839	145,920	1,441,599
2009	1,180	493	883	8,038	161,842	637,637	416,434	47,021	143,872	1,417,402

SUB-INDUSTRIES – 2007 INDUSTRY ESTIMATES

Sub-Industries	Total Establishments	Total Employment	Total Sales ($M)
Department stores	4,728	413,235	60,613
Department stores, discount	5,285	811,926	274,059
Department stores, non-discount	1,366	241,917	64,479

WAREHOUSE CLUBS & SUPERSTORES INDUSTRY (NAICS 45291)

INDUSTRY DEFINITION

NAICS 45291: Warehouse Clubs and Superstores This industry comprises establishments known as warehouse clubs, superstores or supercenters primarily engaged in retailing a general line of groceries in combination with general lines of new merchandise, such as apparel, furniture, and appliances.

INDUSTRY ESTABLISHMENTS, SALES & EMPLOYMENT TRENDS

	Year					Percent Change Year-to-Year			
	2005	2006	2007	2008	2009	05-06	06-07	07-08	08-09
Establishments	3,654	3,934	4,214	4,550	4,912	7.7%	7.1%	8.0%	8.0%
Sales ($Millions)	234,141	277,592	311,001	348,788	390,647	18.6%	12.0%	12.2%	12.0%
Employment	839,476	933,999	1,000,341	1,079,983	1,166,114	11.3%	7.1%	8.0%	8.0%

INDUSTRY RATIOS

	Year					Percent Change Year-to-Year			
(Industry Averages)	2005	2006	2007	2008	2009	05-06	06-07	07-08	08-09
Sales ($M)/Estab.	64.08	70.57	73.81	76.66	79.52	10.1%	4.6%	3.9%	3.7%
Sales ($) per Emp.	278,913	297,208	310,895	322,957	334,999	6.6%	4.6%	3.9%	3.7%
Emps. per Estab.	229.7	237.4	237.4	237.4	237.4	3.3%	0.0%	0.0%	0.0%

WAREHOUSE CLUBS & SUPERSTORES INDUSTRY (NAICS 45291)

SIZE OF FIRM INDUSTRY ESTIMATES

Year	Establishments by Size of Firm									
	1-4 Emps.	5-9 Emps.	10-19 Emps.	20-49 Emps.	50-99 Emps.	100-249 Emps.	250-499 Emps.	500+ Emps.	Unknown Emps.	Total
2006	25	4	12	84	121	1,205	1,733	402	624	4,214
2008	27	4	13	91	131	1,301	1,871	434	674	4,550
2009	29	4	14	98	141	1,404	2,020	469	727	4,912
	Sales ($Millions) by Size of Firm									Total
2006	42	15	86	591	1,333	19,881	123,909	163,632	1,511	311,001
2008	47	17	96	663	1,495	22,297	138,966	183,516	1,690	348,788
2009	52	19	108	743	1,675	24,973	155,643	205,540	1,894	390,647
	Employment by Size of Firm									Total
2006	76	22	180	2,939	8,119	180,689	550,936	217,445	39,936	1,000,341
2008	82	23	194	3,174	8,766	195,095	594,860	234,781	43,008	1,079,983
2009	88	25	210	3,427	9,465	210,649	642,286	253,499	46,464	1,166,114

SUB-INDUSTRIES – 2007 INDUSTRY ESTIMATES

Sub-Industries	Total Establishments	Total Employment	Total Sales ($M)
Department stores	1,740	257,110	45,977
Department stores, discount	1,970	600,124	216,303
Department stores, non-discount	503	143,108	48,721

OFFICE SUPPLIES & STATIONERY STORES INDUSTRY (NAICS 45321)

INDUSTRY DEFINITION

NAICS 45321: Office Supplies and Stationery Stores . This industry comprises establishments primarily engaged in one or more of the following: (1) retailing new stationery, school supplies, and office supplies; (2) selling a combination of new office equipment, furniture, and supplies; and (3) selling new office equipment, furniture, and supplies in combination with selling new computers.

INDUSTRY ESTABLISHMENTS, SALES & EMPLOYMENT TRENDS

	Year					Percent Change Year-to-Year			
	2005	2006	2007	2008	2009	05-06	06-07	07-08	08-09
Establishments	10,131	10,379	10,627	10,902	11,183	2.4%	2.4%	2.6%	2.6%
Sales ($Millions)	20,529	21,493	22,214	22,878	23,589	4.7%	3.4%	3.0%	3.1%
Employment	173,965	179,489	183,785	188,366	193,680	3.2%	2.4%	2.5%	2.8%

INDUSTRY RATIOS

(Industry Averages)	Year					Percent Change Year-to-Year			
	2005	2006	2007	2008	2009	05-06	06-07	07-08	08-09
Sales ($M)/Estab.	2.03	2.07	2.09	2.10	2.11	2.2%	0.9%	0.4%	0.5%
Sales ($) per Emp.	118,009	119,744	120,869	121,455	121,797	1.5%	0.9%	0.5%	0.3%
Emps. per Estab.	17.2	17.3	17.3	17.3	17.3	0.7%	0.0%	-0.1%	0.2%

OFFICE SUPPLIES & STATIONERY STORES INDUSTRY (NAICS 45321)

SIZE OF FIRM INDUSTRY ESTIMATES

Year	Establishments by Size of Firm									
	1-4 Emps.	5-9 Emps.	10-19 Emps.	20-49 Emps.	50-99 Emps.	100-249 Emps.	250-499 Emps.	500+ Emps.	Unknown Emps.	Total
2006	3,829	1,761	1,275	2,990	73	13	4	1	681	10,627
2008	3,928	1,806	1,308	3,068	75	13	4	1	698	10,902
2009	4,029	1,853	1,341	3,147	77	14	5	1	716	11,183
Sales ($Millions) by Size of Firm										**Total**
2006	785	1,263	2,483	13,793	858	438	487	221	1,885	22,214
2008	809	1,302	2,558	14,209	884	452	502	228	1,934	22,878
2009	833	1,341	2,635	14,639	911	465	517	235	2,013	23,589
Employment by Size of Firm										**Total**
2006	11,486	10,566	20,397	89,710	4,261	1,854	1,543	386	43,584	183,785
2008	11,783	10,838	20,923	92,027	4,371	1,902	1,583	396	44,544	188,366
2009	12,087	11,118	21,464	94,403	4,484	1,951	1,623	406	46,144	193,680

SUB-INDUSTRIES – 2007 INDUSTRY ESTIMATES

Sub-Industries	Total Establishments	Total Employment	Total Sales ($M)
Stationery stores	2,618	29,902	1,042
Notary and corporate seals	79	684	38
Office forms and supplies	6,758	144,813	20,665
School supplies	761	6,216	352
Writing supplies	412	2,171	117

ELECTRONIC SHOPPING & MAIL ORDER HOUSES (NAICS 45411)

INDUSTRY DEFINITION

NAICS 45411: Electronic Shopping and Mail-Order Houses This industry comprises establishments primarily engaged in retailing all types of merchandise by means of mail or by electronic media, such as interactive television or computer. Included in this industry are establishments primarily engaged in retailing from catalogue showrooms of mail-order houses.

INDUSTRY ESTABLISHMENTS, SALES & EMPLOYMENT TRENDS

	Year					Percent Change Year-to-Year			
	2005	2006	2007	2008	2009	05-06	06-07	07-08	08-09
Establishments	16,125	17,306	18,487	19,828	21,267	7.3%	6.8%	7.3%	7.3%
Sales ($Millions)	143,174	162,677	173,161	184,025	195,728	13.6%	6.4%	6.3%	6.4%
Employment	259,910	291,071	311,067	333,509	357,958	12.0%	6.9%	7.2%	7.3%

INDUSTRY RATIOS

(Industry Averages)	Year					Percent Change Year-to-Year			
	2005	2006	2007	2008	2009	05-06	06-07	07-08	08-09
Sales ($M)/Estab.	8.88	9.40	9.37	9.28	9.20	5.9%	-0.4%	-0.9%	-0.8%
Sales ($) per Emp.	550,858	558,891	556,668	551,784	546,789	1.5%	-0.4%	-0.9%	-0.9%
Emps. per Estab.	16.1	16.8	16.8	16.8	16.8	4.3%	0.0%	0.0%	0.1%

ELECTRONIC SHOPPING & MAIL ORDER HOUSES (NAICS 45411)

SIZE OF FIRM INDUSTRY ESTIMATES

Year	Establishments by Size of Firm									
	1-4 Emps.	5-9 Emps.	10-19 Emps.	20-49 Emps.	50-99 Emps.	100-249 Emps.	250-499 Emps.	500+ Emps.	Unknown Emps.	Total
2006	10,885	3,219	1,965	1,238	433	311	122	83	234	18,487
2008	11,675	3,452	2,108	1,328	465	333	130	89	251	19,828
2009	12,523	3,703	2,261	1,425	499	358	140	95	269	21,267
Sales ($Millions) by Size of Firm										**Total**
2006	8,693	6,426	7,847	22,253	23,495	25,873	24,259	47,934	6,381	173,161
2008	9,241	6,831	8,342	23,656	24,977	27,505	25,788	50,957	6,728	184,025
2009	9,824	7,262	8,867	25,147	26,551	29,239	27,414	54,169	7,255	195,728
Employment by Size of Firm										**Total**
2006	32,656	19,313	27,512	40,868	28,608	40,401	36,452	70,217	15,040	311,067
2008	35,026	20,714	29,508	43,834	30,684	43,333	39,097	75,312	16,000	333,509
2009	37,568	22,217	31,650	47,015	32,911	46,477	41,934	80,778	17,408	357,958

SUB-INDUSTRIES — 2007 INDUSTRY ESTIMATES

Sub-Industries	Total Establishments	Total Employment	Total Sales ($M)
Catalog and mail-order houses	3,929	67,850	11,930
Food, mail order	434	7,581	1,853
Computer equipment and electronics,	930	15,340	11,423
Book and record clubs	708	15,648	9,204
Stamps, coins, and other collectibles,	1,938	8,866	844
Arts and crafts equipment and supplies,	376	2,440	457
Automotive supplies and equipment,	340	3,930	632
Books, mail order (except book clubs)	580	5,424	379
Cards, mail order	95	2,012	284
Catalog sales	1,462	41,555	15,579
Clothing, mail order (except women's)	223	5,779	709
Cosmetics and perfumes, mail order	278	3,024	598
Educational supplies and equipment,	320	2,319	431
Fishing, hunting and camping	132	4,307	1,754
Fitness and sporting goods, mail order	251	4,014	748
Flowers, plants and bulbs: mail order	151	1,206	148
Furniture and furnishings, mail order	155	1,216	254
Other mail order merchandise	6,184	118,557	115,932

SCHEDULED AIR TRANSPORTATION INDUSTRY (NAICS 48111)

INDUSTRY DEFINITION

NAICS 48111: Scheduled Air Transportation Industry. This industry comprises establishments primarily engaged in providing air transportation of passengers and/or cargo over regular routes and on regular schedules. Establishments in this industry operate flights even if partially loaded. Establishments primarily engaged in providing scheduled air transportation of mail on a contract basis are included in this industry.

INDUSTRY ESTABLISHMENTS, SALES & EMPLOYMENT TRENDS

	Year					Percent Change Year-to-Year			
	2005	2006	2007	2008	2009	05-06	06-07	07-08	08-09
Establishments	3,716	3,737	3,758	3,719	3,641	0.6%	0.6%	-1.0%	-2.1%
Sales ($Millions)	169,295	158,690	153,899	145,838	136,552	-6.3%	-3.0%	-5.2%	-6.4%
Employment	267,602	264,401	265,975	263,109	257,786	-1.2%	0.6%	-1.1%	-2.0%

INDUSTRY RATIOS

(Industry Averages)	Year					Percent Change Year-to-Year			
	2005	2006	2007	2008	2009	05-06	06-07	07-08	08-09
Sales ($M)/Estab.	45.56	42.47	40.96	39.22	37.51	-6.8%	-3.6%	-4.2%	-4.4%
Sales ($) per Emp.	632,637	600,187	578,621	554,287	529,712	-5.1%	-3.6%	-4.2%	-4.4%
Emps. per Estab.	72.0	70.8	70.8	70.8	70.8	-1.7%	0.0%	0.0%	0.1%

SCHEDULED AIR TRANSPORTATION INDUSTRY
(NAICS 48111)

SIZE OF FIRM INDUSTRY ESTIMATES

Year	Establishments by Size of Firm									Total
	1-4 Emps.	5-9 Emps.	10-19 Emps.	20-49 Emps.	50-99 Emps.	100-249 Emps.	250-499 Emps.	500+ Emps.	Unknown Emps.	
2006	960	413	496	597	292	173	86	122	616	3,758
2008	950	408	491	590	289	171	85	121	610	3,719
2009	930	400	481	578	283	167	84	119	597	3,641
Sales ($Millions) by Size of Firm										**Total**
2006	1,779	1,530	3,126	8,404	9,584	7,919	21,510	86,873	13,174	153,899
2008	1,686	1,450	2,963	7,966	9,084	7,506	20,388	82,341	12,455	145,838
2009	1,578	1,357	2,773	7,456	8,502	7,025	19,082	77,068	11,711	136,552
Employment by Size of Firm										**Total**
2006	2,879	2,475	7,936	19,090	18,695	24,338	29,517	121,492	39,552	265,975
2008	2,849	2,450	7,854	18,891	18,501	24,085	29,210	120,229	39,040	263,109
2009	2,790	2,398	7,690	18,496	18,114	23,582	28,599	117,716	38,400	257,786

SUB-INDUSTRIES – 2007 INDUSTRY ESTIMATES

Sub-Industries	Total Establishments	Total Employment	Total Sales ($M)
Air transportation, scheduled	1,593	57,680	4,214
Air cargo carrier, scheduled	564	29,919	2,398
Air passenger carrier, scheduled	1,481	174,617	146,645
Helicopter carrier, scheduled	120	3,759	641

LOCAL FREIGHT TRUCKING INDUSTRY (NAICS 48411)

INDUSTRY DEFINITION

NAICS 48411: Freight Trucking, Local. This industry comprises establishments primarily engaged in providing local general freight trucking. General freight establishments handle a wide variety of commodities, generally palletized and transported in a container or van trailer. Local general freight trucking establishments usually provide trucking within a metropolitan area which may cross state lines. Generally the trips are same-day return.

INDUSTRY ESTABLISHMENTS, SALES & EMPLOYMENT TRENDS

	Year					Percent Change Year-to-Year			
	2005	2006	2007	2008	2009	05-06	06-07	07-08	08-09
Establishments	26,622	27,941	29,260	30,909	32,652	5.0%	4.7%	5.6%	5.6%
Sales ($Millions)	18,066	20,069	21,278	22,663	23,942	11.1%	6.0%	6.5%	5.6%
Employment	232,464	254,154	265,961	281,079	296,938	9.3%	4.6%	5.7%	5.6%

INDUSTRY RATIOS

(Industry Averages)	Year					Percent Change Year-to-Year			
	2005	2006	2007	2008	2009	05-06	06-07	07-08	08-09
Sales ($M)/Estab.	0.68	0.72	0.73	0.73	0.73	5.8%	1.2%	0.8%	0.0%
Sales ($) per Emp.	77,716	78,964	80,003	80,630	80,629	1.6%	1.3%	0.8%	0.0%
Emps. per Estab.	8.7	9.1	9.1	9.1	9.1	4.2%	-0.1%	0.0%	0.0%

LOCAL FREIGHT TRUCKING INDUSTRY
(NAICS 48411)

SIZE OF FIRM INDUSTRY ESTIMATES

Year	Establishments by Size of Firm									Total
	1-4 Emps.	5-9 Emps.	10-19 Emps.	20-49 Emps.	50-99 Emps.	100-249 Emps.	250-499 Emps.	500+ Emps.	Unknown Emps.	Total
2006	20,022	3,679	2,703	1,909	531	188	25	8	196	29,260
2008	21,150	3,886	2,856	2,016	560	198	26	9	207	30,909
2009	22,343	4,105	3,017	2,130	592	210	28	9	219	32,652
Sales ($Millions) by Size of Firm										**Total**
2006	3,483	1,694	3,043	4,882	3,420	2,517	830	566	842	21,278
2008	3,708	1,803	3,240	5,198	3,642	2,680	884	603	905	22,663
2009	3,917	1,905	3,422	5,491	3,847	2,831	933	637	957	23,942
Employment by Size of Firm										**Total**
2006	60,065	22,072	37,846	61,076	33,426	24,979	7,814	6,138	12,544	265,961
2008	63,451	23,317	39,980	64,519	35,310	26,387	8,255	6,484	13,376	281,079
2009	67,028	24,631	42,233	68,156	37,300	27,874	8,720	6,849	14,144	296,938

SUB-INDUSTRIES — 2007 INDUSTRY ESTIMATES

Sub-Industries	Total Establishments	Total Employment	Total Sales ($M)
Local trucking, without storage	18,288	142,649	12,590
Animal and farm product transportation	596	4,715	358
Liquid transfer services	640	10,757	1,364
Lumber and timber trucking	379	3,245	225
Moving services	2,032	21,255	1,206
Baggage transfer	21	576	22
Coal haulage, local	119	1,726	171
Delivery service, vehicular	2,790	29,630	1,737
Draying, local: without storage	30	553	76
Dump truck haulage	1,658	14,636	1,155
Garbage collection and transport, no	692	15,850	914
Hazardous waste transport	106	2,810	224
Heavy machinery transport, local	125	1,632	167
Light haulage and cartage, local	1,253	7,335	408
Mail carriers, contract	207	5,035	358
Star routes, local	3	83	8
Steel hauling, local	66	500	50
Truck rental with drivers	255	2,973	245

FREIGHT TRUCKING LONG DISTANCE INDUSTRY (NAICS 48412)

INDUSTRY DEFINITION

NAICS 48412: Freight Trucking, Long-Distance. This industry comprises establishments primarily engaged in providing long-distance general freight trucking. General freight establishments handle a wide variety of commodities, generally palletized and transported in a container or van trailer. Long-distance general freight trucking establishments usually provide trucking between metropolitan areas which may cross North American country borders. Included in this industry are establishments operating as truckload (TL) or less than truckload (LTL) carriers.

INDUSTRY ESTABLISHMENTS, SALES & EMPLOYMENT TRENDS

	Year					Percent Change Year-to-Year			
	2005	2006	2007	2008	2009	05-06	06-07	07-08	08-09
Establishments	39,370	40,002	40,634	41,366	42,173	1.6%	1.6%	1.8%	2.0%
Sales ($Millions)	142,186	141,144	142,677	143,836	146,618	-0.7%	1.1%	0.8%	1.9%
Employment	839,400	847,895	861,124	876,774	893,573	1.0%	1.6%	1.8%	1.9%

INDUSTRY RATIOS

(Industry Averages)	Year					Percent Change Year-to-Year			
	2005	2006	2007	2008	2009	05-06	06-07	07-08	08-09
Sales ($M)/Estab.	3.61	3.53	3.51	3.48	3.48	-2.3%	-0.5%	-1.0%	0.0%
Sales ($) per Emp.	169,390	166,464	165,687	164,051	164,080	-1.7%	-0.5%	-1.0%	0.0%
Emps. per Estab.	21.3	21.2	21.2	21.2	21.2	-0.6%	0.0%	0.0%	0.0%

FREIGHT TRUCKING LONG DISTANCE INDUSTRY (NAICS 48412)

SIZE OF FIRM INDUSTRY ESTIMATES

Year	Establishments by Size of Firm									Total
	1-4 Emps.	5-9 Emps.	10-19 Emps.	20-49 Emps.	50-99 Emps.	100-249 Emps.	250-499 Emps.	500+ Emps.	Unknown Emps.	Total
2006	23,494	4,556	4,163	4,137	1,777	1,000	303	205	999	40,634
2008	23,917	4,638	4,238	4,212	1,809	1,018	308	208	1,017	41,366
2009	24,384	4,728	4,321	4,294	1,845	1,038	314	212	1,037	42,173
Sales ($Millions) by Size of Firm										Total
2006	6,960	3,599	6,989	17,975	15,796	22,712	23,617	39,903	5,125	142,677
2008	7,016	3,628	7,046	18,120	15,924	22,895	23,807	40,224	5,176	143,836
2009	7,153	3,699	7,183	18,474	16,234	23,341	24,272	41,009	5,253	146,618
Employment by Size of Firm										Total
2006	46,988	27,334	62,450	136,521	111,974	138,995	96,572	176,418	63,872	861,124
2008	47,835	27,827	63,576	138,981	113,992	141,501	98,312	179,598	65,152	876,774
2009	48,768	28,370	64,817	141,694	116,217	144,262	100,231	183,103	66,112	893,573

SUB-INDUSTRIES — 2007 INDUSTRY ESTIMATES

Sub-Industries	Total Establishments	Total Employment	Total Sales ($M)
Trucking, except local	26,571	545,043	83,988
Automobiles, transport and delivery	1,587	18,608	3,711
Building materials transport	282	7,656	816
Contract haulers	5,214	143,783	13,301
Heavy hauling, nec	2,769	31,115	3,132
Heavy machinery transport	291	6,471	935
Household goods transport	1,184	32,390	9,965
Less-than-truckload (LTL)	275	26,117	19,877
Liquid petroleum transport, non-local	375	15,055	2,045
Mobile homes transport	1,011	5,268	328
Refrigerated products transport	895	27,888	4,351
Trailer or container on flat car	181	1,729	228

GENERAL WAREHOUSING & STORAGE INDUSTRY (NAICS 49311)

INDUSTRY DEFINITION

NAICS 49311: General Warehousing and Storage . This industry comprises establishments primarily engaged in operating merchandise warehousing and storage facilities. These establishments generally handle goods in containers, such as boxes, barrels, and/or drums, using equipment, such as forklifts, pallets, and racks. They are not specialized in handling bulk products of any particular type, size, or quantity of goods or products.

INDUSTRY ESTABLISHMENTS, SALES & EMPLOYMENT TRENDS

	Year					Percent Change Year-to-Year			
	2005	2006	2007	2008	2009	05-06	06-07	07-08	08-09
Establishments	9,728	10,944	12,161	13,966	16,038	12.5%	11.1%	14.8%	14.8%
Sales ($Millions)	65,448	71,170	77,464	86,657	96,871	8.7%	8.8%	11.9%	11.8%
Employment	418,714	467,242	519,208	596,432	685,059	11.6%	11.1%	14.9%	14.9%

INDUSTRY RATIOS

	Year					Percent Change Year-to-Year			
(Industry Averages)	2005	2006	2007	2008	2009	05-06	06-07	07-08	08-09
Sales ($M)/Estab.	6.73	6.50	6.37	6.21	6.04	-3.3%	-2.0%	-2.6%	-2.7%
Sales ($) per Emp.	156,307	152,320	149,196	145,293	141,406	-2.6%	-2.1%	-2.6%	-2.7%
Emps. per Estab.	43.0	42.7	42.7	42.7	42.7	-0.8%	0.0%	0.0%	0.0%

GENERAL WAREHOUSING & STORAGE INDUSTRY (NAICS 49311)

SIZE OF FIRM INDUSTRY ESTIMATES

Year	Establishments by Size of Firm									Total
	1-4 Emps.	5-9 Emps.	10-19 Emps.	20-49 Emps.	50-99 Emps.	100-249 Emps.	250-499 Emps.	500+ Emps.	Unknown Emps.	
2006	3,686	1,846	1,932	1,853	885	597	275	196	887	12,161
2008	4,233	2,120	2,218	2,128	1,017	685	316	225	1,018	13,966
2009	4,862	2,434	2,548	2,444	1,168	787	363	259	1,169	16,038
	Sales ($Millions) by Size of Firm									Total
2006	705	1,059	2,772	6,559	8,470	17,122	14,462	24,283	2,032	77,464
2008	789	1,185	3,101	7,337	9,475	19,152	16,177	27,163	2,279	86,657
2009	882	1,325	3,466	8,202	10,591	21,409	18,083	30,363	2,551	96,871
	Employment by Size of Firm									Total
2006	7,373	11,074	28,977	57,451	54,899	77,563	82,466	142,766	56,640	519,208
2008	8,467	12,717	33,277	65,977	63,046	89,074	94,704	163,953	65,216	596,432
2009	9,723	14,605	38,216	75,769	72,402	102,293	108,759	188,284	75,008	685,059

SUB-INDUSTRIES — 2007 INDUSTRY ESTIMATES

Sub-Industries	Total Establishments	Total Employment	Total Sales ($M)
General warehousing and storage	5,277	349,532	39,153
General warehousing	9,575	155,582	5,376
Miniwarehouse, warehousing	4,152	11,003	488
Warehousing, self storage	9,710	39,040	1,635

NEWSPAPER PUBLISHING INDUSTRY
(NAICS 51111)

INDUSTRY DEFINITION

NAICS 51111: Newspaper Publishers . Establishments primarily engaged in publishing newspapers, or in publishing and printing newspapers.
These establishments carry on the various operations necessary for issuing newspapers, including the gathering of news and the preparation of editorials and advertisements, but may or may not perform their own printing.

INDUSTRY ESTABLISHMENTS, SALES & EMPLOYMENT TRENDS

	Year					Percent Change Year-to-Year			
	2005	2006	2007	2008	2009	05-06	06-07	07-08	08-09
Establishments	8,598	8,587	8,576	8,558	8,541	-0.1%	-0.1%	-0.2%	-0.2%
Sales ($Millions)	61,737	63,172	64,892	66,239	67,572	2.3%	2.7%	2.1%	2.0%
Employment	362,770	362,162	361,714	360,995	360,213	-0.2%	-0.1%	-0.2%	-0.2%

INDUSTRY RATIOS

(Industry Averages)	Year					Percent Change Year-to-Year			
	2005	2006	2007	2008	2009	05-06	06-07	07-08	08-09
Sales ($M)/Estab.	7.18	7.36	7.57	7.74	7.91	2.5%	2.9%	2.3%	2.2%
Sales ($) per Emp.	170,181	174,429	179,401	183,491	187,590	2.5%	2.9%	2.3%	2.2%
Emps. per Estab.	42.2	42.2	42.2	42.2	42.2	0.0%	0.0%	0.0%	0.0%

Newspaper Publishing Industry
(NAICS 51111)

Size of Firm Industry Estimates

Year	Establishments by Size of Firm									Total
	1-4 Emps.	5-9 Emps.	10-19 Emps.	20-49 Emps.	50-99 Emps.	100-249 Emps.	250-499 Emps.	500+ Emps.	Unknown Emps.	
2006	2,790	1,666	1,362	1,323	531	427	143	133	199	8,576
2008	2,785	1,663	1,360	1,320	530	426	143	133	198	8,558
2009	2,779	1,659	1,357	1,317	529	425	142	133	198	8,541
	Sales ($Millions) by Size of Firm									Total
2006	883	1,055	2,874	6,976	7,173	13,062	9,050	22,094	1,726	64,892
2008	901	1,076	2,934	7,120	7,321	13,332	9,237	22,552	1,765	66,239
2009	919	1,098	2,993	7,264	7,469	13,601	9,424	23,008	1,796	67,572
	Employment by Size of Firm									Total
2006	8,371	9,998	20,437	43,651	34,533	63,198	47,762	120,836	12,928	361,714
2008	8,354	9,977	20,395	43,561	34,462	63,067	47,663	120,587	12,928	360,995
2009	8,337	9,957	20,353	43,471	34,391	62,937	47,565	120,339	12,864	360,213

Sub-Industries – 2007 Industry Estimates

Sub-Industries	Total Establishments	Total Employment	Total Sales ($M)
Newspapers	7,508	131,489	9,015
Newspapers, publishing and printing	4,195	202,994	49,799
Commercial printing and newspaper	702	36,315	13,813
Job printing and newspaper publishing	472	8,358	470
Newspapers: publishing only, not	3,045	82,926	8,966

PERIODICAL PUBLISHING INDUSTRY
(NAICS 51112)

INDUSTRY DEFINITION

NAICS 51112: Periodical Publishing . Establishments primarily engaged in publishing periodicals, or in publishing and printing periodicals. These establishments carry on the various operations necessary for issuing periodicals, but may or may not perform their own printing. Establishments not engaged in publishing periodicals, but which print periodicals for publishers, are classified in SIC 2752-2759.

INDUSTRY ESTABLISHMENTS, SALES & EMPLOYMENT TRENDS

	Year					Percent Change Year-to-Year			
	2005	2006	2007	2008	2009	05-06	06-07	07-08	08-09
Establishments	8,047	8,498	8,949	9,410	9,894	5.6%	5.3%	5.1%	5.1%
Sales ($Millions)	40,331	43,467	47,420	51,351	55,536	7.8%	9.1%	8.3%	8.1%
Employment	165,599	174,123	183,468	193,057	202,837	5.1%	5.4%	5.2%	5.1%

INDUSTRY RATIOS

(Industry Averages)	Year					Percent Change Year-to-Year			
	2005	2006	2007	2008	2009	05-06	06-07	07-08	08-09
Sales ($M)/Estab.	5.01	5.11	5.30	5.46	5.61	2.1%	3.6%	3.0%	2.9%
Sales ($) per Emp.	243,544	249,636	258,466	265,988	273,795	2.5%	3.5%	2.9%	2.9%
Emps. per Estab.	20.6	20.5	20.5	20.5	20.5	-0.4%	0.1%	0.1%	-0.1%

Periodical Publishing Industry
(NAICS 51112)

Size of Firm Industry Estimates

Year	Establishments by Size of Firm									Total
	1-4 Emps.	5-9 Emps.	10-19 Emps.	20-49 Emps.	50-99 Emps.	100-249 Emps.	250-499 Emps.	500+ Emps.	Unknown Emps.	Total
2006	4,354	1,583	1,218	883	372	205	73	32	229	8,949
2008	4,578	1,665	1,281	929	391	216	77	34	241	9,410
2009	4,813	1,750	1,347	977	411	227	81	36	254	9,894
	Sales ($Millions) by Size of Firm									Total
2006	1,397	1,185	3,910	7,559	5,169	7,974	8,341	10,739	1,146	47,420
2008	1,513	1,283	4,233	8,184	5,596	8,633	9,030	11,626	1,253	51,351
2009	1,636	1,388	4,579	8,853	6,053	9,338	9,768	12,577	1,342	55,536
	Employment by Size of Firm									Total
2006	8,707	9,499	17,056	28,267	23,788	28,749	24,596	28,214	14,592	183,468
2008	9,155	9,988	17,934	29,722	25,013	30,228	25,862	29,666	15,488	193,057
2009	9,627	10,502	18,858	31,252	26,300	31,784	27,193	31,193	16,128	202,837

Sub-Industries – 2007 Industry Estimates

Sub-Industries	Total Establishments	Total Employment	Total Sales ($M)
Periodicals	4,641	48,249	11,050
Periodicals, publishing only	728	15,764	2,165
Comic books: publishing only, not	57	775	690
Magazines: publishing only, not printed	2,770	61,220	15,133
Statistical reports (periodicals):	72	4,445	576
Television schedules: publishing only,	14	191	10
Trade journals: publishing only, not	534	12,615	8,017
Periodicals, publishing and printing	238	6,882	1,346
Comic books: publishing and printing	82	255	34
Magazines: publishing and printing	1,654	23,401	3,325
Statistical reports (periodicals):	57	2,254	659
Television schedules: publishing and	8	561	3
Trade journals: publishing and printing	244	4,143	414

BOOK PUBLISHING INDUSTRY
(NAICS 51113)

INDUSTRY DEFINITION

NAICS 51113: Book Publishers . This U.S. industry comprises establishments known as book publishers. Establishments in this industry carry out design, editing, and marketing activities necessary for producing and distributing books. These establishments may publish books in print, electronic, or audio form.

INDUSTRY ESTABLISHMENTS, SALES & EMPLOYMENT TRENDS

	Year					Percent Change Year-to-Year			
	2005	2006	2007	2008	2009	05-06	06-07	07-08	08-09
Establishments	3,400	3,624	3,847	4,044	4,251	6.6%	6.2%	5.1%	5.1%
Sales ($Millions)	31,862	32,988	34,444	35,411	36,397	3.5%	4.4%	2.8%	2.8%
Employment	82,308	87,792	93,223	97,962	103,065	6.7%	6.2%	5.1%	5.2%

INDUSTRY RATIOS

(Industry Averages)	Year					Percent Change Year-to-Year			
	2005	2006	2007	2008	2009	05-06	06-07	07-08	08-09
Sales ($M)/Estab.	9.37	9.10	8.95	8.76	8.56	-2.9%	-1.7%	-2.2%	-2.2%
Sales ($) per Emp.	387,101	375,745	369,480	361,480	353,147	-2.9%	-1.7%	-2.2%	-2.3%
Emps. per Estab.	24.2	24.2	24.2	24.2	24.2	0.1%	0.0%	0.0%	0.1%

Book Publishing Industry
(NAICS 51113)

Size of Firm Industry Estimates

Year	Establishments by Size of Firm									Total
	1-4 Emps.	5-9 Emps.	10-19 Emps.	20-49 Emps.	50-99 Emps.	100-249 Emps.	250-499 Emps.	500+ Emps.	Unknown Emps.	
2006	2,218	556	375	317	143	120	48	24	53	3,847
2008	2,331	585	394	334	150	127	51	25	56	4,044
2009	2,451	615	414	351	158	133	53	26	58	4,251
Sales ($Millions) by Size of Firm										**Total**
2006	855	1,180	1,627	3,092	3,654	5,808	7,002	10,986	241	34,444
2008	880	1,213	1,673	3,179	3,756	5,971	7,199	11,295	245	35,411
2009	904	1,247	1,719	3,267	3,860	6,136	7,398	11,607	259	36,397
Employment by Size of Firm										**Total**
2006	6,654	3,337	5,249	10,477	9,294	17,227	15,928	21,985	3,072	93,223
2008	6,994	3,508	5,517	11,013	9,769	18,108	16,742	23,109	3,200	97,962
2009	7,352	3,687	5,799	11,577	10,269	19,034	17,599	24,291	3,456	103,065

Sub-Industries – 2007 Industry Estimates

Sub-Industries	Total Establishments	Total Employment	Total Sales ($M)
Book publishing	6,525	44,461	5,073
Books, publishing only	2,539	43,070	26,512
Book clubs: publishing only, not printed	71	453	35
Book music: publishing only, not printed	87	499	91
Pamphlets: publishing only, not printed	157	1,217	192
Textbooks: publishing only, not printed	289	6,575	2,297
Books, publishing and printing	602	12,166	6,242
Book clubs: publishing and printing	92	454	17
Book music: publishing and printing	126	494	49
Pamphlets: publishing and printing	179	2,607	428
Textbooks: publishing and printing	147	4,227	432

Database & Directory Publishing Industry (NAICS 51114)

Industry Definition

NAICS 51114: Database and Directory Publishers . This U.S. industry comprises establishments primarily engaged in publishing compilations and collections of information or facts that are logically organized to facilitate their use. These collections may be published in print or electronic form. Electronic versions may be provided directly to customers by the establishment or offered through on-line services or third-party vendors.

Industry Establishments, Sales & Employment Trends

	Year					Percent Change Year-to-Year			
	2005	2006	2007	2008	2009	05-06	06-07	07-08	08-09
Establishments	1,848	2,131	2,414	2,649	2,906	15.3%	13.3%	9.7%	9.7%
Sales ($Millions)	10,412	13,046	15,030	16,692	18,525	25.3%	15.2%	11.1%	11.0%
Employment	56,031	69,609	78,838	86,597	94,951	24.2%	13.3%	9.8%	9.6%

Industry Ratios

(Industry Averages)	Year					Percent Change Year-to-Year			
	2005	2006	2007	2008	2009	05-06	06-07	07-08	08-09
Sales ($M)/Estab.	5.63	6.12	6.23	6.30	6.37	8.7%	1.7%	1.2%	1.1%
Sales ($) per Emp.	185,817	187,421	190,644	192,758	195,097	0.9%	1.7%	1.1%	1.2%
Emps. per Estab.	30.3	32.7	32.7	32.7	32.7	7.7%	0.0%	0.1%	-0.1%

DATABASE & DIRECTORY PUBLISHING INDUSTRY (NAICS 51114)

SIZE OF FIRM INDUSTRY ESTIMATES

Year	Establishments by Size of Firm									Total
	1-4 Emps.	5-9 Emps.	10-19 Emps.	20-49 Emps.	50-99 Emps.	100-249 Emps.	250-499 Emps.	500+ Emps.	Unknown Emps.	
2006	950	342	403	345	193	93	36	21	37	2,414
2008	1,043	376	442	379	212	102	39	23	41	2,649
2009	1,144	412	485	415	232	112	43	25	45	2,906
	Sales ($Millions) by Size of Firm									Total
2006	294	212	1,079	1,922	1,772	3,073	3,848	2,678	152	15,030
2008	326	235	1,198	2,133	1,967	3,411	4,272	2,973	175	16,692
2009	362	261	1,330	2,368	2,184	3,787	4,742	3,300	190	18,525
	Employment by Size of Firm									Total
2006	2,851	2,054	6,038	11,042	12,356	13,035	12,710	16,448	2,304	78,838
2008	3,128	2,254	6,625	12,115	13,557	14,302	13,945	18,046	2,624	86,597
2009	3,432	2,473	7,269	13,293	14,875	15,693	15,300	19,800	2,816	94,951

SUB-INDUSTRIES – 2007 INDUSTRY ESTIMATES

Sub-Industries	Total Establishments	Total Employment	Total Sales ($M)
Miscellaneous publishing	1,455	28,295	4,273
Art copy and poster publishing	85	1,459	224
Atlas, map, and guide publishing	90	3,747	825
Telephone and other directory	116	4,808	483
Directories, nec: publishing and printing	37	3,435	1,614
Directories, nec: publishing only, not	52	4,448	963
Directories, telephone: publishing and	19	1,898	442
Directories, telephone: publishing only,	32	5,228	1,635
Music book and sheet music publishing	163	2,449	338
Newsletter publishing	126	2,763	586
Business service newsletters: publishing	76	2,050	178
Shopping news: publishing and printing	27	2,281	1,358
Shopping news: publishing only, not	25	3,716	338
Technical manual and paper publishing	55	3,568	655
Catalogs: publishing and printing	12	785	105
Catalogs: publishing only, not printed on	13	3,118	420
Other printed materials	31	4,788	594

SOFTWARE PUBLISHING INDUSTRY (NAICS 51121)

INDUSTRY DEFINITION

NAICS 51121: Software Publishers . This industry comprises establishments primarily engaged in computer software publishing or publishing and reproduction. Establishments in this industry carry out operations necessary for producing and distributing computer software, such as designing, providing documentation, assisting in installation, and providing support services to software purchasers. These establishments may design, develop, and publish, or publish only.

INDUSTRY ESTABLISHMENTS, SALES & EMPLOYMENT TRENDS

	Year					Percent Change Year-to-Year			
	2005	2006	2007	2008	2009	05-06	06-07	07-08	08-09
Establishments	9,122	8,744	8,366	8,044	7,733	-4.1%	-4.3%	-3.9%	-3.9%
Sales ($Millions)	117,345	131,113	142,958	153,662	163,292	11.7%	9.0%	7.5%	6.3%
Employment	307,780	299,065	286,221	275,337	264,595	-2.8%	-4.3%	-3.8%	-3.9%

INDUSTRY RATIOS

	Year					Percent Change Year-to-Year			
(Industry Averages)	2005	2006	2007	2008	2009	05-06	06-07	07-08	08-09
Sales ($M)/Estab.	12.86	14.99	17.09	19.10	21.11	16.6%	14.0%	11.8%	10.5%
Sales ($) per Emp.	381,264	438,410	499,467	558,085	617,139	15.0%	13.9%	11.7%	10.6%
Emps. per Estab.	33.7	34.2	34.2	34.2	34.2	1.4%	0.0%	0.1%	0.0%

Software Publishing Industry
(NAICS 51121)

Size of Firm Industry Estimates

Year	Establishments by Size of Firm									Total
	1-4 Emps.	5-9 Emps.	10-19 Emps.	20-49 Emps.	50-99 Emps.	100-249 Emps.	250-499 Emps.	500+ Emps.	Unknown Emps.	Total
2006	3,637	1,191	1,122	1,105	479	341	118	79	293	8,366
2008	3,497	1,145	1,079	1,063	460	328	114	76	282	8,044
2009	3,362	1,101	1,037	1,022	443	315	109	73	271	7,733
	Sales ($Millions) by Size of Firm									Total
2006	1,413	1,850	2,907	7,731	9,925	22,095	30,611	64,133	2,292	142,958
2008	1,519	1,989	3,124	8,308	10,666	23,747	32,899	68,926	2,484	153,662
2009	1,614	2,114	3,320	8,830	11,336	25,238	34,965	73,254	2,621	163,292
	Employment by Size of Firm									Total
2006	7,274	7,144	15,712	36,479	30,174	50,501	39,119	80,937	18,880	286,221
2008	6,994	6,869	15,106	35,072	29,011	48,554	37,611	77,817	18,304	275,337
2009	6,724	6,604	14,524	33,720	27,892	46,682	36,161	74,817	17,472	264,595

Sub-Industries — 2007 Industry Estimates

Sub-Industries	Total Establishments	Total Employment	Total Sales ($M)
Prepackaged software	17,680	158,751	84,626
Application computer software	942	41,613	16,112
Business oriented computer software	1,174	51,328	20,007
Educational computer software	492	6,462	1,193
Home entertainment computer software	89	2,270	4,512
Operating systems computer software	174	3,488	721
Publisher's computer software	371	3,511	714
Utility computer software	71	2,457	1,829
Word processing computer software	38	187	22

MOTION PICTURES & VIDEO PRODUCTION INDUSTRY (NAICS 51211)

INDUSTRY DEFINITION

NAICS 51211: Motion Picture and Video Production Industry . This industry comprises establishments primarily engaged in producing, or producing and distributing motion pictures, videos, television programs, or television and video commercials.

INDUSTRY ESTABLISHMENTS, SALES & EMPLOYMENT TRENDS

	Year					Percent Change Year-to-Year			
	2005	2006	2007	2008	2009	05-06	06-07	07-08	08-09
Establishments	12,496	12,928	13,361	13,888	14,435	3.5%	3.3%	3.9%	3.9%
Sales ($Millions)	50,094	54,599	60,803	67,460	74,568	9.0%	11.4%	10.9%	10.5%
Employment	103,732	108,312	111,950	116,407	121,094	4.4%	3.4%	4.0%	4.0%

INDUSTRY RATIOS

	Year					Percent Change Year-to-Year			
(Industry Averages)	2005	2006	2007	2008	2009	05-06	06-07	07-08	08-09
Sales ($M)/Estab.	4.01	4.22	4.55	4.86	5.17	5.3%	7.8%	6.7%	6.3%
Sales ($) per Emp.	482,921	504,089	543,129	579,519	615,786	4.4%	7.7%	6.7%	6.3%
Emps. per Estab.	8.3	8.4	8.4	8.4	8.4	0.9%	0.0%	0.0%	0.1%

Motion Pictures & Video Production Industry (NAICS 51211)

Size of Firm Industry Estimates

Year	Establishments by Size of Firm									Total
	1-4 Emps.	5-9 Emps.	10-19 Emps.	20-49 Emps.	50-99 Emps.	100-249 Emps.	250-499 Emps.	500+ Emps.	Unknown Emps.	
2006	10,687	1,231	642	439	150	73	24	29	90	13,361
2008	11,108	1,280	667	457	156	76	25	31	94	13,888
2009	11,546	1,331	693	475	162	79	26	32	98	14,435
Sales ($Millions) by Size of Firm										**Total**
2006	6,186	2,852	3,418	4,071	5,219	6,776	5,494	25,115	1,673	60,803
2008	6,862	3,163	3,791	4,515	5,789	7,517	6,094	27,859	1,869	67,460
2009	7,582	3,495	4,189	4,989	6,397	8,305	6,733	30,780	2,099	74,568
Employment by Size of Firm										**Total**
2006	21,373	7,389	8,984	14,063	9,316	10,134	7,165	28,086	5,440	111,950
2008	22,216	7,680	9,338	14,618	9,684	10,534	7,448	29,194	5,696	116,407
2009	23,092	7,983	9,707	15,195	10,065	10,949	7,741	30,345	6,016	121,094

Sub-Industries — 2007 Industry Estimates

Sub-Industries	Total Establishments	Total Employment	Total Sales ($M)
Motion picture and video production	6,505	35,559	17,616
Motion picture production	490	10,038	5,469
Cartoon motion picture production	66	996	267
Educational motion picture production	75	832	60
Educational motion picture production,	46	753	87
Industrial motion picture production	29	367	82
Motion picture production and	188	19,805	25,770
Motion picture production and	86	2,492	3,562
Non-theatrical motion picture production	21	137	16
Non-theatrical motion picture	21	610	117
Religious motion picture production	11	233	10
Television film production	1,049	12,354	2,476
Training motion picture production	30	237	29
Video production	2,510	10,515	1,212
Music video production	290	1,164	208
Video tape production	773	6,662	1,906
Audio-visual program production	832	5,202	656
Other television productions	341	3,995	1,260

MUSIC PUBLISHING INDUSTRY
(NAICS 51223)

INDUSTRY DEFINITION

NAICS 51223: Music Publishers . This U.S. industry comprises
establishments known as music publishers. Establishments in this
industry carry out design, editing, and marketing activities necessary
for producing and distributing music books. These establishments may publish
books in print, electronic, or audio form.

INDUSTRY ESTABLISHMENTS, SALES & EMPLOYMENT TRENDS

	Year					Percent Change Year-to-Year			
	2005	2006	2007	2008	2009	05-06	06-07	07-08	08-09
Establishments	653	630	607	596	586	-3.5%	-3.7%	-1.7%	-1.7%
Sales ($Millions)	1,388	1,885	2,051	2,235	2,414	35.8%	8.8%	9.0%	8.0%
Employment	5,209	5,908	5,710	5,622	5,535	13.4%	-3.4%	-1.5%	-1.5%

INDUSTRY RATIOS

	Year					Percent Change Year-to-Year			
(Industry Averages)	2005	2006	2007	2008	2009	05-06	06-07	07-08	08-09
Sales ($M)/Estab.	2.13	2.99	3.38	3.75	4.12	40.8%	12.9%	10.9%	9.8%
Sales ($) per Emp.	266,461	319,067	359,128	397,604	436,058	19.7%	12.6%	10.7%	9.7%
Emps. per Estab.	8.0	9.4	9.4	9.4	9.4	17.6%	0.3%	0.2%	0.2%

MUSIC PUBLISHING INDUSTRY
(NAICS 51223)

SIZE OF FIRM INDUSTRY ESTIMATES

Year	Establishments by Size of Firm									Total
	1-4 Emps.	5-9 Emps.	10-19 Emps.	20-49 Emps.	50-99 Emps.	100-249 Emps.	250-499 Emps.	500+ Emps.	Unknown Emps.	
2006	462	61	38	20	6	11	1	0	10	607
2008	455	60	37	19	6	11	1	0	10	596
2009	447	59	36	19	6	11	1	0	10	586
Sales ($Millions) by Size of Firm										**Total**
2006	234	140	214	253	199	688	175	0	150	2,051
2008	255	152	233	275	216	749	190	0	166	2,235
2009	275	164	251	296	233	807	205	0	182	2,414
Employment by Size of Firm										**Total**
2006	1,387	368	526	652	385	1,554	325	0	512	5,710
2008	1,364	361	517	641	379	1,528	320	0	512	5,622
2009	1,341	355	508	630	372	1,502	314	0	512	5,535

SUB-INDUSTRIES — 2007 INDUSTRY ESTIMATES

Sub-Industries	Total Establishments	Total Employment	Total Sales ($M)
Book publishing	394	2,499	274
Books, publishing only	153	2,421	1,430
Book clubs: publishing only, not printed	4	25	2
Book music: publishing only, not printed	5	28	5
Books, publishing and printing	36	684	337
Book clubs: publishing and printing	6	25	1
Book music: publishing and printing	8	28	3

RADIO BROADCASTING INDUSTRY
(NAICS 51511)

INDUSTRY DEFINITION

NAICS 51511: Radio Broadcasting . This industry comprises establishments primarily engaged in broadcasting audio signals. These establishments operate radio broadcasting studios and facilities for the transmission of aural programming by radio to the public, to affiliates, or to subscribers. The radio programs may include entertainment, news, talk shows, business data, or religious services.

INDUSTRY ESTABLISHMENTS, SALES & EMPLOYMENT TRENDS

	Year					Percent Change Year-to-Year			
	2005	2006	2007	2008	2009	05-06	06-07	07-08	08-09
Establishments	8,793	9,101	9,408	9,657	9,913	3.5%	3.4%	2.6%	2.6%
Sales ($Millions)	18,041	21,207	24,109	26,867	29,753	17.6%	13.7%	11.4%	10.7%
Employment	197,388	210,331	217,609	223,244	228,977	6.6%	3.5%	2.6%	2.6%

INDUSTRY RATIOS

	Year					Percent Change Year-to-Year			
(Industry Averages)	2005	2006	2007	2008	2009	05-06	06-07	07-08	08-09
Sales ($M)/Estab.	2.05	2.33	2.56	2.78	3.00	13.6%	10.0%	8.6%	7.9%
Sales ($) per Emp.	91,397	100,826	110,789	120,348	129,939	10.3%	9.9%	8.6%	8.0%
Emps. per Estab.	22.4	23.1	23.1	23.1	23.1	3.0%	0.1%	-0.1%	-0.1%

Radio Broadcasting Industry
(NAICS 51511)

Size of Firm Industry Estimates

Year	Establishments by Size of Firm									Total
	1-4 Emps.	5-9 Emps.	10-19 Emps.	20-49 Emps.	50-99 Emps.	100-249 Emps.	250-499 Emps.	500+ Emps.	Unknown Emps.	
2006	2,890	1,664	1,719	1,362	415	139	12	7	1,205	9,408
2008	2,966	1,708	1,764	1,398	426	143	12	7	1,237	9,657
2009	3,045	1,753	1,811	1,435	437	147	13	7	1,270	9,913
Sales ($Millions) by Size of Firm										Total
2006	697	1,003	5,180	6,566	3,504	3,472	581	1,506	1,601	24,109
2008	777	1,118	5,773	7,318	3,905	3,869	648	1,678	1,781	26,867
2009	860	1,238	6,394	8,105	4,325	4,286	717	1,858	1,969	29,753
Employment by Size of Firm										Total
2006	8,669	11,647	25,780	43,571	25,740	17,946	3,374	3,635	77,248	217,609
2008	8,898	11,956	26,462	44,724	26,421	18,421	3,463	3,731	79,168	223,244
2009	9,134	12,272	27,163	45,907	27,120	18,908	3,555	3,829	81,088	228,977

Sub-Industries – 2007 Industry Estimates

Sub-Industries	Total Establishments	Total Employment	Total Sales ($M)
Radio broadcasting stations	7,408	190,290	22,940
Radio broadcasting stations, music	149	3,972	179
Classical	40	687	24
Contemporary	268	5,902	187
Radio broadcasting stations, except	83	815	34
Educational	978	9,549	463
News	53	1,943	61
Religious	251	2,203	126
Sports	134	1,687	74
Talk	44	560	20

TELEVISION BROADCASTING SERVICES INDUSTRY
(NAICS 51512)

INDUSTRY DEFINITION

NAICS 51512: Television Broadcasting . This industry comprises establishments primarily engaged in broadcasting images together with sound. These establishments operate television broadcasting studios and facilities for the programming and transmission of programs to the public. These establishments also produce or transmit visual programming to affiliated broadcast television stations, which in turn broadcast the programs to the public on a predetermined schedule. Programming may originate in their own studios, from an affiliated network, or from external sources.

INDUSTRY ESTABLISHMENTS, SALES & EMPLOYMENT TRENDS

	Year					Percent Change Year-to-Year			
	2005	2006	2007	2008	2009	05-06	06-07	07-08	08-09
Establishments	2,506	2,492	2,479	2,472	2,466	-0.5%	-0.5%	-0.2%	-0.2%
Sales ($Millions)	61,546	58,447	59,430	60,155	60,951	-5.0%	1.7%	1.2%	1.3%
Employment	153,023	147,828	147,197	146,787	146,505	-3.4%	-0.4%	-0.3%	-0.2%

INDUSTRY RATIOS

(Industry Averages)	Year					Percent Change Year-to-Year			
	2005	2006	2007	2008	2009	05-06	06-07	07-08	08-09
Sales ($M)/Estab.	24.56	23.45	23.98	24.33	24.71	-4.5%	2.2%	1.5%	1.6%
Sales ($) per Emp.	402,202	395,373	403,740	409,809	416,034	-1.7%	2.1%	1.5%	1.5%
Emps. per Estab.	61.1	59.3	59.4	59.4	59.4	-2.9%	0.1%	0.0%	0.1%

TELEVISION BROADCASTING SERVICES INDUSTRY (NAICS 51512)

SIZE OF FIRM INDUSTRY ESTIMATES

Year	Establishments by Size of Firm									Total
	1-4 Emps.	5-9 Emps.	10-19 Emps.	20-49 Emps.	50-99 Emps.	100-249 Emps.	250-499 Emps.	500+ Emps.	Unknown Emps.	
2006	515	218	202	331	323	314	48	12	514	2,479
2008	514	217	201	330	322	313	48	12	513	2,472
2009	512	217	201	329	322	313	47	12	511	2,466
	Sales ($Millions) by Size of Firm									Total
2006	1,025	1,301	1,332	2,706	5,655	13,136	4,121	11,768	18,385	59,430
2008	1,038	1,317	1,349	2,740	5,726	13,302	4,173	11,917	18,591	60,155
2009	1,051	1,333	1,366	2,775	5,798	13,468	4,225	12,065	18,869	60,951
	Employment by Size of Firm									Total
2006	1,545	1,306	3,027	11,257	21,649	45,870	14,890	14,629	33,024	147,197
2008	1,541	1,303	3,020	11,229	21,596	45,756	14,853	14,593	32,896	146,787
2009	1,537	1,300	3,012	11,201	21,542	45,643	14,816	14,557	32,896	146,505

SUB-INDUSTRIES – 2007 INDUSTRY ESTIMATES

Sub-Industries	Total Establishments	Total Employment	Total Sales ($M)
Television broadcasting stations	2,425	143,103	59,099
Television translator station	53	4,094	330

CABLE TELEVISION NETWORKS INDUSTRY
(NAICS 51521)

INDUSTRY DEFINITION

NAICS 51521: Cable Networks . This industry comprises establishments primarily engaged in operating studios and facilities for the broadcasting of programs on a subscription or fee basis. The broadcast programming is typically narrowcast in nature (e.g., limited format, such as news, sports, education, or youth-oriented). These establishments produce programming in their own facilities or acquire programming from external sources. The programming material is usually delivered to a third party, such as cable systems or direct-to-home satellite systems, for transmission to viewers.

INDUSTRY ESTABLISHMENTS, SALES & EMPLOYMENT TRENDS

	Year					Percent Change Year-to-Year			
	2005	2006	2007	2008	2009	05-06	06-07	07-08	08-09
Establishments	857	863	869	848	828	0.7%	0.7%	-2.4%	-2.4%
Sales ($Millions)	26,720	31,073	33,462	34,610	35,669	16.3%	7.7%	3.4%	3.1%
Employment	45,527	48,938	49,307	48,133	46,916	7.5%	0.8%	-2.4%	-2.5%

INDUSTRY RATIOS

	Year					Percent Change Year-to-Year			
(Industry Averages)	2005	2006	2007	2008	2009	05-06	06-07	07-08	08-09
Sales ($M)/Estab.	31.18	36.01	38.52	40.81	43.09	15.5%	7.0%	6.0%	5.6%
Sales ($) per Emp.	586,904	634,949	678,639	719,043	760,273	8.2%	6.9%	6.0%	5.7%
Emps. per Estab.	53.1	56.7	56.8	56.8	56.7	6.8%	0.1%	0.0%	-0.2%

CABLE TELEVISION NETWORKS INDUSTRY
(NAICS 51521)

SIZE OF FIRM INDUSTRY ESTIMATES

Year	Establishments by Size of Firm									Total
	1-4 Emps.	5-9 Emps.	10-19 Emps.	20-49 Emps.	50-99 Emps.	100-249 Emps.	250-499 Emps.	500+ Emps.	Unknown Emps.	
2006	285	107	82	69	43	40	18	17	209	869
2008	278	105	80	67	42	39	17	16	204	848
2009	271	102	79	66	41	38	17	16	199	828
	Sales ($Millions) by Size of Firm									Total
2006	262	247	568	1,583	2,458	4,557	6,116	14,796	2,874	33,462
2008	271	256	588	1,637	2,543	4,713	6,326	15,304	2,972	34,610
2009	279	263	606	1,688	2,622	4,860	6,523	15,780	3,048	35,669
	Employment by Size of Firm									Total
2006	854	644	1,236	2,271	2,565	5,627	5,779	16,890	13,440	49,307
2008	834	629	1,206	2,217	2,504	5,493	5,642	16,488	13,120	48,133
2009	814	614	1,178	2,164	2,445	5,363	5,508	16,095	12,736	46,916

SUB-INDUSTRIES — 2007 INDUSTRY ESTIMATES

Sub-Industries	Total Establishments	Total Employment	Total Sales ($M)
Cable and other pay television services	246	15,698	6,401
Cable television services	525	28,685	26,062
Closed circuit television services	5	229	63
Direct broadcast satellite services	31	2,991	249
Multipoint distribution systems services	5	121	14
Satellite master antenna systems	47	948	169
Subscription television services	8	634	504

WIRED TELECOMMUNICATIONS CARRIERS INDUSTRY (NAICS 51711)

INDUSTRY DEFINITION

NAICS 51711: Wired Telecommunications Carriers . This industry comprises establishments engaged in (1) operating and maintaining switching and transmission facilities to provide direct communications via landlines, microwave, or a combination of landlines and satellite linkups or (2) furnishing telegraph and other nonvocal communications using their own facilities.

INDUSTRY ESTABLISHMENTS, SALES & EMPLOYMENT TRENDS

	Year					Percent Change Year-to-Year			
	2005	2006	2007	2008	2009	05-06	06-07	07-08	08-09
Establishments	30,748	31,869	32,989	33,501	34,021	3.6%	3.5%	1.6%	1.6%
Sales ($Millions)	427,233	481,891	485,563	477,072	468,199	12.8%	0.8%	-1.7%	-1.9%
Employment	922,154	1,017,956	1,054,017	1,070,315	1,086,803	10.4%	3.5%	1.5%	1.5%

INDUSTRY RATIOS

	Year					Percent Change Year-to-Year			
(Industry Averages)	2005	2006	2007	2008	2009	05-06	06-07	07-08	08-09
Sales ($M)/Estab.	13.89	15.12	14.72	14.24	13.76	8.8%	-2.7%	-3.2%	-3.4%
Sales ($) per Emp.	463,299	473,391	460,679	445,730	430,804	2.2%	-2.7%	-3.2%	-3.3%
Emps. per Estab.	30.0	31.9	32.0	31.9	31.9	6.5%	0.0%	0.0%	0.0%

WIRED TELECOMMUNICATIONS CARRIERS INDUSTRY (NAICS 51711)

SIZE OF FIRM INDUSTRY ESTIMATES

Year	Establishments by Size of Firm									Total
	1-4 Emps.	5-9 Emps.	10-19 Emps.	20-49 Emps.	50-99 Emps.	100-249 Emps.	250-499 Emps.	500+ Emps.	Unknown Emps.	
2006	15,025	4,252	3,301	3,048	1,585	994	355	252	4,176	32,989
2008	15,258	4,318	3,352	3,095	1,609	1,009	360	256	4,241	33,501
2009	15,494	4,385	3,404	3,143	1,634	1,025	366	259	4,307	34,021
Sales ($Millions) by Size of Firm										**Total**
2006	7,095	7,229	18,707	34,539	40,264	51,628	100,575	192,768	32,759	485,563
2008	6,971	7,103	18,380	33,935	39,560	50,726	98,817	189,400	32,180	477,072
2009	6,842	6,971	18,039	33,305	38,825	49,784	96,982	185,883	31,569	468,199
Employment by Size of Firm										**Total**
2006	45,074	25,514	46,217	100,568	99,844	140,142	115,010	214,193	267,456	1,054,017
2008	45,773	25,910	46,934	102,128	101,393	142,316	116,794	217,516	271,552	1,070,315
2009	46,483	26,312	47,662	103,712	102,966	144,523	118,606	220,890	275,648	1,086,803

SUB-INDUSTRIES – 2007 INDUSTRY ESTIMATES

Sub-Industries	Total Establishments	Total Employment	Total Sales ($M)
Telephone communication, except radio	9,670	440,128	168,507
Local and long distance telephone	2,913	137,121	155,209
Data telephone communications	407	19,285	4,508
Local telephone communications	1,676	125,492	82,542
Long distance telephone	1,573	94,880	14,792
Voice telephone communications	455	9,388	1,365
Online service providers	5,257	65,692	43,940
Internet connectivity services	3,258	63,990	4,841
Internet host services	6,029	63,700	5,579
Proprietary online service networks	804	16,066	1,993
Telephone cable service, land or	137	3,038	233
Wire telephone	108	3,273	111
Telephone/video communications	120	3,897	680
Telephone communications broker	582	8,067	1,264

WIRELESS TELECOMMUNICATIONS CARRIERS (NAICS 51721)

INDUSTRY DEFINITION

NAICS 51721: Wireless Telecommunications Carriers. This industry comprises establishments primarily engaged in providing two-way radiotelephone communications services, such as cellular telephone services. This business also includes establishments primarily engaged in providing telephone paging and beeper services and those engaged in leasing telephone lines or other methods of telephone transmission, such as optical fiber lines and microwave or satellite facilities, and reselling the use of such methods to others.

INDUSTRY ESTABLISHMENTS, SALES & EMPLOYMENT TRENDS

	Year					Percent Change Year-to-Year			
	2005	2006	2007	2008	2009	05-06	06-07	07-08	08-09
Establishments	14,917	16,025	17,132	18,281	19,506	7.4%	6.9%	6.7%	6.7%
Sales ($Millions)	104,715	133,574	149,156	165,160	182,628	27.6%	11.7%	10.7%	10.6%
Employment	286,453	342,862	366,679	391,419	417,735	19.7%	6.9%	6.7%	6.7%

INDUSTRY RATIOS

(Industry Averages)	Year					Percent Change Year-to-Year			
	2005	2006	2007	2008	2009	05-06	06-07	07-08	08-09
Sales ($M)/Estab.	7.02	8.34	8.71	9.03	9.36	18.7%	4.4%	3.8%	3.6%
Sales ($) per Emp.	365,558	389,586	406,775	421,953	437,186	6.6%	4.4%	3.7%	3.6%
Emps. per Estab.	19.2	21.4	21.4	21.4	21.4	11.4%	0.0%	0.0%	0.0%

WIRELESS TELECOMMUNICATIONS CARRIERS
(NAICS 51721)

SIZE OF FIRM INDUSTRY ESTIMATES

Year	Establishments by Size of Firm									Total
	1-4 Emps.	5-9 Emps.	10-19 Emps.	20-49 Emps.	50-99 Emps.	100-249 Emps.	250-499 Emps.	500+ Emps.	Unknown Emps.	
2006	7,388	4,307	2,773	1,000	312	201	95	143	917	17,132
2008	7,883	4,596	2,959	1,067	333	214	101	152	978	18,281
2009	8,411	4,904	3,157	1,139	356	228	108	162	1,044	19,506
	Sales ($Millions) by Size of Firm									Total
2006	4,017	5,152	10,554	13,052	7,850	13,564	15,452	69,742	9,773	149,156
2008	4,447	5,704	11,685	14,450	8,690	15,017	17,107	77,212	10,847	165,160
2009	4,917	6,307	12,920	15,977	9,609	16,604	18,915	85,372	12,008	182,628
	Employment by Size of Firm									Total
2006	22,163	25,842	38,821	32,006	19,061	26,670	28,892	114,534	58,688	366,679
2008	23,648	27,575	41,424	34,151	20,339	28,458	30,829	122,211	62,784	391,419
2009	25,233	29,423	44,200	36,440	21,702	30,366	32,895	130,403	67,072	417,735

SUB-INDUSTRIES — 2007 INDUSTRY ESTIMATES

Sub-Industries	Total Establishments	Total Employment	Total Sales ($M)
Radiotelephone communication	3,937	141,843	61,332
Cellular telephone services	11,948	199,245	83,634
Paging services	984	21,282	3,955
Radio pager (beeper) communication	263	4,309	235

DATA PROCESSING SERVICES INDUSTRY
(NAICS 51821)

INDUSTRY DEFINITION

NAICS 51821: Data Processing Services. This industry comprises establishments primarily engaged in providing computer processing and data preparation services. The service may consist of complete processing and preparation of reports from data supplied by the customer or a specialized service, such as data entry or making data processing equipment available on an hourly or time-sharing basis.

INDUSTRY ESTABLISHMENTS, SALES & EMPLOYMENT TRENDS

	Year					Percent Change Year-to-Year			
	2005	2006	2007	2008	2009	05-06	06-07	07-08	08-09
Establishments	14,863	16,730	18,598	20,345	22,256	12.6%	11.2%	9.4%	9.4%
Sales ($Millions)	59,893	70,051	78,074	85,210	93,003	17.0%	11.5%	9.1%	9.1%
Employment	363,824	419,332	466,154	510,060	558,182	15.3%	11.2%	9.4%	9.4%

INDUSTRY RATIOS

	Year					Percent Change Year-to-Year			
(Industry Averages)	2005	2006	2007	2008	2009	05-06	06-07	07-08	08-09
Sales ($M)/Estab.	4.03	4.19	4.20	4.19	4.18	3.9%	0.3%	-0.2%	-0.2%
Sales ($) per Emp.	164,621	167,055	167,485	167,059	166,618	1.5%	0.3%	-0.3%	-0.3%
Emps. per Estab.	24.5	25.1	25.1	25.1	25.1	2.4%	0.0%	0.0%	0.0%

DATA PROCESSING SERVICES INDUSTRY
(NAICS 51821)

SIZE OF FIRM INDUSTRY ESTIMATES

Year	Establishments by Size of Firm									Total
	1-4 Emps.	5-9 Emps.	10-19 Emps.	20-49 Emps.	50-99 Emps.	100-249 Emps.	250-499 Emps.	500+ Emps.	Unknown Emps.	
2006	10,269	2,329	1,964	1,854	817	612	240	127	388	18,598
2008	11,234	2,548	2,149	2,028	894	670	262	139	425	20,345
2009	12,289	2,787	2,350	2,219	978	733	287	152	465	22,256
	Sales ($Millions) by Size of Firm									Total
2006	2,058	1,634	3,543	9,290	9,825	14,116	10,658	25,673	1,277	78,074
2008	2,246	1,783	3,867	10,139	10,722	15,405	11,631	28,018	1,399	85,210
2009	2,452	1,946	4,220	11,065	11,701	16,812	12,693	30,577	1,537	93,003
	Employment by Size of Firm									Total
2006	30,808	13,975	27,496	59,327	49,833	81,446	73,051	105,515	24,704	466,154
2008	33,702	15,287	30,079	64,900	54,515	89,098	79,914	115,428	27,136	510,060
2009	36,868	16,724	32,905	70,998	59,636	97,468	87,422	126,272	29,888	558,182

SUB-INDUSTRIES – 2007 INDUSTRY ESTIMATES

Sub-Industries	Total Establishments	Total Employment	Total Sales ($M)
Data processing and preparation	3,088	133,965	9,569
Computer processing services	269	14,738	2,606
Calculating service (computer)	34	369	48
Computer graphics service	12,203	81,390	3,273
Computer time-sharing	70	3,307	340
Service bureau, computer	227	10,219	253
Data entry service	368	17,345	3,286
Data processing service	2,128	200,091	58,455
Data verification service	63	1,668	47
Keypunch service	19	747	29
Optical scanning data service	115	1,881	151
Tabulating service	12	432	16

COMMERCIAL BANKING INDUSTRY (NAICS 52211)

INDUSTRY DEFINITION

NAICS 52211: Commercial Banking. This industry comprises commercial banks and trust companies (accepting deposits) chartered under the National Bank Act. Trust companies engaged in fiduciary business, but not regularly engaged in deposit banking, are classified in 6091.

INDUSTRY ESTABLISHMENTS, SALES & EMPLOYMENT TRENDS

	Year					Percent Change Year-to-Year			
	2005	2006	2007	2008	2009	05-06	06-07	07-08	08-09
Establishments	90,781	93,833	96,885	98,944	101,046	3.4%	3.3%	2.1%	2.1%
Sales ($Millions)	588,938	619,443	641,166	653,118	665,299	5.2%	3.5%	1.9%	1.9%
Employment	2,074,975	2,154,185	2,224,357	2,271,603	2,319,899	3.8%	3.3%	2.1%	2.1%

INDUSTRY RATIOS

	Year					Percent Change Year-to-Year			
(Industry Averages)	2005	2006	2007	2008	2009	05-06	06-07	07-08	08-09
Sales ($M)/Estab.	6.49	6.60	6.62	6.60	6.58	1.8%	0.2%	-0.3%	-0.3%
Sales ($) per Emp.	283,829	287,553	288,248	287,514	286,779	1.3%	0.2%	-0.3%	-0.3%
Emps. per Estab.	22.9	23.0	23.0	23.0	23.0	0.4%	0.0%	0.0%	0.0%

COMMERCIAL BANKING INDUSTRY
(NAICS 52211)

SIZE OF FIRM INDUSTRY ESTIMATES

Year	Establishments by Size of Firm									Total
	1-4 Emps.	5-9 Emps.	10-19 Emps.	20-49 Emps.	50-99 Emps.	100-249 Emps.	250-499 Emps.	500+ Emps.	Unknown Emps.	
2006	19,693	30,080	22,673	10,688	2,396	1,137	387	358	9,475	96,885
2008	20,112	30,719	23,154	10,915	2,447	1,161	396	366	9,676	98,944
2009	20,539	31,372	23,646	11,147	2,499	1,186	404	373	9,882	101,046
	Sales ($Millions) by Size of Firm									Total
2006	9,865	39,178	74,961	80,310	52,815	68,349	77,631	181,104	56,952	641,166
2008	10,049	39,908	76,359	81,808	53,799	69,623	79,079	184,481	58,011	653,118
2009	10,237	40,653	77,783	83,333	54,802	70,922	80,553	187,921	59,096	665,299
	Employment by Size of Firm									Total
2006	59,080	180,480	317,417	342,010	146,164	151,221	118,164	303,484	606,336	2,224,357
2008	60,335	184,315	324,162	349,278	149,270	154,435	120,675	309,933	619,200	2,271,603
2009	61,617	188,232	331,051	356,700	152,442	157,716	123,239	316,519	632,384	2,319,899

SUB-INDUSTRIES – 2007 INDUSTRY ESTIMATES

Sub-Industries	Total Establishments	Total Employment	Total Sales ($M)
National commercial banks	90,785	2,088,848	627,378
National trust companies with deposits,	6,100	135,508	13,788

MORTGAGE & NON-MORTGAGE LOAN BROKERS (NAICS 52231)

INDUSTRY DEFINITION

NAICS 52231: Mortgage & Non-Mortgage Loan Brokers. This industry comprises establishments primarily engaged in arranging loans for others. These establishments operate mostly on a commission or fee basis and do not ordinarily have any continuing relationship with either borrower or lender.

INDUSTRY ESTABLISHMENTS, SALES & EMPLOYMENT TRENDS

	Year					Percent Change Year-to-Year			
	2005	2006	2007	2008	2009	05-06	06-07	07-08	08-09
Establishments	22,885	26,665	30,444	34,650	39,437	16.5%	14.2%	13.8%	13.8%
Sales ($Millions)	36,635	43,737	50,656	58,181	66,850	19.4%	15.8%	14.9%	14.9%
Employment	201,312	241,511	275,802	313,893	357,572	20.0%	14.2%	13.8%	13.9%

INDUSTRY RATIOS

	Year					Percent Change Year-to-Year			
(Industry Averages)	2005	2006	2007	2008	2009	05-06	06-07	07-08	08-09
Sales ($M)/Estab.	1.60	1.64	1.66	1.68	1.70	2.5%	1.4%	0.9%	1.0%
Sales ($) per Emp.	181,981	181,096	183,669	185,352	186,955	-0.5%	1.4%	0.9%	0.9%
Emps. per Estab.	8.8	9.1	9.1	9.1	9.1	3.0%	0.0%	0.0%	0.1%

Mortgage & Non-Mortgage Loan Brokers (NAICS 52231)

Size of Firm Industry Estimates

| Year | Establishments by Size of Firm | | | | | | | | | Total |
	1-4 Emps.	5-9 Emps.	10-19 Emps.	20-49 Emps.	50-99 Emps.	100-249 Emps.	250-499 Emps.	500+ Emps.	Unknown Emps.	
2006	20,136	4,908	2,748	1,398	310	124	24	11	783	30,444
2008	22,918	5,586	3,128	1,591	353	141	28	13	891	34,650
2009	26,084	6,357	3,560	1,811	402	160	31	15	1,014	39,437
Sales ($Millions) by Size of Firm										**Total**
2006	8,262	5,538	6,766	9,750	4,774	4,878	2,978	2,891	4,819	50,656
2008	9,490	6,360	7,772	11,198	5,484	5,602	3,421	3,320	5,534	58,181
2009	10,899	7,305	8,926	12,861	6,298	6,434	3,929	3,813	6,386	66,850
Employment by Size of Firm										**Total**
2006	60,408	29,446	38,479	44,727	18,928	16,470	7,380	9,851	50,112	275,802
2008	68,754	33,514	43,795	50,907	21,543	18,745	8,400	11,212	57,024	313,893
2009	78,253	38,145	49,845	57,940	24,519	21,335	9,560	12,761	65,216	357,572

Sub-Industries – 2007 Industry Estimates

Sub-Industries	Total Establishments	Total Employment	Total Sales ($M)
Loan brokers	4,070	34,493	6,665
Agents, farm or business loan	106	753	92
Brokers, farm or business loan	173	1,491	191
Loan agents	830	11,563	909
Mortgage brokers arranging for loans,	25,266	227,502	42,799

INVESTMENT BANKING & SECURITIES DEALING (NAICS 52311)

INDUSTRY DEFINITION

NAICS 52311: Investment Banking & Securities Dealing. This industry compromises establishments primarily engaged in the purchase, sale, and brokerage of securities; and those, generally known as investment bankers, primarily engaged in originating, underwriting, and distributing issues of securities. Establishments primarily engaged in issuing shares of mutual and money market funds, unit investment trusts, and face amount certificates are classified in 6722 or 6726.

INDUSTRY ESTABLISHMENTS, SALES & EMPLOYMENT TRENDS

	Year					Percent Change Year-to-Year			
	2005	2006	2007	2008	2009	05-06	06-07	07-08	08-09
Establishments	5,742	5,854	5,966	5,881	5,797	1.9%	1.9%	-1.4%	-1.4%
Sales ($Millions)	118,629	89,487	84,636	76,511	68,620	-24.6%	-5.4%	-9.6%	-10.3%
Employment	115,136	95,557	97,437	95,946	94,664	-17.0%	2.0%	-1.5%	-1.3%

INDUSTRY RATIOS

(Industry Averages)	Year					Percent Change Year-to-Year			
	2005	2006	2007	2008	2009	05-06	06-07	07-08	08-09
Sales ($M)/Estab.	20.66	15.29	14.19	13.01	11.84	-26.0%	-7.2%	-8.3%	-9.0%
Sales ($) per Emp.	1,030,338	936,476	868,627	797,441	724,877	-9.1%	-7.2%	-8.2%	-9.1%
Emps. per Estab.	20.1	16.3	16.3	16.3	16.3	-18.6%	0.1%	-0.1%	0.1%

Investment Banking & Securities Dealing (NAICS 52311)

Size of Firm Industry Estimates

Year	Establishments by Size of Firm									Total
	1-4 Emps.	5-9 Emps.	10-19 Emps.	20-49 Emps.	50-99 Emps.	100-249 Emps.	250-499 Emps.	500+ Emps.	Unknown Emps.	
2006	4,215	604	445	287	99	93	18	37	171	5,966
2008	4,154	596	439	283	98	91	17	37	168	5,881
2009	4,095	587	433	279	97	90	17	36	166	5,797
	Sales ($Millions) by Size of Firm									Total
2006	7,236	2,593	3,823	3,948	3,754	9,536	4,517	48,069	1,161	84,636
2008	6,542	2,344	3,456	3,570	3,394	8,622	4,084	43,460	1,039	76,511
2009	5,866	2,102	3,099	3,201	3,044	7,731	3,662	38,973	940	68,620
	Employment by Size of Firm									Total
2006	12,644	3,625	6,235	9,199	6,063	12,312	5,350	31,193	10,816	97,437
2008	12,463	3,573	6,146	9,068	5,977	12,137	5,274	30,749	10,560	95,946
2009	12,286	3,522	6,058	8,938	5,891	11,964	5,198	30,310	10,496	94,664

Sub-Industries — 2007 Industry Estimates

Sub-Industries	Total Establishments	Total Employment	Total Sales ($M)
Security brokers and dealers	2,669	34,404	33,188
Security brokers and dealers	845	15,742	7,435
Bond dealers and brokers	62	1,325	310
Brokers, security	956	17,971	19,996
Dealers, security	79	4,323	2,778
Floor traders, security	4	48	18
Note brokers	19	84	11
Stock brokers and dealers	367	6,861	2,048
Stock option dealers	10	124	37
Tax certificate dealers	4	24	2
Traders, security	30	691	220
Flotation companies	20	370	87
Distributors, security	14	86	15
Investment bankers	322	7,857	14,712
Investment certificate sales	9	68	38
Investment firm, general brokerage	505	7,057	3,652
Securities flotation companies	39	277	42
Syndicate shares (real estate,	13	123	48

SECURITIES BROKERAGE INDUSTRY (NAICS 52312)

INDUSTRY DEFINITION

NAICS 52312: Securities Brokerage Industry. This industry comprises establishments primarily engaged in the purchase, sale, and brokerage of securities; and those, generally known as investment bankers, primarily engaged in originating, underwriting, and distributing issues of securities. Establishments primarily engaged in issuing shares of mutual and money market funds, unit investment trusts, and face amount certificates are classified in 6722 or 6726.

INDUSTRY ESTABLISHMENTS, SALES & EMPLOYMENT TRENDS

	Year					Percent Change Year-to-Year			
	2005	2006	2007	2008	2009	05-06	06-07	07-08	08-09
Establishments	29,824	33,124	36,424	37,422	38,447	11.1%	10.0%	2.7%	2.7%
Sales ($Millions)	102,616	105,275	117,096	121,065	125,136	2.6%	11.2%	3.4%	3.4%
Employment	369,806	387,618	426,410	438,182	450,045	4.8%	10.0%	2.8%	2.7%

INDUSTRY RATIOS

	Year					Percent Change Year-to-Year			
(Industry Averages)	2005	2006	2007	2008	2009	05-06	06-07	07-08	08-09
Sales ($M)/Estab.	3.44	3.18	3.21	3.24	3.25	-7.6%	1.2%	0.6%	0.6%
Sales ($) per Emp.	277,486	271,594	274,609	276,290	278,051	-2.1%	1.1%	0.6%	0.6%
Emps. per Estab.	12.4	11.7	11.7	11.7	11.7	-5.6%	0.0%	0.0%	0.0%

SECURITIES BROKERAGE INDUSTRY
(NAICS 52312)

SIZE OF FIRM INDUSTRY ESTIMATES

Year	Establishments by Size of Firm									Total
	1-4 Emps.	5-9 Emps.	10-19 Emps.	20-49 Emps.	50-99 Emps.	100-249 Emps.	250-499 Emps.	500+ Emps.	Unknown Emps.	Total
2006	23,747	5,537	2,825	2,215	817	370	76	46	788	36,424
2008	24,398	5,689	2,902	2,276	839	380	78	48	810	37,422
2009	25,066	5,845	2,982	2,338	862	390	80	49	832	38,447
Sales ($Millions) by Size of Firm										**Total**
2006	12,108	8,470	8,642	15,814	12,491	22,634	10,803	19,698	6,437	117,096
2008	12,517	8,756	8,934	16,348	12,913	23,399	11,168	20,364	6,666	121,065
2009	12,940	9,052	9,236	16,901	13,349	24,190	11,545	21,051	6,872	125,136
Employment by Size of Firm										**Total**
2006	71,241	33,225	39,549	70,892	49,812	49,201	23,079	38,915	50,496	426,410
2008	73,193	34,135	40,633	72,835	51,176	50,549	23,711	39,982	51,968	438,182
2009	75,199	35,070	41,746	74,831	52,579	51,934	24,361	41,077	53,248	450,045

SUB-INDUSTRIES — 2007 INDUSTRY ESTIMATES

Sub-Industries	Total Establishments	Total Employment	Total Sales ($M)
Security brokers and dealers	16,294	150,560	45,916
Security brokers and dealers	5,161	68,893	10,286
Bond dealers and brokers	379	5,797	429
Brokers, security	5,835	78,647	27,665
Dealers, security	485	18,919	3,843
Floor traders, security	24	210	25
Note brokers	118	369	15
Stock brokers and dealers	2,239	30,025	2,834
Stock option dealers	64	541	51
Tax certificate dealers	23	107	3
Traders, security	180	3,024	305
Flotation companies	121	1,620	120
Distributors, security	84	378	21
Investment bankers	1,964	34,386	20,354
Investment certificate sales	52	299	53
Investment firm, general brokerage	3,084	30,885	5,052
Securities flotation companies	238	1,212	58
Syndicate shares (real estate,	79	540	66

LIFE INSURANCE CARRIERS INDUSTRY (NAICS 524113)

INDUSTRY DEFINITION

NAICS 524113: Life Insurance Carriers. This industry comprises establishments primarily engaged in underwriting life insurance. These establishments are operated by enterprises that may be owned by stockholders, policyholders, or other carriers.

INDUSTRY ESTABLISHMENTS, SALES & EMPLOYMENT TRENDS

	Year					Percent Change Year-to-Year			
	2005	2006	2007	2008	2009	05-06	06-07	07-08	08-09
Establishments	9,157	8,564	7,970	7,596	7,239	-6.5%	-6.9%	-4.7%	-4.7%
Sales ($Millions)	604,172	627,006	638,036	657,478	673,652	3.8%	1.8%	3.0%	2.5%
Employment	321,912	307,702	286,196	272,881	260,141	-4.4%	-7.0%	-4.7%	-4.7%

INDUSTRY RATIOS

(Industry Averages)	Year					Percent Change Year-to-Year			
	2005	2006	2007	2008	2009	05-06	06-07	07-08	08-09
Sales ($M)/Estab.	65.98	73.22	80.05	86.56	93.05	11.0%	9.3%	8.1%	7.5%
Sales ($) per Emp.	1,876,822	2,037,708	2,229,368	2,409,390	2,589,569	8.6%	9.4%	8.1%	7.5%
Emps. per Estab.	35.2	35.9	35.9	35.9	35.9	2.2%	-0.1%	0.0%	0.0%

LIFE INSURANCE CARRIERS INDUSTRY
(NAICS 524113)

SIZE OF FIRM INDUSTRY ESTIMATES

Year	Establishments by Size of Firm									Total
	1-4 Emps.	5-9 Emps.	10-19 Emps.	20-49 Emps.	50-99 Emps.	100-249 Emps.	250-499 Emps.	500+ Emps.	Unknown Emps.	
2006	3,507	1,007	989	1,176	448	231	97	115	401	7,970
2008	3,342	959	943	1,120	427	220	93	110	382	7,596
2009	3,185	914	899	1,068	407	210	88	105	364	7,239
	Sales ($Millions) by Size of Firm									Total
2006	10,459	7,925	19,476	61,284	47,586	71,511	101,403	287,698	30,693	638,036
2008	10,776	8,164	20,065	63,137	49,025	73,672	104,469	296,395	31,775	657,478
2009	11,039	8,364	20,556	64,681	50,224	75,474	107,024	303,644	32,647	673,652
	Employment by Size of Firm									Total
2006	10,521	6,039	13,852	37,617	27,340	30,770	29,683	104,646	25,728	286,196
2008	10,027	5,756	13,202	35,852	26,056	29,326	28,290	99,733	24,640	272,881
2009	9,556	5,485	12,582	34,169	24,833	27,949	26,962	95,052	23,552	260,141

SUB-INDUSTRIES — 2007 INDUSTRY ESTIMATES

Sub-Industries	Total Establishments	Total Employment	Total Sales ($M)
Life insurance	5,645	127,155	222,628
Mutual association life insurance	107	6,809	11,220
Cooperative life insurance organizations	36	1,846	2,552
Fraternal life insurance organizations	382	5,031	7,125
Fraternal protective associations	21	107	17
Assessment life insurance agents	114	658	458
Benevolent insurance associations	24	169	59
Burial insurance societies	15	77	18
Funeral insurance	38	414	103
Legal reserve life insurance	32	458	536
Life insurance carriers	1,448	132,826	383,586
Life insurance funds, savings bank	18	49	1,021
Life reinsurance carriers	90	10,597	8,715

HEALTH & MEDICAL INSURANCE CARRIERS (NAICS 524114)

INDUSTRY DEFINITION

NAICS 524114: Health & Medical Insurance Carrier. This industry comprises establishments primarily engaged in providing hospital, medical, and other health services to subscribers or members in accordance with prearranged agreements or service plans, generally in return for specified subscription charges. The plans may be through a contract with a participating hospital or physician. Other plans provide for partial indemnity and service benefits. Includes separate establishments of HMOs which provide insurance.

INDUSTRY ESTABLISHMENTS, SALES & EMPLOYMENT TRENDS

	Year					Percent Change Year-to-Year			
	2005	2006	2007	2008	2009	05-06	06-07	07-08	08-09
Establishments	4,625	4,833	5,040	5,262	5,494	4.5%	4.3%	4.4%	4.4%
Sales ($Millions)	434,521	508,677	561,214	615,380	673,018	17.1%	10.3%	9.7%	9.4%
Employment	383,450	422,352	440,222	459,740	479,770	10.1%	4.2%	4.4%	4.4%

INDUSTRY RATIOS

(Industry Averages)	Year					Percent Change Year-to-Year			
	2005	2006	2007	2008	2009	05-06	06-07	07-08	08-09
Sales ($M)/Estab.	93.95	105.26	111.35	116.95	122.50	12.0%	5.8%	5.0%	4.8%
Sales ($) per Emp.	1,133,188	1,204,390	1,274,844	1,338,539	1,402,794	6.3%	5.8%	5.0%	4.8%
Emps. per Estab.	82.9	87.4	87.3	87.4	87.3	5.4%	-0.1%	0.0%	0.0%

HEALTH & MEDICAL INSURANCE CARRIERS (NAICS 524114)

SIZE OF FIRM INDUSTRY ESTIMATES

Year	Establishments by Size of Firm									Total
	1-4 Emps.	5-9 Emps.	10-19 Emps.	20-49 Emps.	50-99 Emps.	100-249 Emps.	250-499 Emps.	500+ Emps.	Unknown Emps.	
2006	1,747	529	429	450	317	372	241	250	703	5,040
2008	1,824	552	448	470	331	388	252	261	734	5,262
2009	1,904	577	467	490	346	405	263	273	767	5,494
Sales ($Millions) by Size of Firm										**Total**
2006	5,852	3,545	7,179	10,045	19,468	72,630	122,758	293,800	25,939	561,214
2008	6,415	3,886	7,871	11,014	21,344	79,630	134,590	322,116	28,515	615,380
2009	7,018	4,251	8,610	12,048	23,348	87,106	147,226	352,359	31,052	673,018
Employment by Size of Firm										**Total**
2006	5,241	3,175	6,001	14,396	19,338	49,439	73,541	224,035	45,056	440,222
2008	5,472	3,315	6,265	15,030	20,190	51,617	76,780	233,904	47,168	459,740
2009	5,713	3,461	6,541	15,692	21,080	53,890	80,162	244,207	49,024	479,770

SUB-INDUSTRIES – 2007 INDUSTRY ESTIMATES

Sub-Industries	Total Establishments	Total Employment	Total Sales ($M)
Hospital and medical service plans	2,500	217,084	211,226
Dental insurance	430	18,909	16,409
Group hospitalization plans	544	77,544	143,637
Health Maintenance Organization	1,566	126,685	189,943

PROPERTY & CASUALTY INSURANCE CARRIERS (NAICS 524126)

INDUSTRY DEFINITION

NAICS 524126: Property & Casualty Insurance Carriers. This industry comprises establishments primarily engaged in underwriting fire, marine, and casualty insurance. These establishments are operated by enterprises that may be owned by stockholders, policyholders, or other carriers.

INDUSTRY ESTABLISHMENTS, SALES & EMPLOYMENT TRENDS

	Year					Percent Change Year-to-Year			
	2005	2006	2007	2008	2009	05-06	06-07	07-08	08-09
Establishments	14,167	13,701	13,235	13,091	12,949	-3.3%	-3.4%	-1.1%	-1.1%
Sales ($Millions)	690,217	820,747	893,497	978,995	1,062,525	18.9%	8.9%	9.6%	8.5%
Employment	481,967	509,816	492,720	487,340	482,013	5.8%	-3.4%	-1.1%	-1.1%

INDUSTRY RATIOS

(Industry Averages)	Year					Percent Change Year-to-Year			
	2005	2006	2007	2008	2009	05-06	06-07	07-08	08-09
Sales ($M)/Estab.	48.72	59.90	67.51	74.78	82.05	23.0%	12.7%	10.8%	9.7%
Sales ($) per Emp.	1,432,084	1,609,890	1,813,395	2,008,854	2,204,347	12.4%	12.6%	10.8%	9.7%
Emps. per Estab.	34.0	37.2	37.2	37.2	37.2	9.4%	0.0%	0.0%	0.0%

Property & Casualty Insurance Carriers (NAICS 524126)

Size of Firm Industry Estimates

Year	Establishments by Size of Firm									Total
	1-4 Emps.	5-9 Emps.	10-19 Emps.	20-49 Emps.	50-99 Emps.	100-249 Emps.	250-499 Emps.	500+ Emps.	Unknown Emps.	
2006	6,784	1,642	1,288	1,257	692	565	220	195	593	13,235
2008	6,710	1,624	1,274	1,243	685	559	218	193	586	13,091
2009	6,638	1,607	1,260	1,229	677	553	215	190	580	12,949
Sales ($Millions) by Size of Firm										**Total**
2006	68,703	31,182	48,898	106,574	78,866	133,094	125,371	258,403	42,406	893,497
2008	75,280	34,167	53,580	116,777	86,416	145,836	137,374	283,142	46,423	978,995
2009	81,708	37,084	58,154	126,747	93,794	158,287	149,103	307,315	50,332	1,062,525
Employment by Size of Firm										**Total**
2006	20,352	9,853	18,026	40,209	42,226	75,179	67,125	181,671	38,080	492,720
2008	20,131	9,746	17,830	39,773	41,768	74,363	66,397	179,700	37,632	487,340
2009	19,913	9,640	17,637	39,341	41,314	73,556	65,676	177,751	37,184	482,013

Sub-Industries – 2007 Industry Estimates

Sub-Industries	Total Establishments	Total Employment	Total Sales ($M)
Fire, marine, and casualty insurance	5,401	169,531	226,073
Agricultural insurance	172	1,014	569
Federal Crop Insurance Corporation	95	154	27
Fire, marine and casualty insurance and	1,064	85,016	81,053
Associated factory mutuals, fire and	10	51	13
Fire, marine, and casualty insurance:	748	22,317	45,714
Fire, marine, and casualty insurance:	150	17,544	63,331
Assessment associations: fire, marine	93	1,836	18,552
Automobile insurance	2,524	69,108	106,017
Boiler insurance	16	256	730
Burglary and theft insurance	14	156	140
Contact lens insurance	10	29	20
Plate glass insurance	4	31	3
Property damage insurance	1,640	90,993	316,280
Reciprocal interinsurance exchanges:	34	1,198	2,234
Workers' compensation insurance	1,260	33,488	32,740

INSURANCE AGENCIES & BROKERAGES INDUSTRY (NAICS 52421)

INDUSTRY DEFINITION

NAICS 52421: Insurance Agencies & Brokerages. This industry comprises establishments primarily representing one or more insurance carriers, or brokers not representing any particular carriers primarily engaged as independent contractors in the sale or placement of insurance contracts with carriers, but not employees of the insurance carriers they represent. This business also includes independent organizations concerned with insurance services.

INDUSTRY ESTABLISHMENTS, SALES & EMPLOYMENT TRENDS

	Year					Percent Change Year-to-Year			
	2005	2006	2007	2008	2009	05-06	06-07	07-08	08-09
Establishments	132,308	133,867	135,426	137,339	139,280	1.2%	1.2%	1.4%	1.4%
Sales ($Millions)	153,764	166,527	180,163	193,723	207,630	8.3%	8.2%	7.5%	7.2%
Employment	902,802	915,745	926,212	939,343	952,638	1.4%	1.1%	1.4%	1.4%

INDUSTRY RATIOS

(Industry Averages)	Year					Percent Change Year-to-Year			
	2005	2006	2007	2008	2009	05-06	06-07	07-08	08-09
Sales ($M)/Estab.	1.16	1.24	1.33	1.41	1.49	7.0%	6.9%	6.0%	5.7%
Sales ($) per Emp.	170,319	181,849	194,516	206,233	217,953	6.8%	7.0%	6.0%	5.7%
Emps. per Estab.	6.8	6.8	6.8	6.8	6.8	0.3%	0.0%	0.0%	0.0%

INSURANCE AGENCIES & BROKERAGES INDUSTRY
(NAICS 52421)

SIZE OF FIRM INDUSTRY ESTIMATES

Year	Establishments by Size of Firm									Total
	1-4 Emps.	5-9 Emps.	10-19 Emps.	20-49 Emps.	50-99 Emps.	100-249 Emps.	250-499 Emps.	500+ Emps.	Unknown Emps.	
2006	99,248	21,781	7,799	3,554	865	390	89	45	1,655	135,426
2008	100,651	22,089	7,909	3,604	877	395	90	46	1,678	137,339
2009	102,073	22,401	8,021	3,655	890	401	92	46	1,702	139,280
Sales ($Millions) by Size of Firm										**Total**
2006	33,966	34,786	20,464	20,272	14,801	15,553	12,185	14,944	13,192	180,163
2008	36,522	37,403	22,003	21,797	15,914	16,724	13,101	16,069	14,190	193,723
2009	39,143	40,088	23,582	23,362	17,057	17,924	14,042	17,222	15,211	207,630
Employment by Size of Firm										**Total**
2006	297,745	130,685	109,189	113,730	52,762	51,809	27,148	37,417	105,728	926,212
2008	301,953	132,532	110,732	115,337	53,508	52,541	27,531	37,946	107,264	939,343
2009	306,220	134,405	112,297	116,967	54,264	53,284	27,920	38,482	108,800	952,638

SUB-INDUSTRIES — 2007 INDUSTRY ESTIMATES

Sub-Industries	Total Establishments	Total Employment	Total Sales ($M)
Insurance agents, brokers, and service	93,113	495,210	62,799
Insurance information and consulting	2,060	19,735	5,046
Advisory services, insurance	361	5,442	2,025
Education services, insurance	61	830	89
Information bureaus, insurance	94	1,317	92
Pension and retirement plan consultants	1,305	11,494	1,401
Policyholders' consulting service	65	454	44
Insurance adjusters	1,963	15,825	1,785
Insurance claim adjusters, not	1,667	13,858	1,513
Insurance agents and brokers	4,917	48,203	41,173
Insurance agents, nec	20,316	178,633	29,508
Insurance brokers, nec	3,378	53,878	21,702
Life insurance agents	2,058	19,110	2,740
Real estate insurance agents	558	2,882	264
Property and casualty insurance agent	1,108	20,301	5,897
Title insurance agents	163	1,668	205
Other insurance services	2,237	37,372	3,882

OFFICES OF REAL ESTATE AGENTS & BROKERS (NAICS 53121)

INDUSTRY DEFINITION

NAICS 53121: Real Estate Agents & Brokers. This industry comprises establishments primarily engaged in renting, buying, selling, managing, and appraising real estate for others.

INDUSTRY ESTABLISHMENTS, SALES & EMPLOYMENT TRENDS

	Year					Percent Change Year-to-Year			
	2005	2006	2007	2008	2009	05-06	06-07	07-08	08-09
Establishments	108,055	105,166	102,277	103,313	105,346	-2.7%	-2.7%	1.0%	2.0%
Sales ($Millions)	62,854	65,891	66,413	69,455	73,215	4.8%	0.8%	4.6%	5.4%
Employment	555,126	560,469	545,031	550,759	561,383	1.0%	-2.8%	1.1%	1.9%

INDUSTRY RATIOS

(Industry Averages)	Year					Percent Change Year-to-Year			
	2005	2006	2007	2008	2009	05-06	06-07	07-08	08-09
Sales ($M)/Estab.	0.58	0.63	0.65	0.67	0.69	7.7%	3.6%	3.5%	3.4%
Sales ($) per Emp.	113,224	117,564	121,852	126,108	130,419	3.8%	3.6%	3.5%	3.4%
Emps. per Estab.	5.1	5.3	5.3	5.3	5.3	3.7%	0.0%	0.0%	0.0%

OFFICES OF REAL ESTATE AGENTS & BROKERS (NAICS 53121)

SIZE OF FIRM INDUSTRY ESTIMATES

Year	Establishments by Size of Firm									Total
	1-4 Emps.	5-9 Emps.	10-19 Emps.	20-49 Emps.	50-99 Emps.	100-249 Emps.	250-499 Emps.	500+ Emps.	Unknown Emps.	Total
2006	85,440	10,179	3,660	1,410	415	154	30	16	971	102,277
2008	86,306	10,282	3,697	1,424	419	156	31	16	981	103,313
2009	88,004	10,484	3,770	1,452	428	159	31	17	1,000	105,346
Sales ($Millions) by Size of Firm										**Total**
2006	25,698	7,654	6,683	6,512	4,461	4,474	3,147	4,769	3,015	66,413
2008	26,871	8,003	6,988	6,809	4,664	4,678	3,291	4,987	3,163	69,455
2009	28,330	8,438	7,368	7,179	4,918	4,932	3,469	5,258	3,324	73,215
Employment by Size of Firm										**Total**
2006	256,321	61,074	51,237	45,113	25,332	20,514	9,211	14,277	61,952	545,031
2008	258,919	61,693	51,756	45,570	25,588	20,722	9,305	14,421	62,784	550,759
2009	264,013	62,907	52,775	46,466	26,092	21,130	9,488	14,705	63,808	561,383

SUB-INDUSTRIES – 2007 INDUSTRY ESTIMATES

Sub-Industries	Total Establishments	Total Employment	Total Sales ($M)
Real estate agents and managers	52,141	258,533	22,965
Real estate brokers and agents	36,764	214,007	32,803
Broker of manufactured homes, on site	227	1,286	148
Buying agent, real estate	856	3,299	310
Escrow agent, real estate	431	3,296	246
Real estate agent, commercial	5,179	32,280	7,059
Real estate agent, residential	5,650	25,937	2,377
Selling agent, real estate	1,029	6,393	506

REAL ESTATE PROPERTY MANAGERS INDUSTRY (NAICS 53131)

INDUSTRY DEFINITION

NAICS 53131: Real Estate Property Managers. This industry comprises establishments primarily engaged in renting, buying, selling, managing, and appraising real estate for others.

INDUSTRY ESTABLISHMENTS, SALES & EMPLOYMENT TRENDS

	Year					Percent Change Year-to-Year			
	2005	2006	2007	2008	2009	05-06	06-07	07-08	08-09
Establishments	45,594	44,463	43,332	42,142	41,020	-2.5%	-2.5%	-2.7%	-2.7%
Sales ($Millions)	47,291	48,665	49,256	49,686	50,100	2.9%	1.2%	0.9%	0.8%
Employment	530,651	527,375	514,126	500,215	487,132	-0.6%	-2.5%	-2.7%	-2.6%

INDUSTRY RATIOS

(Industry Averages)	Year					Percent Change Year-to-Year			
	2005	2006	2007	2008	2009	05-06	06-07	07-08	08-09
Sales ($M)/Estab.	1.04	1.09	1.14	1.18	1.22	5.5%	3.9%	3.7%	3.6%
Sales ($) per Emp.	89,119	92,277	95,806	99,329	102,847	3.5%	3.8%	3.7%	3.5%
Emps. per Estab.	11.6	11.9	11.9	11.9	11.9	1.9%	0.0%	0.0%	0.0%

REAL ESTATE PROPERTY MANAGERS INDUSTRY
(NAICS 53131)

SIZE OF FIRM INDUSTRY ESTIMATES

Year	Establishments by Size of Firm									
	1-4 Emps.	5-9 Emps.	10-19 Emps.	20-49 Emps.	50-99 Emps.	100-249 Emps.	250-499 Emps.	500+ Emps.	Unknown Emps.	Total
2006	26,469	7,717	4,364	2,638	973	559	150	53	405	43,332
2008	25,742	7,505	4,244	2,565	947	543	146	51	394	42,142
2009	25,056	7,305	4,131	2,497	921	529	142	50	383	41,020
	Sales ($Millions) by Size of Firm									Total
2006	4,281	3,328	4,705	7,111	5,772	7,829	7,718	7,235	1,276	49,256
2008	4,317	3,357	4,746	7,171	5,822	7,896	7,784	7,297	1,297	49,686
2009	4,352	3,384	4,784	7,229	5,869	7,959	7,847	7,356	1,320	50,100
	Employment by Size of Firm									Total
2006	79,406	46,302	61,094	84,408	59,374	74,282	45,672	37,477	26,112	514,126
2008	77,225	45,030	59,417	82,090	57,744	72,242	44,418	36,448	25,600	500,215
2009	75,169	43,832	57,835	79,905	56,207	70,319	43,236	35,478	25,152	487,132

SUB-INDUSTRIES – 2007 INDUSTRY ESTIMATES

Sub-Industries	Total Establishments	Total Employment	Total Sales ($M)
Real estate managers	36,049	436,960	43,839
Cemetery management service	315	3,749	484
Condominium manager	6,023	59,844	3,723
Cooperative apartment manager	945	13,572	1,211

OFFICES OF LAWYERS INDUSTRY
(NAICS 54111)

INDUSTRY DEFINITION

NAICS 54111: Offices of Lawyers. This industry comprises offices of legal practitioners known as lawyers or attorneys (i.e., counselors-at-law) primarily engaged in the practice of law. Establishments in this industry may provide expertise in a range or in specific areas of law, such as criminal law, corporate law, family and estate law, patent law, real estate law, or tax law.

INDUSTRY ESTABLISHMENTS, SALES & EMPLOYMENT TRENDS

	Year					Percent Change Year-to-Year			
	2005	2006	2007	2008	2009	05-06	06-07	07-08	08-09
Establishments	176,339	176,922	177,505	178,695	179,894	0.3%	0.3%	0.7%	0.7%
Sales ($Millions)	132,398	145,676	157,651	169,508	181,503	10.0%	8.2%	7.5%	7.1%
Employment	1,229,742	1,261,562	1,265,995	1,274,449	1,282,700	2.6%	0.4%	0.7%	0.6%

INDUSTRY RATIOS

(Industry Averages)	Year					Percent Change Year-to-Year			
	2005	2006	2007	2008	2009	05-06	06-07	07-08	08-09
Sales ($M)/Estab.	0.75	0.82	0.89	0.95	1.01	9.7%	7.9%	6.8%	6.4%
Sales ($) per Emp.	107,663	115,472	124,527	133,005	141,501	7.3%	7.8%	6.8%	6.4%
Emps. per Estab.	7.0	7.1	7.1	7.1	7.1	2.2%	0.0%	0.0%	0.0%

OFFICES OF LAWYERS INDUSTRY
(NAICS 54111)

SIZE OF FIRM INDUSTRY ESTIMATES

Year	Establishments by Size of Firm									Total
	1-4 Emps.	5-9 Emps.	10-19 Emps.	20-49 Emps.	50-99 Emps.	100-249 Emps.	250-499 Emps.	500+ Emps.	Unknown Emps.	
2006	127,206	26,915	12,592	6,461	1,734	874	216	82	1,425	177,505
2008	128,059	27,096	12,677	6,505	1,746	880	217	83	1,434	178,695
2009	128,918	27,278	12,762	6,548	1,757	886	219	84	1,444	179,894
	Sales ($Millions) by Size of Firm									Total
2006	29,513	15,611	17,529	22,487	14,080	19,164	16,491	18,134	4,642	157,651
2008	31,733	16,786	18,848	24,178	15,139	20,606	17,732	19,498	4,989	169,508
2009	33,982	17,975	20,183	25,892	16,212	22,066	18,988	20,880	5,325	181,503
	Employment by Size of Firm									Total
2006	254,412	161,491	176,291	213,228	109,236	123,245	71,404	65,232	91,456	1,265,995
2008	256,119	162,575	177,473	214,658	109,969	124,071	71,883	65,670	92,032	1,274,449
2009	257,837	163,665	178,664	216,098	110,706	124,904	72,365	66,110	92,352	1,282,700

SUB-INDUSTRIES — 2007 INDUSTRY ESTIMATES

Sub-Industries	Total Establishments	Total Employment	Total Sales ($M)
Legal services	51,438	272,791	27,069
Specialized legal services	1,342	10,215	1,387
Specialized law offices, attorneys	6,174	42,711	5,758
Administrative and government law	216	2,296	391
Antitrust and trade regulation law	37	689	137
Bankrupcy law	771	4,319	463
Corporate, partnership and business law	1,027	15,774	2,284
Criminal law	1,605	6,139	634
Debt collection law	151	1,491	261
Divorce and family law	1,378	5,123	540
Environmental law	149	1,005	99
Immigration and naturalization law	834	3,403	367
Labor and employment law	757	4,350	466
Malpractice and negligence law	504	4,564	932
Other specialized law offices	3,749	19,787	2,388
General practice attorney, lawyer	83,676	500,075	56,267
General practice law office	22,971	362,008	56,614
Legal aid service	723	9,256	1,595

OFFICES OF CERTIFIED PUBLIC ACCOUNTANTS (NAICS 541211)

INDUSTRY DEFINITION

NAICS 541211: Offices of Certified Public Accountants This U.S. industry comprises establishments of accountants that are certified to audit the accounting records of public and private organizations and to attest to compliance with generally accepted accounting practices. Offices of certified public accountants (CPAs) may provide one or more of the following accounting services: (1) auditing financial statements; (2) designing accounting systems; (3) preparing financial statements; (4) developing budgets; and (5) providing advice on matters related to accounting. These establishments may also provide related services, such as bookkeeping, tax return preparation, and payroll processing.

INDUSTRY ESTABLISHMENTS, SALES & EMPLOYMENT TRENDS

	Year					Percent Change Year-to-Year			
	2005	2006	2007	2008	2009	05-06	06-07	07-08	08-09
Establishments	57,614	58,336	59,057	59,643	60,234	1.3%	1.2%	1.0%	1.0%
Sales ($Millions)	47,056	49,179	51,916	54,347	56,790	4.5%	5.6%	4.7%	4.5%
Employment	487,974	494,321	500,382	505,642	510,434	1.3%	1.2%	1.1%	0.9%

INDUSTRY RATIOS

	Year					Percent Change Year-to-Year			
(Industry Averages)	2005	2006	2007	2008	2009	05-06	06-07	07-08	08-09
Sales ($M)/Estab.	0.82	0.84	0.88	0.91	0.94	3.2%	4.3%	3.7%	3.5%
Sales ($) per Emp.	96,431	99,487	103,753	107,481	111,258	3.2%	4.3%	3.6%	3.5%
Emps. per Estab.	8.5	8.5	8.5	8.5	8.5	0.0%	0.0%	0.1%	0.0%

OFFICES OF CERTIFIED PUBLIC ACCOUNTANTS
(NAICS 541211)

SIZE OF FIRM INDUSTRY ESTIMATES

Year	Establishments by Size of Firm									Total
	1-4 Emps.	5-9 Emps.	10-19 Emps.	20-49 Emps.	50-99 Emps.	100-249 Emps.	250-499 Emps.	500+ Emps.	Unknown Emps.	
2006	38,583	11,346	5,310	2,257	574	244	64	38	644	59,057
2008	38,965	11,458	5,363	2,280	580	247	65	38	650	59,643
2009	39,352	11,572	5,416	2,302	586	249	66	39	657	60,234
Sales ($Millions) by Size of Firm										**Total**
2006	7,531	6,152	6,910	8,077	4,546	5,031	3,839	7,468	2,363	51,916
2008	7,881	6,437	7,231	8,452	4,757	5,265	4,018	7,815	2,491	54,347
2009	8,237	6,728	7,558	8,834	4,972	5,503	4,199	8,168	2,590	56,790
Employment by Size of Firm										**Total**
2006	115,748	68,075	79,653	74,485	37,900	34,433	21,179	27,885	41,024	500,382
2008	116,896	68,751	80,443	75,224	38,276	34,775	21,389	28,161	41,728	505,642
2009	118,055	69,432	81,241	75,970	38,656	35,119	21,601	28,440	41,920	510,434

SUB-INDUSTRIES — 2007 INDUSTRY ESTIMATES

Sub-Industries	Total Establishments	Total Employment	Total Sales ($M)
Accounting, auditing, and bookkeeping	19,362	121,834	5,660
Auditing services	938	8,985	675
Certified public accountant	27,490	225,644	32,497
Accounting services, except auditing	4,460	52,007	6,112
Calculating and statistical service	91	650	21
Payroll accounting service	1,155	30,907	3,297
Billing and bookkeeping service	5,561	60,356	3,654

ARCHITECTURAL SERVICES INDUSTRY (NAICS 54131)

INDUSTRY DEFINITION

NAICS 54131: Architectural Services. This industry comprises establishments primarily engaged in planning and designing residential, institutional, leisure, commercial, and industrial buildings and structures by applying knowledge of design, construction procedures, zoning regulations, building codes, and building materials.

INDUSTRY ESTABLISHMENTS, SALES & EMPLOYMENT TRENDS

	Year					Percent Change Year-to-Year			
	2005	2006	2007	2008	2009	05-06	06-07	07-08	08-09
Establishments	24,834	25,326	25,819	26,388	26,970	2.0%	1.9%	2.2%	2.2%
Sales ($Millions)	21,527	23,492	25,552	27,638	29,800	9.1%	8.8%	8.2%	7.8%
Employment	205,805	211,090	215,194	219,939	224,789	2.6%	1.9%	2.2%	2.2%

INDUSTRY RATIOS

(Industry Averages)	Year					Percent Change Year-to-Year			
	2005	2006	2007	2008	2009	05-06	06-07	07-08	08-09
Sales ($M)/Estab.	0.87	0.93	0.99	1.05	1.10	7.0%	6.7%	5.8%	5.5%
Sales ($) per Emp.	104,599	111,289	118,741	125,664	132,570	6.4%	6.7%	5.8%	5.5%
Emps. per Estab.	8.3	8.3	8.3	8.3	8.3	0.6%	0.0%	0.0%	0.0%

ARCHITECTURAL SERVICES INDUSTRY
(NAICS 54131)

SIZE OF FIRM INDUSTRY ESTIMATES

Year	Establishments by Size of Firm									Total
	1-4 Emps.	5-9 Emps.	10-19 Emps.	20-49 Emps.	50-99 Emps.	100-249 Emps.	250-499 Emps.	500+ Emps.	Unknown Emps.	
2006	15,713	5,199	2,761	1,404	376	167	19	0	183	25,819
2008	16,060	5,313	2,822	1,435	385	170	20	0	187	26,388
2009	16,414	5,430	2,884	1,466	393	174	20	0	191	26,970
	Sales ($Millions) by Size of Firm									Total
2006	3,569	2,952	4,077	5,261	3,335	4,279	1,429	0	651	25,552
2008	3,860	3,193	4,409	5,689	3,607	4,628	1,546	0	708	27,638
2009	4,162	3,442	4,754	6,135	3,889	4,990	1,667	0	763	29,800
	Employment by Size of Firm									Total
2006	47,139	31,192	38,657	44,919	24,095	22,841	6,351	0	0	215,194
2008	48,179	31,880	39,509	45,910	24,626	23,345	6,491	0	0	219,939
2009	49,241	32,583	40,380	46,922	25,169	23,860	6,634	0	0	224,789

SUB-INDUSTRIES — 2007 INDUSTRY ESTIMATES

Sub-Industries	Total Establishments	Total Employment	Total Sales ($M)
Architectural services	22,294	173,126	19,630
Architectural engineering	424	4,353	459
Architectural engineering	1,756	33,032	5,066
House designer	1,345	4,683	398

ENGINEERING SERVICES INDUSTRY
(NAICS 54133)

INDUSTRY DEFINITION

NAICS 54133: Engineering Services. This industry comprises establishments primarily engaged in applying physical laws and principles of engineering in the design, development, and utilization of machines, materials, instruments, structures, processes, and systems. The assignments undertaken by these establishments may involve any of the following activities: provision of advice, preparation of feasibility studies, preparation of preliminary and final plans and designs, provision of technical services during the construction or installation phase, inspection and evaluation of engineering projects, and related services.

INDUSTRY ESTABLISHMENTS, SALES & EMPLOYMENT TRENDS

	Year					Percent Change Year-to-Year			
	2005	2006	2007	2008	2009	05-06	06-07	07-08	08-09
Establishments	57,139	57,236	57,333	57,692	58,053	0.2%	0.2%	0.6%	0.6%
Sales ($Millions)	147,808	153,922	162,571	171,215	179,970	4.1%	5.6%	5.3%	5.1%
Employment	941,039	936,357	938,003	943,766	949,626	-0.5%	0.2%	0.6%	0.6%

INDUSTRY RATIOS

(Industry Averages)	Year					Percent Change Year-to-Year			
	2005	2006	2007	2008	2009	05-06	06-07	07-08	08-09
Sales ($M)/Estab.	2.59	2.69	2.84	2.97	3.10	4.0%	5.4%	4.7%	4.5%
Sales ($) per Emp.	157,069	164,384	173,316	181,417	189,517	4.7%	5.4%	4.7%	4.5%
Emps. per Estab.	16.5	16.4	16.4	16.4	16.4	-0.7%	0.0%	0.0%	0.0%

Engineering Services Industry
(NAICS 54133)

Size of Firm Industry Estimates

Year	Establishments by Size of Firm									Total
	1-4 Emps.	5-9 Emps.	10-19 Emps.	20-49 Emps.	50-99 Emps.	100-249 Emps.	250-499 Emps.	500+ Emps.	Unknown Emps.	Total
2006	30,432	8,985	7,676	5,761	1,959	963	220	111	1,224	57,333
2008	30,623	9,041	7,724	5,797	1,971	969	222	112	1,231	57,692
2009	30,814	9,098	7,772	5,833	1,984	975	223	113	1,239	58,053
Sales ($Millions) by Size of Firm										**Total**
2006	6,747	6,972	14,465	28,097	20,847	27,638	21,316	26,576	9,913	162,571
2008	7,106	7,343	15,235	29,594	21,957	29,110	22,451	27,992	10,427	171,215
2009	7,470	7,719	16,015	31,108	23,081	30,600	23,600	29,424	10,954	179,970
Employment by Size of Firm										**Total**
2006	60,864	53,912	115,138	190,104	125,375	132,848	71,809	109,553	78,400	938,003
2008	61,245	54,249	115,858	191,293	126,160	133,680	72,258	110,238	78,784	943,766
2009	61,628	54,588	116,583	192,490	126,949	134,516	72,710	110,928	79,232	949,626

Sub-Industries — 2007 Industry Estimates

Sub-Industries	Total Establishments	Total Employment	Total Sales ($M)
Engineering services	22,501	430,456	69,017
Sanitary engineers	149	2,498	348
Pollution control engineering	207	3,708	1,215
Industrial engineers	556	10,836	5,158
Machine tool design	339	2,417	197
Mechanical engineering	1,575	20,030	1,671
Petroleum, mining, and chemical	763	12,187	1,676
Construction and civil engineering	728	17,948	2,471
Building construction consultant	1,932	14,443	1,840
Civil engineering	4,725	87,371	33,682
Heating and ventilation engineering	288	3,219	374
Structural engineering	1,806	16,395	1,834
Acoustical engineering	261	3,102	143
Aviation and/or aeronautical	799	15,067	2,019
Consulting engineer	15,016	216,773	32,540
Designing: ship, boat, machine, and	897	23,107	2,657
Electrical or electronic engineering	2,295	34,000	3,427
Other engineering services	2,496	24,445	2,302

INTERIOR DESIGN SERVICES INDUSTRY
(NAICS 54141)

INDUSTRY DEFINITION

NAICS 54141: Interior Design Services . This industry comprises establishments primarily engaged in planning, designing, and administering projects in interior spaces to meet the physical and aesthetic needs of people using them, taking into consideration building codes, health and safety regulations, traffic patterns and floor planning, mechanical and electrical needs, and interior fittings and furniture. Interior designers and interior design consultants work in areas, such as hospitality design, health care design, institutional design, commercial and corporate design, and residential design. This industry also includes interior decorating consultants engaged exclusively in providing aesthetic services associated with interior spaces.

INDUSTRY ESTABLISHMENTS, SALES & EMPLOYMENT TRENDS

	Year					Percent Change Year-to-Year			
	2005	2006	2007	2008	2009	05-06	06-07	07-08	08-09
Establishments	12,732	13,064	13,396	13,862	14,344	2.6%	2.5%	3.5%	3.5%
Sales ($Millions)	6,288	6,832	7,307	7,857	8,408	8.7%	6.9%	7.5%	7.0%
Employment	62,971	65,410	67,016	69,499	71,802	3.9%	2.5%	3.7%	3.3%

INDUSTRY RATIOS

(Industry Averages)	Year					Percent Change Year-to-Year			
	2005	2006	2007	2008	2009	05-06	06-07	07-08	08-09
Sales ($M)/Estab.	0.49	0.52	0.55	0.57	0.59	5.9%	4.3%	3.9%	3.4%
Sales ($) per Emp.	99,850	104,453	109,028	113,049	117,100	4.6%	4.4%	3.7%	3.6%
Emps. per Estab.	4.9	5.0	5.0	5.0	5.0	1.2%	-0.1%	0.2%	-0.2%

INTERIOR DESIGN SERVICES INDUSTRY
(NAICS 54141)

SIZE OF FIRM INDUSTRY ESTIMATES

Year	Establishments by Size of Firm									Total
	1-4 Emps.	5-9 Emps.	10-19 Emps.	20-49 Emps.	50-99 Emps.	100-249 Emps.	250-499 Emps.	500+ Emps.	Unknown Emps.	
2006	10,871	1,595	581	213	41	18	1	0	78	13,396
2008	11,249	1,650	602	220	42	18	1	0	80	13,862
2009	11,640	1,707	623	228	44	19	1	0	83	14,344
	Sales ($Millions) by Size of Firm									Total
2006	2,834	1,213	1,074	833	401	463	0	0	489	7,307
2008	3,041	1,301	1,152	894	431	497	0	0	541	7,857
2009	3,259	1,395	1,235	958	462	532	0	0	567	8,408
	Employment by Size of Firm									Total
2006	32,612	9,568	8,141	6,818	2,628	2,450	0	0	4,800	67,016
2008	33,746	9,900	8,424	7,055	2,719	2,535	0	0	5,120	69,499
2009	34,919	10,245	8,717	7,300	2,814	2,624	0	0	5,184	71,802

SUB-INDUSTRIES — 2007 INDUSTRY ESTIMATES

Sub-Industries	Total Establishments	Total Employment	Total Sales ($M)
Interior design services	701	1,711	150
Decoration service for special events	35	163	11
Interior designer	308	959	105
Interior decorating	201	534	52

GRAPHIC DESIGNS SERVICES INDUSTRY
(NAICS 54143)

INDUSTRY DEFINITION

NAICS 54143: Graphic Design Services . This industry comprises establishments primarily engaged in planning, designing, and managing the production of visual communication in order to convey specific messages or concepts, clarify complex information, or project visual identities. These services can include the design of printed materials, packaging, advertising, signage systems, and corporate identification (logos). This industry also includes commercial artists engaged exclusively in generating drawings and illustrations requiring technical accuracy or interpretative skills.

INDUSTRY ESTABLISHMENTS, SALES & EMPLOYMENT TRENDS

	Year					Percent Change Year-to-Year			
	2005	2006	2007	2008	2009	05-06	06-07	07-08	08-09
Establishments	16,566	16,659	16,751	16,938	17,127	0.6%	0.6%	1.1%	1.1%
Sales ($Millions)	7,651	7,728	7,772	7,820	7,868	1.0%	0.6%	0.6%	0.6%
Employment	85,065	85,841	86,300	87,226	88,162	0.9%	0.5%	1.1%	1.1%

INDUSTRY RATIOS

(Industry Averages)	Year					Percent Change Year-to-Year			
	2005	2006	2007	2008	2009	05-06	06-07	07-08	08-09
Sales ($M)/Estab.	0.46	0.46	0.46	0.46	0.46	0.4%	0.0%	-0.5%	-0.5%
Sales ($) per Emp.	89,942	90,024	90,063	89,656	89,250	0.1%	0.0%	-0.5%	-0.5%
Emps. per Estab.	5.1	5.2	5.2	5.1	5.1	0.4%	0.0%	0.0%	0.0%

Graphic Designs Services Industry (NAICS 54143)

Size of Firm Industry Estimates

Year	Establishments by Size of Firm									Total
	1-4 Emps.	5-9 Emps.	10-19 Emps.	20-49 Emps.	50-99 Emps.	100-249 Emps.	250-499 Emps.	500+ Emps.	Unknown Emps.	
2006	13,232	2,152	888	346	57	20	1	1	57	16,751
2008	13,380	2,176	898	350	58	20	1	1	58	16,938
2009	13,529	2,201	908	354	59	20	1	1	59	17,127
	Sales ($Millions) by Size of Firm									Total
2006	2,773	1,289	1,330	1,278	372	395	43	43	249	7,772
2008	2,791	1,297	1,338	1,286	374	398	44	44	248	7,820
2009	2,809	1,305	1,347	1,295	377	401	44	44	247	7,868
	Employment by Size of Firm									Total
2006	39,696	12,914	12,438	10,732	3,556	2,595	409	632	3,328	86,300
2008	40,139	13,058	12,577	10,852	3,596	2,624	413	639	3,328	87,226
2009	40,587	13,204	12,717	10,973	3,636	2,654	418	646	3,328	88,162

Sub-Industries – 2007 Industry Estimates

Sub-Industries	Total Establishments	Total Employment	Total Sales ($M)
Commercial art and graphic design	8,121	35,683	3,215
Art design services	790	3,432	276
Chart and graph design	383	1,390	101
Creative services to advertisers, except	306	1,695	140
Graphic arts and related design	5,274	30,841	2,909
Package design	166	1,964	211
Silk screen design	620	6,719	577
Film strip, slide, and still film production	198	1,152	94
Film strip and slide producer	46	270	21
Still film producer	17	89	7
Commercial art and illustration	831	3,066	221

COMPUTER SYSTEMS DESIGNS SERVICES INDUSTRY (NAICS 54151)

INDUSTRY DEFINITION

NAICS 54151: Computer Systems Design and Related Services .
This industry comprises establishments primarily engaged in providing expertise in the field of information technologies through one or more of the following activities: (1) writing, modifying, testing, and supporting software to meet the needs of a particular customer; (2) planning and designing computer systems that integrate computer hardware, software, and communication technologies; (3) on-site management and operation of clients' computer systems and/or data processing facilities; and (4) other professional and technical computer-related advice and services.

INDUSTRY ESTABLISHMENTS, SALES & EMPLOYMENT TRENDS

	Year					Percent Change Year-to-Year			
	2005	2006	2007	2008	2009	05-06	06-07	07-08	08-09
Establishments	109,633	111,686	113,738	115,876	118,054	1.9%	1.8%	1.9%	1.9%
Sales ($Millions)	146,387	151,715	158,023	163,779	169,705	3.6%	4.2%	3.6%	3.6%
Employment	1,287,107	1,309,553	1,333,670	1,358,624	1,384,260	1.7%	1.8%	1.9%	1.9%

INDUSTRY RATIOS

(Industry Averages)	Year					Percent Change Year-to-Year			
	2005	2006	2007	2008	2009	05-06	06-07	07-08	08-09
Sales ($M)/Estab.	1.34	1.36	1.39	1.41	1.44	1.7%	2.3%	1.7%	1.7%
Sales ($) per Emp.	113,734	115,852	118,487	120,547	122,596	1.9%	2.3%	1.7%	1.7%
Emps. per Estab.	11.7	11.7	11.7	11.7	11.7	-0.1%	0.0%	0.0%	0.0%

COMPUTER SYSTEMS DESIGNS SERVICES INDUSTRY
(NAICS 54151)

SIZE OF FIRM INDUSTRY ESTIMATES

Year	Establishments by Size of Firm									Total
	1-4 Emps.	5-9 Emps.	10-19 Emps.	20-49 Emps.	50-99 Emps.	100-249 Emps.	250-499 Emps.	500+ Emps.	Unknown Emps.	
2006	81,992	11,967	7,670	5,878	2,348	1,285	400	188	2,008	113,738
2008	83,533	12,192	7,814	5,988	2,392	1,309	408	192	2,045	115,876
2009	85,103	12,421	7,961	6,101	2,437	1,334	416	195	2,084	118,054
	Sales ($Millions) by Size of Firm									Total
2006	17,103	6,241	10,400	21,457	18,855	25,462	24,726	28,540	5,238	158,023
2008	17,727	6,468	10,779	22,240	19,543	26,390	25,628	29,580	5,425	163,779
2009	18,368	6,702	11,169	23,044	20,249	27,344	26,554	30,650	5,625	169,705
	Employment by Size of Firm									Total
2006	245,976	71,804	107,381	188,096	143,217	170,886	122,141	155,593	128,576	1,333,670
2008	250,599	73,154	109,399	191,632	145,909	174,098	124,436	158,518	130,880	1,358,624
2009	255,309	74,529	111,455	195,233	148,651	177,370	126,775	161,497	133,440	1,384,260

SUB-INDUSTRIES — 2007 INDUSTRY ESTIMATES

Sub-Industries	Total Establishments	Total Employment	Total Sales ($M)
Custom computer programming	28,872	301,177	26,943
Custom computer programming	3,816	49,096	5,773
Computer software systems analysis	22,367	174,066	18,586
Computer software writing services	1,513	10,715	819
Computer code authors	191	716	64
Computer software writers, freelance	1,049	4,957	370
Computer software development and	11,342	159,364	20,292
Computer software development	41,576	596,920	80,838
Software programming applications	3,012	36,658	4,339

MANAGEMENT CONSULTING SERVICES INDUSTRY (NAICS 54161)

INDUSTRY DEFINITION

NAICS 54161: Management Consulting Services . This industry comprises establishments primarily engaged in providing advice and assistance to businesses and other organizations on management issues, such as strategic and organizational planning; financial planning and budgeting; marketing objectives and policies; human resource policies, practices, and planning; production scheduling; and control planning.

INDUSTRY ESTABLISHMENTS, SALES & EMPLOYMENT TRENDS

	Year					Percent Change Year-to-Year			
	2005	2006	2007	2008	2009	05-06	06-07	07-08	08-09
Establishments	109,271	120,959	132,646	143,556	155,363	10.7%	9.7%	8.2%	8.2%
Sales ($Millions)	116,822	130,565	146,965	162,315	179,211	11.8%	12.6%	10.4%	10.4%
Employment	966,730	1,060,788	1,163,626	1,259,192	1,362,733	9.7%	9.7%	8.2%	8.2%

INDUSTRY RATIOS

	Year					Percent Change Year-to-Year			
(Industry Averages)	2005	2006	2007	2008	2009	05-06	06-07	07-08	08-09
Sales ($M)/Estab.	1.07	1.08	1.11	1.13	1.15	1.0%	2.6%	2.1%	2.0%
Sales ($) per Emp.	120,842	123,083	126,299	128,904	131,509	1.9%	2.6%	2.1%	2.0%
Emps. per Estab.	8.8	8.8	8.8	8.8	8.8	-0.9%	0.0%	0.0%	0.0%

MANAGEMENT CONSULTING SERVICES INDUSTRY (NAICS 54161)

SIZE OF FIRM INDUSTRY ESTIMATES

Year	Establishments by Size of Firm									
	1-4 Emps.	5-9 Emps.	10-19 Emps.	20-49 Emps.	50-99 Emps.	100-249 Emps.	250-499 Emps.	500+ Emps.	Unknown Emps.	Total
2006	105,222	12,208	6,768	4,147	1,453	870	281	164	1,533	132,646
2008	113,877	13,212	7,325	4,488	1,572	942	304	177	1,659	143,556
2009	123,243	14,299	7,928	4,857	1,701	1,019	329	192	1,796	155,363
	Sales ($Millions) by Size of Firm									Total
2006	24,306	8,973	13,503	17,417	13,727	18,270	14,077	27,027	9,664	146,965
2008	26,848	9,911	14,915	19,238	15,162	20,180	15,549	29,853	10,661	162,315
2009	29,643	10,943	16,467	21,241	16,740	22,281	17,167	32,960	11,768	179,211
	Employment by Size of Firm									Total
2006	315,667	73,249	94,758	132,701	92,964	121,801	91,344	142,965	98,176	1,163,626
2008	341,630	79,274	102,552	143,615	100,610	131,819	98,857	154,723	106,112	1,259,192
2009	369,728	85,794	110,986	155,427	108,885	142,660	106,988	167,449	114,816	1,362,733

SUB-INDUSTRIES — 2007 INDUSTRY ESTIMATES

Sub-Industries	Total Establishments	Total Employment	Total Sales ($M)
Management consulting services	39,170	378,878	50,410
Industrial and labor consulting services	4,630	35,768	3,768
Human resource consulting services	9,872	133,498	16,678
Marketing consulting services	22,422	149,675	19,504
Distribution channels consultant	230	2,624	314
Franchising consultant	135	1,171	187
Merchandising consultant	323	3,657	681
New products and services consultants	396	3,055	283
Sales (including sales management)	2,180	13,909	1,140
Industry specialist consultants	21,391	204,302	29,143
Business planning and organizing	1,948	18,058	2,423
Corporate objectives and policies	149	834	82
Corporation organizing consultant	338	3,228	446
Materials mgmt. (purchasing, handling,	280	3,786	323
New business start-up consultant	520	3,493	320
Planning consultant	1,694	12,748	1,329
Administrative services consultant	26,968	194,943	19,935

ADVERTISING AGENCIES INDUSTRY (NAICS 54181)

INDUSTRY DEFINITION

NAICS 54181: Advertising Agencies . This industry comprises establishments primarily engaged in designing and implementing public relations campaigns. These campaigns are designed to promote the interests and image of their clients. Establishments providing lobbying, political consulting, or public relations consulting are included in this industry.

INDUSTRY ESTABLISHMENTS, SALES & EMPLOYMENT TRENDS

	Year					Percent Change Year-to-Year			
	2005	2006	2007	2008	2009	05-06	06-07	07-08	08-09
Establishments	13,540	13,103	12,665	12,505	12,347	-3.2%	-3.3%	-1.3%	-1.3%
Sales ($Millions)	104,381	93,179	97,513	103,197	108,704	-10.7%	4.7%	5.8%	5.3%
Employment	178,957	161,167	155,722	153,860	151,891	-9.9%	-3.4%	-1.2%	-1.3%

INDUSTRY RATIOS

(Industry Averages)	Year					Percent Change Year-to-Year			
	2005	2006	2007	2008	2009	05-06	06-07	07-08	08-09
Sales ($M)/Estab.	7.71	7.11	7.70	8.25	8.80	-7.8%	8.3%	7.2%	6.7%
Sales ($) per Emp.	583,276	578,149	626,198	670,720	715,672	-0.9%	8.3%	7.1%	6.7%
Emps. per Estab.	13.2	12.3	12.3	12.3	12.3	-6.9%	0.0%	0.1%	0.0%

ADVERTISING AGENCIES INDUSTRY
(NAICS 54181)

SIZE OF FIRM INDUSTRY ESTIMATES

Year	Establishments by Size of Firm									Total
	1-4 Emps.	5-9 Emps.	10-19 Emps.	20-49 Emps.	50-99 Emps.	100-249 Emps.	250-499 Emps.	500+ Emps.	Unknown Emps.	Total
2006	7,823	1,987	1,266	850	261	136	41	16	286	12,665
2008	7,724	1,962	1,250	839	258	134	40	16	282	12,505
2009	7,627	1,937	1,234	828	254	133	40	16	279	12,347
	Sales ($Millions) by Size of Firm									Total
2006	3,658	3,020	9,471	13,905	15,255	20,270	11,491	17,918	2,525	97,513
2008	3,871	3,195	10,021	14,713	16,141	21,448	12,159	18,960	2,687	103,197
2009	4,078	3,366	10,557	15,499	17,003	22,593	12,808	19,972	2,827	108,704
	Employment by Size of Firm									Total
2006	23,469	11,920	17,721	27,186	15,919	18,114	12,491	10,470	18,432	155,722
2008	23,173	11,770	17,497	26,842	15,718	17,885	12,333	10,338	18,304	153,860
2009	22,880	11,621	17,276	26,503	15,519	17,659	12,177	10,207	18,048	151,891

SUB-INDUSTRIES — 2007 INDUSTRY ESTIMATES

Sub-Industries	Total Establishments	Total Employment	Total Sales ($M)
Advertising agencies	9,498	134,248	91,147
Advertising consultant	3,168	21,474	6,366

PUBLIC RELATIONS AGENCIES INDUSTRY
(NAICS 54182)

INDUSTRY DEFINITION

NAICS 54182: Public Relations Agencies . This industry comprises establishments primarily engaged in designing and implementing public relations campaigns. These campaigns are designed to promote the interests and image of their clients. Establishments providing lobbying, political consulting, or public relations consulting are included in this industry.

INDUSTRY ESTABLISHMENTS, SALES & EMPLOYMENT TRENDS

	Year					Percent Change Year-to-Year			
	2005	2006	2007	2008	2009	05-06	06-07	07-08	08-09
Establishments	7,289	7,377	7,464	7,626	7,792	1.2%	1.2%	2.2%	2.2%
Sales ($Millions)	6,213	6,522	6,941	7,407	7,890	5.0%	6.4%	6.7%	6.5%
Employment	52,434	52,617	53,254	54,441	55,651	0.3%	1.2%	2.2%	2.2%

INDUSTRY RATIOS

	Year					Percent Change Year-to-Year			
(Industry Averages)	2005	2006	2007	2008	2009	05-06	06-07	07-08	08-09
Sales ($M)/Estab.	0.85	0.88	0.93	0.97	1.01	3.7%	5.2%	4.5%	4.3%
Sales ($) per Emp.	118,492	123,955	130,329	136,055	141,783	4.6%	5.1%	4.4%	4.2%
Emps. per Estab.	7.2	7.1	7.1	7.1	7.1	-0.8%	0.0%	0.1%	0.1%

PUBLIC RELATIONS AGENCIES INDUSTRY
(NAICS 54182)

SIZE OF FIRM INDUSTRY ESTIMATES

Year	Establishments by Size of Firm									Total
	1-4 Emps.	5-9 Emps.	10-19 Emps.	20-49 Emps.	50-99 Emps.	100-249 Emps.	250-499 Emps.	500+ Emps.	Unknown Emps.	
2006	5,365	1,075	582	278	65	21	7	0	74	7,464
2008	5,481	1,099	595	284	66	22	8	0	76	7,626
2009	5,600	1,123	607	290	68	22	8	0	78	7,792
	Sales ($Millions) by Size of Firm									Total
2006	1,479	830	1,219	1,347	572	539	534	27	394	6,941
2008	1,577	885	1,300	1,437	611	576	569	29	423	7,407
2009	1,680	943	1,385	1,530	650	613	606	31	453	7,890
	Employment by Size of Firm									Total
2006	16,094	6,453	8,146	8,885	3,958	2,830	2,271	138	4,480	53,254
2008	16,443	6,593	8,323	9,077	4,044	2,891	2,320	141	4,608	54,441
2009	16,800	6,736	8,504	9,274	4,132	2,954	2,371	144	4,736	55,651

SUB-INDUSTRIES — 2007 INDUSTRY ESTIMATES

Sub-Industries	Total Establishments	Total Employment	Total Sales ($M)
Public relations services	2,896	18,725	2,261
Lobbyist	514	3,006	446
Promotion service	1,681	11,937	1,615
Public relations and publicity	1,057	10,023	1,199
Sales promotion	1,316	9,564	1,419

DIRECT MAIL ADVERTISING INDUSTRY
(NAICS 54186)

INDUSTRY DEFINITION

NAICS 54186: Direct Mail Advertising . This industry comprises establishments primarily engaged in (1) creating and designing advertising campaigns for the purpose of distributing advertising materials (e.g., coupons, flyers, samples) or specialties (e.g., key chains, magnets, pens with customized messages imprinted) by mail or other direct distribution; and/or (2) preparing advertising materials or specialties for mailing or other direct distribution. These establishments may also compile, maintain, sell, and rent mailing lists.

INDUSTRY ESTABLISHMENTS, SALES & EMPLOYMENT TRENDS

	Year					Percent Change Year-to-Year			
	2005	2006	2007	2008	2009	05-06	06-07	07-08	08-09
Establishments	3,466	3,437	3,407	3,371	3,335	-0.9%	-0.9%	-1.1%	-1.1%
Sales ($Millions)	8,777	8,752	9,005	9,196	9,382	-0.3%	2.9%	2.1%	2.0%
Employment	72,304	70,973	70,330	69,623	68,924	-1.8%	-0.9%	-1.0%	-1.0%

INDUSTRY RATIOS

(Industry Averages)	Year					Percent Change Year-to-Year			
	2005	2006	2007	2008	2009	05-06	06-07	07-08	08-09
Sales ($M)/Estab.	2.53	2.55	2.64	2.73	2.81	0.6%	3.8%	3.2%	3.1%
Sales ($) per Emp.	121,386	123,319	128,037	132,079	136,121	1.6%	3.8%	3.2%	3.1%
Emps. per Estab.	20.9	20.7	20.6	20.7	20.7	-1.0%	0.0%	0.1%	0.1%

DIRECT MAIL ADVERTISING INDUSTRY
(NAICS 54186)

SIZE OF FIRM INDUSTRY ESTIMATES

Year	Establishments by Size of Firm									Total
	1-4 Emps.	5-9 Emps.	10-19 Emps.	20-49 Emps.	50-99 Emps.	100-249 Emps.	250-499 Emps.	500+ Emps.	Unknown Emps.	
2006	1,622	554	484	400	165	90	29	10	57	3,407
2008	1,604	548	479	396	163	90	28	10	57	3,371
2009	1,588	543	474	392	161	89	28	10	56	3,335
	Sales ($Millions) by Size of Firm									Total
2006	348	357	1,039	1,418	1,062	1,652	1,842	1,013	273	9,005
2008	356	365	1,061	1,448	1,084	1,687	1,880	1,034	281	9,196
2009	363	372	1,082	1,476	1,106	1,720	1,917	1,055	290	9,382
	Employment by Size of Firm									Total
2006	4,865	3,325	6,772	12,798	10,049	12,031	8,713	8,321	3,456	70,330
2008	4,813	3,290	6,701	12,662	9,943	11,904	8,621	8,233	3,456	69,623
2009	4,763	3,255	6,630	12,529	9,837	11,778	8,530	8,146	3,456	68,924

SUB-INDUSTRIES – 2007 INDUSTRY ESTIMATES

Sub-Industries	Total Establishments	Total Employment	Total Sales ($M)
Direct mail advertising services	1,638	36,264	4,525
Addressing service	45	1,459	112
Addressographing service	2	14	1
Mailing list compilers	169	2,927	494
Mailing service	1,440	27,701	3,603
Mailing list management	26	355	64
Mailing list brokers	87	1,612	205

MARKETING RESEARCH & PUBLIC OPINION POLLING (NAICS 54191)

INDUSTRY DEFINITION

NAICS 54191: Marketing Research & Public Opinion Polling .
This industry comprises establishments primarily engaged in
systematically gathering, recording, tabulating, and presenting
marketing and public opinion data.

INDUSTRY ESTABLISHMENTS, SALES & EMPLOYMENT TRENDS

	Year					Percent Change Year-to-Year			
	2005	2006	2007	2008	2009	05-06	06-07	07-08	08-09
Establishments	5,325	5,643	5,962	6,199	6,445	6.0%	5.6%	4.0%	4.0%
Sales ($Millions)	15,221	16,198	17,670	18,880	20,156	6.4%	9.1%	6.8%	6.8%
Employment	120,863	126,032	133,091	138,492	144,091	4.3%	5.6%	4.1%	4.0%

INDUSTRY RATIOS

	Year					Percent Change Year-to-Year			
(Industry Averages)	2005	2006	2007	2008	2009	05-06	06-07	07-08	08-09
Sales ($M)/Estab.	2.86	2.87	2.96	3.05	3.13	0.4%	3.3%	2.8%	2.7%
Sales ($) per Emp.	125,933	128,519	132,766	136,322	139,884	2.1%	3.3%	2.7%	2.6%
Emps. per Estab.	22.7	22.3	22.3	22.3	22.4	-1.6%	0.0%	0.1%	0.1%

Marketing Research & Public Opinion Polling
(NAICS 54191)

Size of Firm Industry Estimates

Year	Establishments by Size of Firm									Total
	1-4 Emps.	5-9 Emps.	10-19 Emps.	20-49 Emps.	50-99 Emps.	100-249 Emps.	250-499 Emps.	500+ Emps.	Unknown Emps.	Total
2006	3,226	762	693	632	254	208	52	26	113	5,962
2008	3,354	792	720	657	264	216	54	27	118	6,199
2009	3,488	824	749	683	275	225	56	28	122	6,445
	Sales ($Millions) by Size of Firm									Total
2006	686	405	958	3,361	1,759	3,718	1,969	4,123	689	17,670
2008	733	433	1,023	3,589	1,878	3,970	2,103	4,403	747	18,880
2009	782	462	1,092	3,830	2,004	4,236	2,244	4,698	807	20,156
	Employment by Size of Firm									Total
2006	6,452	4,571	9,701	20,853	16,024	28,912	16,432	23,235	6,912	133,091
2008	6,709	4,753	10,087	21,682	16,661	30,061	17,085	24,158	7,296	138,492
2009	6,976	4,942	10,488	22,544	17,323	31,256	17,764	25,119	7,680	144,091

Sub-Industries – 2007 Industry Estimates

Sub-Industries	Total Establishments	Total Employment	Total Sales ($M)
Commercial nonphysical research	942	18,027	1,238
Market analysis, business, and	438	13,245	1,286
Business analysis	92	1,902	925
Business economic service	192	2,533	549
Business research service	323	5,738	658
Economic research	224	2,795	326
Market analysis or research	1,995	54,527	6,997
Merger, acquisition, and reorganization	163	3,567	1,126
Opinion research	46	1,378	70
Research services, except laboratory	787	16,109	2,358
Survey service: marketing, location, etc.	226	3,577	1,348
Commercial sociological and	34	520	34
Educational research	452	8,223	626
Sociological research	48	949	130

TELEMARKETING SERVICES INDUSTRY
(NAICS 561422)

INDUSTRY DEFINITION

NAICS 561422: Telemarketing Services. This industry comprises establishments primarily engaged in providing telemarketing services on a contract or fee basis for others, such as: (1) promoting clients' products or services by telephone, (2) taking orders for clients by telephone, and (3) soliciting contributions or providing information for clients by telephone. These establishments never own the product or provide the services they are representing and generally can originate and/or receive calls for others.

INDUSTRY ESTABLISHMENTS, SALES & EMPLOYMENT TRENDS

	Year					Percent Change Year-to-Year			
	2005	2006	2007	2008	2009	05-06	06-07	07-08	08-09
Establishments	3,224	3,213	3,203	3,138	3,074	-0.3%	-0.3%	-2.0%	-2.0%
Sales ($Millions)	28,432	29,945	30,769	31,054	31,305	5.3%	2.8%	0.9%	0.8%
Employment	269,783	275,643	274,730	269,193	263,688	2.2%	-0.3%	-2.0%	-2.0%

INDUSTRY RATIOS

(Industry Averages)	Year					Percent Change Year-to-Year			
	2005	2006	2007	2008	2009	05-06	06-07	07-08	08-09
Sales ($M)/Estab.	8.82	9.32	9.61	9.90	10.18	5.7%	3.1%	3.0%	2.9%
Sales ($) per Emp.	105,389	108,636	111,999	115,358	118,718	3.1%	3.1%	3.0%	2.9%
Emps. per Estab.	83.7	85.8	85.8	85.8	85.8	2.5%	0.0%	0.0%	0.0%

TELEMARKETING SERVICES INDUSTRY
(NAICS 561422)

SIZE OF FIRM INDUSTRY ESTIMATES

Year	Establishments by Size of Firm									Total
	1-4 Emps.	5-9 Emps.	10-19 Emps.	20-49 Emps.	50-99 Emps.	100-249 Emps.	250-499 Emps.	500+ Emps.	Unknown Emps.	
2006	1,075	325	380	453	292	325	199	144	16	3,203
2008	1,054	318	372	444	286	318	195	141	15	3,138
2009	1,032	312	364	435	280	312	191	138	15	3,074
	Sales ($Millions) by Size of Firm									**Total**
2006	229	173	484	1,253	1,552	4,491	8,651	13,922	14	30,769
2008	231	174	489	1,265	1,566	4,533	8,731	14,051	15	31,054
2009	233	176	492	1,275	1,578	4,569	8,802	14,164	15	31,305
	Employment by Size of Firm									**Total**
2006	3,226	1,950	5,313	14,512	17,809	43,230	60,550	127,628	512	274,730
2008	3,161	1,911	5,206	14,219	17,449	42,357	59,327	125,051	512	269,193
2009	3,096	1,872	5,100	13,927	17,092	41,489	58,112	122,489	512	263,688

SUB-INDUSTRIES — 2007 INDUSTRY ESTIMATES

Sub-Industries	Total Establishments	Total Employment	Total Sales ($M)
Telemarketing services	3,203	274,730	30,769

SECURITY GUARDS & PATROL SERVICES INDUSTRY (NAICS 561612)

INDUSTRY DEFINITION

NAICS 561612: Security Guards & Patrol Services. This industry comprises establishments primarily engaged in providing detective, guard, and armored car services. Establishments primarily engaged in monitoring and maintaining security systems devices, such as burglar and fire alarms, are classified in 7382.

INDUSTRY ESTABLISHMENTS, SALES & EMPLOYMENT TRENDS

	Year					Percent Change Year-to-Year			
	2005	2006	2007	2008	2009	05-06	06-07	07-08	08-09
Establishments	8,085	8,370	8,655	8,977	9,311	3.5%	3.4%	3.7%	3.7%
Sales ($Millions)	16,748	19,044	21,504	24,076	26,809	13.7%	12.9%	12.0%	11.4%
Employment	519,398	534,641	552,859	573,421	594,741	2.9%	3.4%	3.7%	3.7%

INDUSTRY RATIOS

(Industry Averages)	Year					Percent Change Year-to-Year			
	2005	2006	2007	2008	2009	05-06	06-07	07-08	08-09
Sales ($M)/Estab.	2.07	2.28	2.48	2.68	2.88	9.8%	9.2%	7.9%	7.4%
Sales ($) per Emp.	32,245	35,620	38,895	41,986	45,077	10.5%	9.2%	7.9%	7.4%
Emps. per Estab.	64.2	63.9	63.9	63.9	63.9	-0.6%	0.0%	0.0%	0.0%

SECURITY GUARDS & PATROL SERVICES INDUSTRY
(NAICS 561612)

SIZE OF FIRM INDUSTRY ESTIMATES

Year	Establishments by Size of Firm									Total
	1-4 Emps.	5-9 Emps.	10-19 Emps.	20-49 Emps.	50-99 Emps.	100-249 Emps.	250-499 Emps.	500+ Emps.	Unknown Emps.	Total
2006	2,296	1,040	1,126	1,446	929	1,134	421	182	83	8,655
2008	2,382	1,079	1,168	1,500	963	1,176	436	189	87	8,977
2009	2,470	1,119	1,211	1,556	999	1,219	452	196	90	9,311
	Sales ($Millions) by Size of Firm									Total
2006	273	247	803	2,579	2,540	6,066	4,500	4,218	276	21,504
2008	306	277	899	2,888	2,844	6,791	5,038	4,723	309	24,076
2009	340	308	1,001	3,216	3,167	7,563	5,611	5,259	343	26,809
	Employment by Size of Firm									Total
2006	6,888	6,241	15,761	46,278	56,663	150,767	128,254	136,695	5,312	552,859
2008	7,145	6,473	16,348	47,999	58,771	156,376	133,025	141,781	5,504	573,421
2009	7,410	6,714	16,956	49,785	60,957	162,193	137,974	147,055	5,696	594,741

SUB-INDUSTRIES – 2007 INDUSTRY ESTIMATES

Sub-Industries	Total Establishments	Total Employment	Total Sales ($M)
Detective and armored car services	1,125	65,940	3,241
Guard services	803	37,240	1,380
Armored car services	260	20,841	681
Burglary protection service	16	2,691	75
Guard dog rental	20	651	11
Protective services, guard	404	48,568	1,391
Security guard service	2,114	281,635	12,728
Detective services	855	18,113	451
Detective agency	501	21,170	388
Fingerprint service	41	1,329	13
Lie detection service	92	1,818	25
Private investigator	2,422	52,861	1,120

COLLEGES & UNIVERSITIES INDUSTRY (NAICS 61131)

INDUSTRY DEFINITION

NAICS 61131: Colleges & Universities. This industry comprises establishments primarily furnishing academic courses and granting academic degrees. The requirement for admission is at least a high school diploma or equivalent general academic training.

INDUSTRY ESTABLISHMENTS, SALES & EMPLOYMENT TRENDS

	Year					Percent Change Year-to-Year			
	2005	2006	2007	2008	2009	05-06	06-07	07-08	08-09
Establishments	4,435	4,516	4,598	4,707	4,820	1.8%	1.8%	2.4%	2.4%
Sales ($Millions)	176,337	194,814	208,657	223,213	238,333	10.5%	7.1%	7.0%	6.8%
Employment	912,501	962,995	980,051	1,003,433	1,027,278	5.5%	1.8%	2.4%	2.4%

INDUSTRY RATIOS

(Industry Averages)	Year					Percent Change Year-to-Year			
	2005	2006	2007	2008	2009	05-06	06-07	07-08	08-09
Sales ($M)/Estab.	39.76	43.13	45.38	47.42	49.45	8.5%	5.2%	4.5%	4.3%
Sales ($) per Emp.	193,245	202,300	212,905	222,449	232,005	4.7%	5.2%	4.5%	4.3%
Emps. per Estab.	205.7	213.2	213.2	213.2	213.1	3.6%	0.0%	0.0%	0.0%

COLLEGES & UNIVERSITIES INDUSTRY
(NAICS 61131)

SIZE OF FIRM INDUSTRY ESTIMATES

Year	Establishments by Size of Firm									Total
	1-4 Emps.	5-9 Emps.	10-19 Emps.	20-49 Emps.	50-99 Emps.	100-249 Emps.	250-499 Emps.	500+ Emps.	Unknown Emps.	Total
2006	820	349	353	388	278	419	376	737	880	4,598
2008	839	357	362	398	285	429	385	755	901	4,707
2009	859	366	370	407	292	439	394	773	923	4,820
	Sales ($Millions) by Size of Firm									Total
2006	271	193	741	2,101	3,043	13,838	34,648	147,312	6,510	208,657
2008	290	206	793	2,248	3,255	14,804	37,065	157,588	6,964	223,213
2009	310	220	846	2,400	3,476	15,807	39,578	168,272	7,424	238,333
	Employment by Size of Firm									Total
2006	2,459	2,093	4,944	12,428	16,980	55,751	114,763	714,313	56,320	980,051
2008	2,518	2,143	5,062	12,724	17,385	57,081	117,501	731,356	57,664	1,003,433
2009	2,578	2,194	5,183	13,028	17,799	58,443	120,304	748,805	58,944	1,027,278

SUB-INDUSTRIES — 2007 INDUSTRY ESTIMATES

Sub-Industries	Total Establishments	Total Employment	Total Sales ($M)
Colleges and universities	1,813	237,448	23,034
Colleges and universities	312	35,185	5,123
College, except junior	342	123,147	27,702
University	1,937	557,722	147,005
Professional schools	94	15,239	3,573
Service academy	23	4,679	930
Theological seminary	78	6,631	1,291

EXAM PREPARATION & TUTORING INDUSTRY (NAICS 611691)

INDUSTRY DEFINITION

NAICS 6111691: Exam Preparation & Tutoring. This industry comprises establishments primarily engaged in offering educational courses and services, not elsewhere classified. Includes music schools, drama schools, language schools, short-term examination preparatory schools, student exchange programs, curriculum development, and vocational counseling, except rehabilitation counseling. Dance schools are classified in 7911, and rehabilitation counseling is classified in 8331.

INDUSTRY ESTABLISHMENTS, SALES & EMPLOYMENT TRENDS

	Year					Percent Change Year-to-Year			
	2005	2006	2007	2008	2009	05-06	06-07	07-08	08-09
Establishments	5,927	6,691	7,455	8,270	9,173	12.9%	11.4%	10.9%	10.9%
Sales ($Millions)	3,040	3,448	4,000	4,597	5,285	13.5%	16.0%	14.9%	15.0%
Employment	80,001	89,245	99,211	110,014	122,339	11.6%	11.2%	10.9%	11.2%

INDUSTRY RATIOS

(Industry Averages)	Year					Percent Change Year-to-Year			
	2005	2006	2007	2008	2009	05-06	06-07	07-08	08-09
Sales ($M)/Estab.	0.51	0.52	0.54	0.56	0.58	0.5%	4.1%	3.6%	3.7%
Sales ($) per Emp.	37,993	38,641	40,322	41,782	43,202	1.7%	4.3%	3.6%	3.4%
Emps. per Estab.	13.5	13.3	13.3	13.3	13.3	-1.2%	-0.2%	0.0%	0.3%

EXAM PREPARATION & TUTORING INDUSTRY (NAICS 611691)

SIZE OF FIRM INDUSTRY ESTIMATES

Year	Establishments by Size of Firm									
	1-4 Emps.	5-9 Emps.	10-19 Emps.	20-49 Emps.	50-99 Emps.	100-249 Emps.	250-499 Emps.	500+ Emps.	Unknown Emps.	Total
2006	3,467	1,279	1,277	1,107	211	42	7	4	66	7,455
2008	3,845	1,419	1,416	1,228	234	47	8	5	73	8,270
2009	4,265	1,574	1,571	1,362	259	52	8	5	81	9,173
	Sales ($Millions) by Size of Firm									Total
2006	301	277	692	1,320	616	335	148	206	104	4,000
2008	346	319	795	1,518	708	385	170	237	119	4,597
2009	397	366	913	1,742	813	442	196	272	145	5,285
	Employment by Size of Firm									Total
2006	10,400	7,677	17,874	35,431	12,841	5,636	2,085	3,430	3,840	99,211
2008	11,536	8,515	19,826	39,301	14,244	6,251	2,312	3,804	4,224	110,014
2009	12,796	9,445	21,992	43,595	15,800	6,934	2,565	4,220	4,992	122,339

SUB-INDUSTRIES – 2007 INDUSTRY ESTIMATES

Sub-Industries	Total Establishments	Total Employment	Total Sales ($M)
Educational services	5,368	73,472	3,251
Educational service, nondegree	668	14,263	555
Tutoring school	1,419	11,477	194

EDUCATIONAL SUPPORT SERVICES INDUSTRY
(NAICS 61171)

INDUSTRY DEFINITION

NAICS 61171: Educational Support Services. This industry comprises establishments primarily engaged in offering educational courses and services, not elsewhere classified. Includes music schools, drama schools, language schools, short-term examination preparatory schools, student exchange programs, curriculum development, and vocational counseling, except rehabilitation counseling. Dance schools are classified in 7911, and rehabilitation counseling is classified in 8331.

INDUSTRY ESTABLISHMENTS, SALES & EMPLOYMENT TRENDS

	Year					Percent Change Year-to-Year			
	2005	2006	2007	2008	2009	05-06	06-07	07-08	08-09
Establishments	6,310	6,830	7,350	7,903	8,498	8.2%	7.6%	7.5%	7.5%
Sales ($Millions)	5,806	6,396	7,267	8,192	9,222	10.2%	13.6%	12.7%	12.6%
Employment	70,301	74,097	79,605	85,578	92,233	5.4%	7.4%	7.5%	7.8%

INDUSTRY RATIOS

(Industry Averages)	Year					Percent Change Year-to-Year			
	2005	2006	2007	2008	2009	05-06	06-07	07-08	08-09
Sales ($M)/Estab.	0.92	0.94	0.99	1.04	1.09	1.8%	5.6%	4.8%	4.7%
Sales ($) per Emp.	82,582	86,325	91,288	95,723	99,983	4.5%	5.8%	4.9%	4.5%
Emps. per Estab.	11.1	10.8	10.8	10.8	10.9	-2.6%	-0.2%	0.0%	0.2%

EDUCATIONAL SUPPORT SERVICES INDUSTRY
(NAICS 61171)

SIZE OF FIRM INDUSTRY ESTIMATES

Year	Establishments by Size of Firm									Total
	1-4 Emps.	5-9 Emps.	10-19 Emps.	20-49 Emps.	50-99 Emps.	100-249 Emps.	250-499 Emps.	500+ Emps.	Unknown Emps.	Total
2006	5,092	944	606	402	133	66	22	11	73	7,350
2008	5,475	1,015	652	433	143	71	24	12	79	7,903
2009	5,887	1,091	701	465	154	76	25	13	85	8,498
Sales ($Millions) by Size of Firm										**Total**
2006	850	420	607	1,074	801	1,065	1,102	1,224	125	7,267
2008	958	473	684	1,211	903	1,201	1,242	1,380	140	8,192
2009	1,078	533	770	1,362	1,015	1,351	1,397	1,552	164	9,222
Employment by Size of Firm										**Total**
2006	15,276	5,663	8,490	12,872	8,129	8,781	6,712	9,202	4,480	79,605
2008	16,426	6,089	9,129	13,840	8,741	9,441	7,217	9,895	4,800	85,578
2009	17,662	6,547	9,816	14,882	9,399	10,152	7,760	10,640	5,376	92,233

SUB-INDUSTRIES — 2007 INDUSTRY ESTIMATES

Sub-Industries	Total Establishments	Total Employment	Total Sales ($M)
Schools and educational services, nec	1,154	5,579	204
Arts and crafts schools	97	1,122	402
Art school, except commercial	119	2,570	197
Ceramic school	38	150	5
Floral arrangement instruction	72	183	7
Educational services	2,228	33,237	3,775
Educational service, nondegree	277	6,452	645
Tutoring school	589	5,192	225
Music and drama schools	845	6,090	277
Vehicle driving school	490	2,976	120
Automobile driving instruction	131	1,263	59
Truck driving training	52	724	88
Reading and speaking schools	92	793	35
Diction school	3	37	2
Language school	223	2,492	365
Public speaking school	72	752	64
Reading school, including speed	53	676	31
Other schools and educational services	814	9,318	765

OFFICES OF PHYSICIANS INDUSTRY
(NAICS 62111)

INDUSTRY DEFINITION

NAICS 62111: Offices of Physicians. This industry comprises establishments primarily of licensed practitioners having the degree of M.D. and engaged in the practice of general or specialized medicine and surgery. Establishments operating as clinics of physicians are included in this business. Osteopathic physicians are classified in 8031.

INDUSTRY ESTABLISHMENTS, SALES & EMPLOYMENT TRENDS

	Year					Percent Change Year-to-Year			
	2005	2006	2007	2008	2009	05-06	06-07	07-08	08-09
Establishments	215,513	219,516	223,519	227,402	231,351	1.9%	1.8%	1.7%	1.7%
Sales ($Millions)	215,290	239,515	264,374	288,539	313,447	11.3%	10.4%	9.1%	8.6%
Employment	2,240,118	2,313,624	2,355,832	2,396,836	2,438,256	3.3%	1.8%	1.7%	1.7%

INDUSTRY RATIOS

	Year					Percent Change Year-to-Year			
(Industry Averages)	2005	2006	2007	2008	2009	05-06	06-07	07-08	08-09
Sales ($M)/Estab.	1.00	1.09	1.18	1.27	1.35	9.2%	8.4%	7.3%	6.8%
Sales ($) per Emp.	96,107	103,524	112,221	120,383	128,554	7.7%	8.4%	7.3%	6.8%
Emps. per Estab.	10.4	10.5	10.5	10.5	10.5	1.4%	0.0%	0.0%	0.0%

OFFICES OF PHYSICIANS INDUSTRY
(NAICS 62111)

SIZE OF FIRM INDUSTRY ESTIMATES

Year	Establishments by Size of Firm									
	1-4 Emps.	5-9 Emps.	10-19 Emps.	20-49 Emps.	50-99 Emps.	100-249 Emps.	250-499 Emps.	500+ Emps.	Unknown Emps.	Total
2006	113,711	53,290	32,058	17,512	3,351	1,189	273	140	1,995	223,519
2008	115,686	54,216	32,615	17,816	3,409	1,209	278	142	2,030	227,402
2009	117,696	55,158	33,181	18,125	3,469	1,230	283	145	2,065	231,351
	Sales ($Millions) by Size of Firm									Total
2006	26,650	31,224	45,080	61,563	27,096	24,379	19,198	21,933	7,251	264,374
2008	29,086	34,077	49,200	67,189	29,572	26,607	20,952	23,937	7,919	288,539
2009	31,598	37,021	53,449	72,992	32,127	28,905	22,762	26,004	8,589	313,447
	Employment by Size of Firm									Total
2006	341,134	319,742	448,809	560,376	204,419	158,111	83,279	112,218	127,744	2,355,832
2008	347,059	325,296	456,604	570,109	207,969	160,857	84,726	114,167	130,048	2,396,836
2009	353,087	330,946	464,535	580,012	211,581	163,651	86,197	116,150	132,096	2,438,256

SUB-INDUSTRIES — 2007 INDUSTRY ESTIMATES

Sub-Industries	Total Establishments	Total Employment	Total Sales ($M)
Offices and clinics of medical doctors	79,406	688,956	63,068
Internal medicine practitioners	24,005	274,514	26,077
Medical centers	14,307	317,389	37,127
Medical insurance associations	1,302	46,703	36,956
Psychiatrists and psychoanalysts	5,726	39,463	3,959
Specialized medical practitioners,	45,735	530,663	50,672
General and family practice,	36,193	290,844	29,517
Occupational and industrial specialist,	643	9,163	893
Physical medicine, physician/surgeon	3,025	23,300	1,757
Physicians' office, including specialists	7,995	83,144	10,003

OFFICES OF DENTISTS INDUSTRY
(NAICS 62121)

INDUSTRY DEFINITION

NAICS 62121: Offices of Dentists. This industry comprises establishments primarily of licensed practitioners having the degree of D.M.D. or D.D.S. (or D.D.Sc.) and engaged in the practice of general or specialized dentistry, including dental surgery. Establishments operating as clinics of dentists are included in this business.

INDUSTRY ESTABLISHMENTS, SALES & EMPLOYMENT TRENDS

	Year					Percent Change Year-to-Year			
	2005	2006	2007	2008	2009	05-06	06-07	07-08	08-09
Establishments	123,908	124,881	125,855	127,158	128,474	0.8%	0.8%	1.0%	1.0%
Sales ($Millions)	40,706	45,747	50,113	54,439	58,850	12.4%	9.5%	8.6%	8.1%
Employment	900,990	934,480	942,028	951,743	961,616	3.7%	0.8%	1.0%	1.0%

INDUSTRY RATIOS

	Year					Percent Change Year-to-Year			
(Industry Averages)	2005	2006	2007	2008	2009	05-06	06-07	07-08	08-09
Sales ($M)/Estab.	0.33	0.37	0.40	0.43	0.46	11.5%	8.7%	7.5%	7.0%
Sales ($) per Emp.	45,179	48,954	53,197	57,199	61,199	8.4%	8.7%	7.5%	7.0%
Emps. per Estab.	7.3	7.5	7.5	7.5	7.5	2.9%	0.0%	0.0%	0.0%

OFFICES OF DENTISTS INDUSTRY
(NAICS 62121)

SIZE OF FIRM INDUSTRY ESTIMATES

Year	Establishments by Size of Firm									Total
	1-4 Emps.	5-9 Emps.	10-19 Emps.	20-49 Emps.	50-99 Emps.	100-249 Emps.	250-499 Emps.	500+ Emps.	Unknown Emps.	Total
2006	50,585	48,994	21,453	3,573	191	30	2	1	1,020	125,855
2008	51,108	49,501	21,676	3,610	193	30	2	1	1,030	127,158
2009	51,638	50,014	21,900	3,647	195	30	2	1	1,041	128,474
Sales ($Millions) by Size of Firm										**Total**
2006	8,939	17,316	15,164	5,892	1,325	700	54	0	722	50,113
2008	9,711	18,811	16,474	6,401	1,439	761	58	0	784	54,439
2009	10,497	20,335	17,808	6,920	1,556	823	63	0	848	58,850
Employment by Size of Firm										**Total**
2006	151,754	293,965	300,348	114,325	11,626	3,973	628	0	65,408	942,028
2008	153,325	297,008	303,457	115,508	11,746	4,015	635	0	66,048	951,743
2009	154,913	300,083	306,599	116,704	11,868	4,056	641	0	66,752	961,616

SUB-INDUSTRIES — 2007 INDUSTRY ESTIMATES

Sub-Industries	Total Establishments	Total Employment	Total Sales ($M)
Offices and clinics of dentists	67,971	467,295	23,643
Specialized dental practitioners	1,101	8,972	512
Dental surgeon	4,040	30,524	1,617
Endodontist	1,155	8,452	457
Maxillofacial specialist	746	6,372	335
Oral pathologist	503	4,077	226
Orthodontist	5,718	49,359	3,002
Pedodontist	639	6,800	333
Periodontist	1,988	16,456	906
Prosthodontist	889	6,104	324
Dental clinics and offices	2,232	19,318	1,235
Dental clinic	2,567	22,670	1,415
Dentists' office	35,788	288,493	15,138
Dental insurance plan	269	3,759	807
Group and corporate practice, dentist	250	3,376	162

MEDICAL LABORATORIES INDUSTRY (NAICS 621511)

INDUSTRY DEFINITION

NAICS 621511: Medical Laboratories. This industry comprises establishments primarily engaged in providing professional analytic or diagnostic services to the medical profession, or to the patient on prescription of a physician.

INDUSTRY ESTABLISHMENTS, SALES & EMPLOYMENT TRENDS

	Year					Percent Change Year-to-Year			
	2005	2006	2007	2008	2009	05-06	06-07	07-08	08-09
Establishments	5,509	5,361	5,213	5,154	5,095	-2.7%	-2.8%	-1.1%	-1.1%
Sales ($Millions)	19,114	19,796	20,812	22,027	23,211	3.6%	5.1%	5.8%	5.4%
Employment	146,057	144,783	140,614	139,066	137,469	-0.9%	-2.9%	-1.1%	-1.1%

INDUSTRY RATIOS

(Industry Averages)	Year					Percent Change Year-to-Year			
	2005	2006	2007	2008	2009	05-06	06-07	07-08	08-09
Sales ($M)/Estab.	3.47	3.69	3.99	4.27	4.56	6.4%	8.1%	7.1%	6.6%
Sales ($) per Emp.	130,866	136,732	148,009	158,395	168,846	4.5%	8.2%	7.0%	6.6%
Emps. per Estab.	26.5	27.0	27.0	27.0	27.0	1.9%	-0.1%	0.0%	0.0%

MEDICAL LABORATORIES INDUSTRY
(NAICS 621511)

SIZE OF FIRM INDUSTRY ESTIMATES

Year	Establishments by Size of Firm									Total
	1-4 Emps.	5-9 Emps.	10-19 Emps.	20-49 Emps.	50-99 Emps.	100-249 Emps.	250-499 Emps.	500+ Emps.	Unknown Emps.	
2006	2,557	818	618	464	201	128	56	44	327	5,213
2008	2,528	809	611	459	199	126	55	43	323	5,154
2009	2,499	799	604	454	197	125	54	43	320	5,095
	Sales ($Millions) by Size of Firm									Total
2006	596	381	792	1,353	1,291	2,625	2,719	10,636	419	20,812
2008	631	404	838	1,431	1,366	2,778	2,878	11,256	445	22,027
2009	665	425	884	1,508	1,439	2,927	3,032	11,861	468	23,211
	Employment by Size of Firm									Total
2006	7,670	4,907	8,647	14,847	12,276	17,009	16,933	37,395	20,928	140,614
2008	7,584	4,852	8,549	14,679	12,137	16,817	16,741	36,972	20,736	139,066
2009	7,498	4,797	8,452	14,513	12,000	16,626	16,551	36,553	20,480	137,469

SUB-INDUSTRIES — 2007 INDUSTRY ESTIMATES

Sub-Industries	Total Establishments	Total Employment	Total Sales ($M)
Medical laboratories	3,710	80,992	9,801
Testing laboratories	439	26,125	6,258
Bacteriological laboratory	10	231	34
Biological laboratory	88	3,214	1,549
Blood analysis laboratory	88	3,240	320
Pathological laboratory	262	11,682	1,380
Urinalysis laboratory	14	348	24
Neurological laboratory	33	755	115
Ultrasound laboratory	141	1,855	195
X-ray laboratory, including dental	427	12,172	1,136

Home Health Care Services Industry
(NAICS 62161)

INDUSTRY DEFINITION

NAICS 62161: Home Health Care Services. This industry comprises establishments primarily engaged in providing skilled nursing or medical care in the home, under supervision of a physician. Registered or practical nurses engaged in the independent practice of their profession are classified in 8049, and nurses' registries are classified in 7361. Selling health care products for personal or household consumption is classified in retail trade and renting or leasing products for health care is classified in 7352.

INDUSTRY ESTABLISHMENTS, SALES & EMPLOYMENT TRENDS

	Year					Percent Change Year-to-Year			
	2005	2006	2007	2008	2009	05-06	06-07	07-08	08-09
Establishments	21,085	21,516	21,946	22,629	23,332	2.0%	2.0%	3.1%	3.1%
Sales ($Millions)	40,803	44,433	48,315	52,657	57,241	8.9%	8.7%	9.0%	8.7%
Employment	880,849	903,325	921,504	949,978	980,050	2.6%	2.0%	3.1%	3.2%

INDUSTRY RATIOS

	Year					Percent Change Year-to-Year			
(Industry Averages)	2005	2006	2007	2008	2009	05-06	06-07	07-08	08-09
Sales ($M)/Estab.	1.94	2.07	2.20	2.33	2.45	6.7%	6.6%	5.7%	5.4%
Sales ($) per Emp.	46,323	49,189	52,431	55,429	58,407	6.2%	6.6%	5.7%	5.4%
Emps. per Estab.	41.8	42.0	42.0	42.0	42.0	0.5%	0.0%	0.0%	0.1%

HOME HEALTH CARE SERVICES INDUSTRY
(NAICS 62161)

SIZE OF FIRM INDUSTRY ESTIMATES

Year	Establishments by Size of Firm									
	1-4 Emps.	5-9 Emps.	10-19 Emps.	20-49 Emps.	50-99 Emps.	100-249 Emps.	250-499 Emps.	500+ Emps.	Unknown Emps.	Total
2006	6,602	2,188	2,912	4,507	2,559	1,618	386	184	992	21,946
2008	6,808	2,256	3,003	4,648	2,639	1,668	398	190	1,023	22,629
2009	7,019	2,326	3,096	4,792	2,721	1,720	410	196	1,055	23,332
	Sales ($Millions) by Size of Firm									Total
2006	748	991	2,145	8,172	8,699	12,830	6,996	6,161	1,572	48,315
2008	815	1,081	2,338	8,907	9,482	13,984	7,626	6,716	1,709	52,657
2009	886	1,174	2,541	9,680	10,305	15,197	8,288	7,299	1,872	57,241
	Employment by Size of Firm									Total
2006	19,807	13,125	40,767	144,238	156,107	215,129	117,702	151,204	63,424	921,504
2008	20,423	13,533	42,035	148,723	160,961	221,819	121,362	155,906	65,216	949,978
2009	21,058	13,954	43,342	153,347	165,966	228,716	125,136	160,753	67,776	980,050

SUB-INDUSTRIES — 2007 INDUSTRY ESTIMATES

Sub-Industries	Total Establishments	Total Employment	Total Sales ($M)
Home health care services	20,730	826,334	43,834
Oxygen tent service	108	1,460	44
Visiting nurse service	1,108	93,710	4,437

MEDICAL & SURGICAL HOSPITALS INDUSTRY (NAICS 62211)

INDUSTRY DEFINITION

NAICS 62211: Medical & Surgical Hospital. This industry comprises establishments primarily engaged in providing general medical and surgical services and other hospital services. Specialty hospitals are classified in 8063 and 8069.

INDUSTRY ESTABLISHMENTS, SALES & EMPLOYMENT TRENDS

	Year					Percent Change Year-to-Year			
	2005	2006	2007	2008	2009	05-06	06-07	07-08	08-09
Establishments	6,290	6,306	6,322	6,277	6,233	0.3%	0.3%	-0.7%	-0.7%
Sales ($Millions)	653,977	690,906	747,214	792,467	837,121	5.6%	8.1%	6.1%	5.6%
Employment	3,214,048	3,145,970	3,153,995	3,131,363	3,109,208	-2.1%	0.3%	-0.7%	-0.7%

INDUSTRY RATIOS

	Year					Percent Change Year-to-Year			
(Industry Averages)	2005	2006	2007	2008	2009	05-06	06-07	07-08	08-09
Sales ($M)/Estab.	103.97	109.56	118.18	126.24	134.31	5.4%	7.9%	6.8%	6.4%
Sales ($) per Emp.	203,475	219,616	236,910	253,074	269,239	7.9%	7.9%	6.8%	6.4%
Emps. per Estab.	511.0	498.9	498.9	498.8	498.8	-2.4%	0.0%	0.0%	0.0%

MEDICAL & SURGICAL HOSPITALS INDUSTRY
(NAICS 62211)

SIZE OF FIRM INDUSTRY ESTIMATES

Year	Establishments by Size of Firm									
	1-4 Emps.	5-9 Emps.	10-19 Emps.	20-49 Emps.	50-99 Emps.	100-249 Emps.	250-499 Emps.	500+ Emps.	Unknown Emps.	Total
2006	233	78	58	152	346	1,062	976	2,542	878	6,322
2008	231	77	57	151	344	1,055	969	2,524	872	6,277
2009	230	77	57	150	341	1,047	963	2,506	865	6,233
	Sales ($Millions) by Size of Firm									Total
2006	1,353	453	1,002	3,532	18,082	86,285	90,643	533,057	12,809	747,214
2008	1,435	480	1,062	3,746	19,178	91,515	96,137	565,371	13,542	792,467
2009	1,515	507	1,122	3,957	20,258	96,668	101,550	597,203	14,341	837,121
	Employment by Size of Firm									Total
2006	699	468	806	4,869	21,122	141,273	297,792	2,630,902	56,064	3,153,995
2008	694	465	800	4,834	20,972	140,267	295,672	2,612,171	55,488	3,131,363
2009	689	462	794	4,800	20,822	139,269	293,567	2,593,573	55,232	3,109,208

SUB-INDUSTRIES – 2007 INDUSTRY ESTIMATES

Sub-Industries	Total Establishments	Total Employment	Total Sales ($M)
General medical and surgical hospitals	5,896	2,755,812	607,311
Hospital, affiliated with AMA residency	92	87,939	22,454
Hospital, med school affiliated with	47	44,047	11,426
Hospital, medical school affiliated with	51	66,107	11,066
Hospital, medical school affiliation	100	81,445	13,452
Hospital, professional nursing school	41	22,422	3,817
Hospital, professional nursing school	10	17,565	5,221
Hospital, AMA approved residency	69	70,634	16,159

NURSING CARE FACILITIES INDUSTRY
(NAICS 62311)

INDUSTRY DEFINITION

NAICS 62311: Nursing Care Facilities. This industry comprises establishments primarily engaged in providing inpatient nursing and rehabilitative services, but not on a continuous basis. Staffing must include 24-hour per day personnel with a licensed nurse on duty full-time during each day shift. At least once a week, consultation from a registered nurse on the delivery of care is required. Included are facilities certified to deliver intermediate care under the Medicaid program.

INDUSTRY ESTABLISHMENTS, SALES & EMPLOYMENT TRENDS

	Year					Percent Change Year-to-Year			
	2005	2006	2007	2008	2009	05-06	06-07	07-08	08-09
Establishments	18,169	18,109	18,050	18,107	18,164	-0.3%	-0.3%	0.3%	0.3%
Sales ($Millions)	64,208	68,284	70,578	72,981	75,409	6.3%	3.4%	3.4%	3.3%
Employment	1,511,764	1,552,301	1,547,184	1,552,073	1,557,168	2.7%	-0.3%	0.3%	0.3%

INDUSTRY RATIOS

(Industry Averages)	Year					Percent Change Year-to-Year			
	2005	2006	2007	2008	2009	05-06	06-07	07-08	08-09
Sales ($M)/Estab.	3.53	3.77	3.91	4.03	4.15	6.7%	3.7%	3.1%	3.0%
Sales ($) per Emp.	42,472	43,989	45,617	47,022	48,427	3.6%	3.7%	3.1%	3.0%
Emps. per Estab.	83.2	85.7	85.7	85.7	85.7	3.0%	0.0%	0.0%	0.0%

NURSING CARE FACILITIES INDUSTRY
(NAICS 62311)

SIZE OF FIRM INDUSTRY ESTIMATES

Year	Establishments by Size of Firm									Total
	1-4 Emps.	5-9 Emps.	10-19 Emps.	20-49 Emps.	50-99 Emps.	100-249 Emps.	250-499 Emps.	500+ Emps.	Unknown Emps.	
2006	1,946	616	706	1,753	4,861	6,569	589	90	921	18,050
2008	1,952	618	709	1,758	4,876	6,589	591	90	924	18,107
2009	1,959	620	711	1,764	4,892	6,610	592	91	927	18,164
	Sales ($Millions) by Size of Firm									Total
2006	417	198	530	2,443	9,903	37,330	13,256	3,835	2,664	70,578
2008	432	205	548	2,526	10,241	38,601	13,707	3,966	2,755	72,981
2009	446	212	566	2,610	10,580	39,881	14,161	4,097	2,855	75,409
	Employment by Size of Firm									Total
2006	5,839	3,698	9,890	56,088	296,520	873,635	179,548	63,086	58,880	1,547,184
2008	5,857	3,710	9,921	56,265	297,456	876,392	180,115	63,285	59,072	1,552,073
2009	5,876	3,721	9,952	56,442	298,395	879,157	180,683	63,485	59,456	1,557,168

SUB-INDUSTRIES – 2007 INDUSTRY ESTIMATES

Sub-Industries	Total Establishments	Total Employment	Total Sales ($M)
Intermediate care facilities	11,725	1,154,943	41,368
Home for the mentally retarded, with	3,006	213,283	20,009
Personal care facility	3,318	178,959	9,200

COMMUNITY CARE FACILITIES FOR THE ELDERLY (NAICS 62331)

INDUSTRY DEFINITION

NAICS 62331: Community Care Facilities for the Elderly. This industry comprises establishments primarily engaged in the provision of residential social and personal care for children, the aged, and special categories of persons with some limits on ability for self-care, but where medical care is not a major element. Included are establishments providing 24-hour year-round care for children. Boarding schools providing elementary and secondary education are classified in 8211.

INDUSTRY ESTABLISHMENTS, SALES & EMPLOYMENT TRENDS

	Year					Percent Change Year-to-Year			
	2005	2006	2007	2008	2009	05-06	06-07	07-08	08-09
Establishments	19,670	19,762	19,854	19,986	20,118	0.5%	0.5%	0.7%	0.7%
Sales ($Millions)	24,664	26,688	29,098	31,448	33,830	8.2%	9.0%	8.1%	7.6%
Employment	637,931	636,061	639,076	643,164	647,406	-0.3%	0.5%	0.6%	0.7%

INDUSTRY RATIOS

(Industry Averages)	Year					Percent Change Year-to-Year			
	2005	2006	2007	2008	2009	05-06	06-07	07-08	08-09
Sales ($M)/Estab.	1.25	1.35	1.47	1.57	1.68	7.7%	8.5%	7.4%	6.9%
Sales ($) per Emp.	38,663	41,959	45,532	48,896	52,255	8.5%	8.5%	7.4%	6.9%
Emps. per Estab.	32.4	32.2	32.2	32.2	32.2	-0.8%	0.0%	0.0%	0.0%

COMMUNITY CARE FACILITIES FOR THE ELDERLY (NAICS 62331)

SIZE OF FIRM INDUSTRY ESTIMATES

Year	Establishments by Size of Firm									
	1-4 Emps.	5-9 Emps.	10-19 Emps.	20-49 Emps.	50-99 Emps.	100-249 Emps.	250-499 Emps.	500+ Emps.	Unknown Emps.	Total
2006	6,172	2,589	2,891	3,929	1,890	1,130	295	36	920	19,854
2008	6,213	2,607	2,910	3,955	1,902	1,138	296	36	926	19,986
2009	6,254	2,624	2,929	3,981	1,915	1,145	298	36	933	20,118
	Sales ($Millions) by Size of Firm									**Total**
2006	725	608	1,698	5,537	5,549	7,167	5,085	1,434	1,297	29,098
2008	783	657	1,835	5,985	5,998	7,746	5,496	1,549	1,398	31,448
2009	843	707	1,974	6,438	6,452	8,333	5,912	1,667	1,504	33,830
	Employment by Size of Firm									**Total**
2006	18,516	15,537	40,476	125,733	115,285	150,299	89,833	24,518	58,880	639,076
2008	18,638	15,639	40,743	126,564	116,047	151,292	90,426	24,680	59,136	643,164
2009	18,761	15,743	41,012	127,400	116,813	152,291	91,023	24,843	59,520	647,406

SUB-INDUSTRIES — 2007 INDUSTRY ESTIMATES

Sub-Industries	Total Establishments	Total Employment	Total Sales ($M)
Geriatric residential care	5,284	133,936	6,156
Aged home	11,207	341,171	16,416
Old soldiers' home	97	6,496	10
Rest home, with health care incidental	3,266	157,474	6,517

MUSICAL GROUPS & ARTISTS INDUSTRY (NAICS 71113)

INDUSTRY DEFINITION

NAICS 71113: Musical Groups and Artists . This industry comprises (1) groups primarily engaged in producing live musical entertainment (except theatrical musical or opera productions) and (2) independent (i.e., freelance) artists primarily engaged in providing live musical entertainment. Musical groups and artists may perform in front of a live audience or in a studio, and may or may not operate their own facilities for staging their shows.

INDUSTRY ESTABLISHMENTS, SALES & EMPLOYMENT TRENDS

	Year					Percent Change Year-to-Year			
	2005	2006	2007	2008	2009	05-06	06-07	07-08	08-09
Establishments	4,531	4,518	4,505	4,498	4,491	-0.3%	-0.3%	-0.2%	-0.2%
Sales ($Millions)	3,259	3,369	3,506	3,630	3,754	3.4%	4.1%	3.5%	3.4%
Employment	43,698	43,518	43,394	43,324	43,255	-0.4%	-0.3%	-0.2%	-0.2%

INDUSTRY RATIOS

(Industry Averages)	Year					Percent Change Year-to-Year			
	2005	2006	2007	2008	2009	05-06	06-07	07-08	08-09
Sales ($M)/Estab.	0.72	0.75	0.78	0.81	0.84	3.7%	4.4%	3.7%	3.6%
Sales ($) per Emp.	74,581	77,408	80,795	83,788	86,782	3.8%	4.4%	3.7%	3.6%
Emps. per Estab.	9.6	9.6	9.6	9.6	9.6	-0.1%	0.0%	0.0%	0.0%

MUSICAL GROUPS & ARTISTS INDUSTRY
(NAICS 71113)

SIZE OF FIRM INDUSTRY ESTIMATES

Year	Establishments by Size of Firm									Total
	1-4 Emps.	5-9 Emps.	10-19 Emps.	20-49 Emps.	50-99 Emps.	100-249 Emps.	250-499 Emps.	500+ Emps.	Unknown Emps.	Total
2006	3,255	631	300	137	77	81	15	4	10	4,505
2008	3,250	630	299	137	77	81	15	4	10	4,498
2009	3,244	629	299	137	77	81	15	4	10	4,491
Sales ($Millions) by Size of Firm										Total
2006	424	206	228	283	351	1,002	617	362	33	3,506
2008	439	213	236	293	364	1,037	639	375	34	3,630
2009	454	220	244	303	376	1,073	661	387	35	3,754
Employment by Size of Firm										Total
2006	8,137	3,789	4,199	4,251	4,771	10,356	5,150	2,419	320	43,394
2008	8,124	3,783	4,192	4,245	4,764	10,339	5,142	2,415	320	43,324
2009	8,111	3,777	4,186	4,238	4,756	10,323	5,134	2,411	320	43,255

SUB-INDUSTRIES — 2007 INDUSTRY ESTIMATES

Sub-Industries	Total Establishments	Total Employment	Total Sales ($M)
Entertainers and entertainment groups	1,189	8,906	657
Musical entertainers	1,099	13,770	1,245
Actor	2,217	20,718	1,604

SPECTATOR SPORTS INDUSTRY
(NAICS 71121)

INDUSTRY DEFINITION

NAICS 71121: Spectator Sports . This industry comprises (1) sports teams or clubs primarily participating in live sporting events before a paying audience; (2) establishments primarily engaged in operating racetracks; (3) independent athletes engaged in participating in live sporting or racing events before a paying audience; (4) owners of racing participants, such as cars, dogs, and horses, primarily engaged in entering them in racing events or other spectator sports events; and (5) establishments, such as sports trainers, primarily engaged in providing specialized services to support participants in sports events or competitions. The sports teams and clubs included in this industry may or may not operate their own arena, stadium, or other facility for presenting their games or other spectator sports events.

INDUSTRY ESTABLISHMENTS, SALES & EMPLOYMENT TRENDS

	Year					Percent Change Year-to-Year			
	2005	2006	2007	2008	2009	05-06	06-07	07-08	08-09
Establishments	4,569	4,514	4,459	4,453	4,447	-1.2%	-1.2%	-0.1%	-0.1%
Sales ($Millions)	13,898	15,378	16,598	17,881	19,176	10.6%	7.9%	7.7%	7.2%
Employment	110,413	111,421	110,111	109,914	109,781	0.9%	-1.2%	-0.2%	-0.1%

INDUSTRY RATIOS

(Industry Averages)	Year					Percent Change Year-to-Year			
	2005	2006	2007	2008	2009	05-06	06-07	07-08	08-09
Sales ($M)/Estab.	3.04	3.41	3.72	4.02	4.31	12.0%	9.3%	7.9%	7.4%
Sales ($) per Emp.	125,870	138,013	150,742	162,684	174,670	9.6%	9.2%	7.9%	7.4%
Emps. per Estab.	24.2	24.7	24.7	24.7	24.7	2.1%	0.0%	-0.1%	0.0%

SPECTATOR SPORTS INDUSTRY
(NAICS 71121)

SIZE OF FIRM INDUSTRY ESTIMATES

Year	Establishments by Size of Firm									Total
	1-4 Emps.	5-9 Emps.	10-19 Emps.	20-49 Emps.	50-99 Emps.	100-249 Emps.	250-499 Emps.	500+ Emps.	Unknown Emps.	
2006	2,773	535	397	309	114	148	81	36	70	4,459
2008	2,769	535	396	309	114	148	81	36	70	4,453
2009	2,766	534	396	308	114	148	81	36	70	4,447
Sales ($Millions) by Size of Firm										Total
2006	659	446	755	1,176	1,629	3,708	3,651	3,603	970	16,598
2008	711	480	814	1,268	1,756	3,998	3,937	3,885	1,032	17,881
2009	762	515	873	1,360	1,883	4,287	4,221	4,166	1,108	19,176
Employment by Size of Firm										Total
2006	5,545	3,212	5,558	9,891	7,305	19,748	25,131	29,369	4,352	110,111
2008	5,538	3,208	5,551	9,878	7,296	19,723	25,099	29,332	4,288	109,914
2009	5,531	3,204	5,544	9,866	7,287	19,699	25,068	29,295	4,288	109,781

SUB-INDUSTRIES — 2007 INDUSTRY ESTIMATES

Sub-Industries	Total Establishments	Total Employment	Total Sales ($M)
Sports clubs, managers, and promoters	2,911	71,928	12,447
Stadium event operator services	562	23,622	1,813
Manager of individual professional	986	14,561	2,338

GOLF COURSES & COUNTRY CLUBS INDUSTRY (NAICS 71391)

INDUSTRY DEFINITION

NAICS 71391: Golf Courses and Country Clubs . This industry comprises (1) establishments primarily engaged in operating golf courses (except miniature) and (2) establishments primarily engaged in operating golf courses, along with dining facilities and other recreational facilities that are known as country clubs. These establishments often provide food and beverage services, equipment rental services, and golf instruction services.

INDUSTRY ESTABLISHMENTS, SALES & EMPLOYMENT TRENDS

	Year					Percent Change Year-to-Year			
	2005	2006	2007	2008	2009	05-06	06-07	07-08	08-09
Establishments	12,880	12,946	13,012	13,049	13,087	0.5%	0.5%	0.3%	0.3%
Sales ($Millions)	15,274	15,614	16,313	16,902	17,495	2.2%	4.5%	3.6%	3.5%
Employment	346,180	344,384	346,099	346,997	347,961	-0.5%	0.5%	0.3%	0.3%

INDUSTRY RATIOS

(Industry Averages)	Year					Percent Change Year-to-Year			
	2005	2006	2007	2008	2009	05-06	06-07	07-08	08-09
Sales ($M)/Estab.	1.19	1.21	1.25	1.30	1.34	1.7%	4.0%	3.3%	3.2%
Sales ($) per Emp.	44,122	45,338	47,135	48,710	50,278	2.8%	4.0%	3.3%	3.2%
Emps. per Estab.	26.9	26.6	26.6	26.6	26.6	-1.0%	0.0%	0.0%	0.0%

GOLF COURSES & COUNTRY CLUBS INDUSTRY
(NAICS 71391)

SIZE OF FIRM INDUSTRY ESTIMATES

Year	Establishments by Size of Firm									Total
	1-4 Emps.	5-9 Emps.	10-19 Emps.	20-49 Emps.	50-99 Emps.	100-249 Emps.	250-499 Emps.	500+ Emps.	Unknown Emps.	
2006	4,316	1,667	1,707	2,358	1,512	513	36	1	903	13,012
2008	4,329	1,672	1,712	2,365	1,516	514	36	1	906	13,049
2009	4,341	1,677	1,716	2,371	1,521	516	36	1	908	13,087
Sales ($Millions) by Size of Firm										**Total**
2006	930	539	1,287	4,827	4,073	3,204	1,168	91	195	16,313
2008	964	558	1,334	5,001	4,220	3,320	1,210	94	202	16,902
2009	998	578	1,380	5,177	4,368	3,436	1,252	97	209	17,495
Employment by Size of Firm										**Total**
2006	12,949	10,005	25,599	73,090	90,718	64,085	11,016	717	57,920	346,099
2008	12,986	10,034	25,673	73,301	90,980	64,271	11,048	719	57,984	346,997
2009	13,024	10,063	25,747	73,513	91,243	64,457	11,080	722	58,112	347,961

SUB-INDUSTRIES – 2007 INDUSTRY ESTIMATES

Sub-Industries	Total Establishments	Total Employment	Total Sales ($M)
Public golf courses	13,012	346,099	16,313

FITNESS & RECREATIONAL SPORTS CENTERS (NAICS 71394)

INDUSTRY DEFINITION

NAICS 71394: Fitness and Recreational Sports Centers . This industry comprises establishments primarily engaged in operating fitness and recreational sports facilities featuring exercise and other active physical fitness conditioning or recreational sports activities, such as swimming, skating, or racquet sports.

INDUSTRY ESTABLISHMENTS, SALES & EMPLOYMENT TRENDS

	Year					Percent Change Year-to-Year			
	2005	2006	2007	2008	2009	05-06	06-07	07-08	08-09
Establishments	32,415	34,473	36,530	38,896	41,416	6.3%	6.0%	6.5%	6.5%
Sales ($Millions)	14,935	16,833	18,752	20,844	23,128	12.7%	11.4%	11.2%	11.0%
Employment	513,601	556,254	589,504	627,851	668,472	8.3%	6.0%	6.5%	6.5%

INDUSTRY RATIOS

(Industry Averages)	Year					Percent Change Year-to-Year			
	2005	2006	2007	2008	2009	05-06	06-07	07-08	08-09
Sales ($M)/Estab.	0.46	0.49	0.51	0.54	0.56	6.0%	5.1%	4.4%	4.2%
Sales ($) per Emp.	29,080	30,262	31,810	33,199	34,599	4.1%	5.1%	4.4%	4.2%
Emps. per Estab.	15.8	16.1	16.1	16.1	16.1	1.8%	0.0%	0.0%	0.0%

FITNESS & RECREATIONAL SPORTS CENTERS (NAICS 71394)

SIZE OF FIRM INDUSTRY ESTIMATES

Year	1-4 Emps.	5-9 Emps.	10-19 Emps.	20-49 Emps.	50-99 Emps.	100-249 Emps.	250-499 Emps.	500+ Emps.	Unknown Emps.	Total
Establishments by Size of Firm										**Total**
2006	17,728	6,190	4,724	4,521	1,933	818	100	12	503	36,530
2008	18,876	6,591	5,030	4,814	2,058	871	106	13	536	38,896
2009	20,099	7,018	5,356	5,126	2,191	927	113	13	571	41,416
Sales ($Millions) by Size of Firm										**Total**
2006	977	1,160	1,822	4,484	3,195	4,685	1,928	446	55	18,752
2008	1,086	1,289	2,025	4,984	3,551	5,208	2,143	496	62	20,844
2009	1,205	1,430	2,247	5,530	3,940	5,778	2,378	550	68	23,128
Employment by Size of Firm										**Total**
2006	53,184	37,141	70,865	135,625	115,967	106,286	29,298	9,011	32,128	589,504
2008	56,629	39,547	75,456	144,410	123,480	113,171	31,196	9,595	34,368	627,851
2009	60,298	42,108	80,344	153,765	131,479	120,502	33,216	10,216	36,544	668,472

SUB-INDUSTRIES – 2007 INDUSTRY ESTIMATES

Sub-Industries	Total Establishments	Total Employment	Total Sales ($M)
Physical fitness facilities	12,861	170,729	6,665
Physical fitness clubs with training	1,742	32,010	981
Athletic club and gymnasiums,	2,428	63,228	1,768
Health club	10,313	224,301	6,973
Spas	3,755	50,158	1,197
Weight reducing clubs	373	4,222	260
Reducing facility	51	553	10
Slenderizing salon	153	919	21
Exercise facilities	964	9,114	215
Aerobic dance and exercise classes	3,527	30,105	577
Exercise salon	362	4,166	86

HOTELS & MOTELS INDUSTRY
(NAICS 72111)

INDUSTRY DEFINITION

NAICS 72111: Hotels (except Casino Hotels) and Motels . This industry comprises establishments primarily engaged in providing short-term lodging in facilities known as hotels, motor hotels, resort hotels, and motels. The establishments in this industry may offer services, such as food and beverage services, recreational services, conference rooms and convention services, laundry services, parking, and other services.

INDUSTRY ESTABLISHMENTS, SALES & EMPLOYMENT TRENDS

	Year					Percent Change Year-to-Year			
	2005	2006	2007	2008	2009	05-06	06-07	07-08	08-09
Establishments	48,995	49,523	50,051	50,593	51,140	1.1%	1.1%	1.1%	1.1%
Sales ($Millions)	140,042	145,142	151,626	157,501	163,493	3.6%	4.5%	3.9%	3.8%
Employment	1,475,209	1,491,261	1,507,174	1,523,401	1,539,988	1.1%	1.1%	1.1%	1.1%

INDUSTRY RATIOS

(Industry Averages)	Year					Percent Change Year-to-Year			
	2005	2006	2007	2008	2009	05-06	06-07	07-08	08-09
Sales ($M)/Estab.	2.86	2.93	3.03	3.11	3.20	2.5%	3.4%	2.8%	2.7%
Sales ($) per Emp.	94,930	97,329	100,603	103,388	106,165	2.5%	3.4%	2.8%	2.7%
Emps. per Estab.	30.1	30.1	30.1	30.1	30.1	0.0%	0.0%	0.0%	0.0%

HOTELS & MOTELS INDUSTRY
(NAICS 72111)

SIZE OF FIRM INDUSTRY ESTIMATES

Year	Establishments by Size of Firm									
	1-4 Emps.	5-9 Emps.	10-19 Emps.	20-49 Emps.	50-99 Emps.	100-249 Emps.	250-499 Emps.	500+ Emps.	Unknown Emps.	Total
2006	16,286	6,813	11,231	9,092	2,677	2,034	585	302	1,030	50,051
2008	16,462	6,887	11,353	9,191	2,706	2,056	592	305	1,041	50,593
2009	16,640	6,962	11,476	9,290	2,735	2,078	598	308	1,053	51,140
	Sales ($Millions) by Size of Firm									Total
2006	3,123	5,081	14,358	22,279	18,535	28,167	24,938	33,170	1,975	151,626
2008	3,244	5,278	14,915	23,142	19,254	29,259	25,904	34,456	2,049	157,501
2009	3,367	5,479	15,482	24,022	19,986	30,371	26,889	35,766	2,131	163,493
	Employment by Size of Firm									Total
2006	48,858	40,881	168,471	290,959	173,988	288,804	188,439	240,853	65,920	1,507,174
2008	49,387	41,323	170,293	294,106	175,870	291,927	190,477	243,458	66,560	1,523,401
2009	49,921	41,770	172,135	297,287	177,772	295,084	192,537	246,091	67,392	1,539,988

SUB-INDUSTRIES — 2007 INDUSTRY ESTIMATES

Sub-Industries	Total Establishments	Total Employment	Total Sales ($M)
Hotels and motels	10,876	304,748	25,298
Motels	16,306	186,686	10,004
Motel, franchised	1,409	48,657	2,484
Vacation lodges	937	8,483	380
Ski lodge	261	13,112	2,144
Tourist camps, cabins, cottages, and	849	5,992	252
Hotels	6,770	393,868	45,790
Casino hotel	558	227,707	45,892
Hotel, franchised	1,138	95,374	7,049
Resort hotel	2,321	140,920	8,018
Resort hotel, franchised	81	13,516	1,680
Seasonal hotel	73	1,697	70
YMCA/YMHA hotel	41	3,171	50
YWCA/YWHA hotel	11	378	7
Inns	2,173	29,359	951
Bed and breakfast inn	5,648	20,039	823
Motor inn	456	10,189	584
Hostels	144	3,282	149

FULL-SERVICE RESTAURANTS INDUSTRY (NAICS 72211)

INDUSTRY DEFINITION

NAICS 72211: Full-Service Restaurants -- This industry comprises establishments primarily engaged in providing food services to patrons who order and are served while seated (i.e. waiter/waitress service) and pay after eating. These establishments may provide this type of food services to patrons in combination with selling alcoholic beverages, providing takeout services, or presenting live nontheatrical entertainment.

INDUSTRY ESTABLISHMENTS, SALES & EMPLOYMENT TRENDS

	Year					Percent Change Year-to-Year			
	2005	2006	2007	2008	2009	05-06	06-07	07-08	08-09
Establishments	214,225	215,005	219,990	223,618	227,306	0.4%	2.3%	1.6%	1.6%
Sales ($Millions)	186,262	195,611	211,075	224,625	238,566	5.0%	7.9%	6.4%	6.2%
Employment	4,586,969	4,601,631	4,708,533	4,786,178	4,864,837	0.3%	2.3%	1.6%	1.6%

INDUSTRY RATIOS

	Year					Percent Change Year-to-Year			
(Industry Averages)	2005	2006	2007	2008	2009	05-06	06-07	07-08	08-09
Sales ($M)/Estab.	0.87	0.91	0.96	1.00	1.05	4.6%	5.5%	4.7%	4.5%
Sales ($) per Emp.	40,607	42,509	44,828	46,932	49,039	4.7%	5.5%	4.7%	4.5%
Emps. per Estab.	21.4	21.4	21.4	21.4	21.4	0.0%	0.0%	0.0%	0.0%

FULL-SERVICE RESTAURANTS INDUSTRY
(NAICS 72211)

SIZE OF FIRM INDUSTRY ESTIMATES

Year	Establishments by Size of Firm									Total
	1-4 Emps.	5-9 Emps.	10-19 Emps.	20-49 Emps.	50-99 Emps.	100-249 Emps.	250-499 Emps.	500+ Emps.	Unknown Emps.	
2006	68,574	38,196	39,030	43,293	21,351	5,190	153	20	4,185	219,990
2008	69,705	38,825	39,674	44,007	21,703	5,275	155	20	4,254	223,618
2009	70,855	39,466	40,328	44,733	22,061	5,362	158	21	4,324	227,306
	Sales ($Millions) by Size of Firm									Total
2006	11,407	14,826	23,807	48,013	47,356	51,801	8,876	4,525	464	211,075
2008	12,140	15,777	25,335	51,095	50,396	55,126	9,446	4,815	494	224,625
2009	12,893	16,757	26,908	54,266	53,524	58,548	10,032	5,114	524	238,566
	Employment by Size of Firm									Total
2006	205,723	229,173	585,456	1,385,388	1,323,740	648,737	47,654	14,695	267,968	4,708,533
2008	209,116	232,953	595,110	1,408,235	1,345,569	659,435	48,440	14,937	272,384	4,786,178
2009	212,564	236,794	604,924	1,431,457	1,367,758	670,309	49,238	15,184	276,608	4,864,837

SUB-INDUSTRIES — 2007 INDUSTRY ESTIMATES

Sub-Industries	Total Establishments	Total Employment	Total Sales ($M)
Eating places	79,930	1,381,505	52,415
Ethnic food restaurants	58,576	1,139,922	44,214
Lunchrooms and cafeterias	4,987	93,460	3,403
Family restaurants	16,547	782,711	41,033
Pizza restaurants	32,625	566,314	26,847
Seafood restaurants	4,627	186,587	17,257
Steak and barbecue restaurants	8,852	333,941	16,775
Buffet (eating places)	1,540	38,092	3,461
Cafe	10,324	126,899	4,237
Caterers	15,638	253,280	11,506
Chicken restaurant	4,195	94,827	2,655
Commissary restaurant	55	2,017	236
Contract food services	861	59,680	28,210
Diner	2,909	53,221	1,764
Dinner theater	110	6,560	213
Health food restaurant	184	2,978	99

FAST FOOD RESTAURANTS INDUSTRY
(NAICS 72221)

INDUSTRY DEFINITION

NAICS 72221: Fast Food Restaurants. This industry comprises establishments primarily engaged in the retail sale of prepared food and drinks for on-premise or immediate consumption. Caterers and industrial and institutional food service establishments are also included in this business.

INDUSTRY ESTABLISHMENTS, SALES & EMPLOYMENT TRENDS

	Year					Percent Change Year-to-Year			
	2005	2006	2007	2008	2009	05-06	06-07	07-08	08-09
Establishments	256,300	263,387	270,475	278,827	287,437	2.8%	2.7%	3.1%	3.1%
Sales ($Millions)	157,659	165,831	169,183	173,291	177,491	5.2%	2.0%	2.4%	2.4%
Employment	4,499,159	4,610,678	4,734,666	4,880,881	5,031,724	2.5%	2.7%	3.1%	3.1%

INDUSTRY RATIOS

(Industry Averages)	Year					Percent Change Year-to-Year			
	2005	2006	2007	2008	2009	05-06	06-07	07-08	08-09
Sales ($M)/Estab.	0.62	0.63	0.63	0.62	0.62	2.4%	-0.7%	-0.6%	-0.6%
Sales ($) per Emp.	35,042	35,967	35,733	35,504	35,274	2.6%	-0.7%	-0.6%	-0.6%
Emps. per Estab.	17.6	17.5	17.5	17.5	17.5	-0.3%	0.0%	0.0%	0.0%

Fast Food Restaurants Industry
(NAICS 72221)

Size of Firm Industry Estimates

Year	Establishments by Size of Firm									Total
	1-4 Emps.	5-9 Emps.	10-19 Emps.	20-49 Emps.	50-99 Emps.	100-249 Emps.	250-499 Emps.	500+ Emps.	Unknown Emps.	
2006	85,249	41,632	57,479	67,807	10,549	1,104	96	24	6,535	270,475
2008	87,882	42,917	59,254	69,901	10,875	1,139	99	25	6,737	278,827
2009	90,595	44,242	61,084	72,059	11,211	1,174	102	25	6,945	287,437
	Sales ($Millions) by Size of Firm									Total
2006	12,939	16,007	31,988	54,888	26,685	14,528	6,692	4,794	661	169,183
2008	13,253	16,396	32,764	56,221	27,333	14,881	6,855	4,911	677	173,291
2009	13,574	16,793	33,559	57,583	27,996	15,242	7,021	5,030	694	177,491
	Employment by Size of Firm									Total
2006	255,747	249,790	804,706	2,169,830	643,505	146,897	29,235	16,780	418,176	4,734,666
2008	263,645	257,504	829,555	2,236,831	663,375	151,433	30,138	17,298	431,104	4,880,881
2009	271,785	265,455	855,170	2,305,901	683,859	156,109	31,068	17,832	444,544	5,031,724

Sub-Industries — 2007 Industry Estimates

Sub-Industries	Total Establishments	Total Employment	Total Sales ($M)
Eating places	116,731	1,548,282	43,581
Ice cream, soft drink and soda fountain	18,816	250,291	6,420
Fast food restaurants and stands	3,076	40,016	1,485
Box lunch stand	113	1,440	30
Carry-out only (except pizza) restaurant	5,520	54,660	971
Chili stand	166	2,503	49
Coffee shop	17,359	151,001	8,233
Delicatessen (eating places)	7,535	68,215	2,164
Drive-in restaurant	5,650	123,395	2,777
Fast-food restaurant, chain	52,106	2,001,394	92,580
Fast-food restaurant, independent	3,465	43,997	1,163
Food bars	226	8,405	56
Grills (eating places)	10,133	150,119	2,663
Hamburger stand	1,664	17,278	444
Hot dog stand	1,933	8,741	190
Sandwiches and submarines shop	24,301	251,454	5,625
Snack bar	1,248	11,456	711
Snack shop	433	2,020	43

DRINKING PLACES & BARS INDUSTRY (NAICS 72241)

INDUSTRY DEFINITION

NAICS 72241: Drinking Places (Alcoholic Beverages) . This industry comprises establishments known as bars, taverns, nightclubs or drinking places primarily engaged in preparing and serving alcoholic beverages for immediate consumption. These establishments may also provide limited food services.

INDUSTRY ESTABLISHMENTS, SALES & EMPLOYMENT TRENDS

	Year					Percent Change Year-to-Year			
	2005	2006	2007	2008	2009	05-06	06-07	07-08	08-09
Establishments	47,359	46,790	46,221	45,587	44,963	-1.2%	-1.2%	-1.4%	-1.4%
Sales ($Millions)	13,686	14,451	15,227	15,886	16,525	5.6%	5.4%	4.3%	4.0%
Employment	391,562	387,996	383,211	377,971	372,864	-0.9%	-1.2%	-1.4%	-1.4%

INDUSTRY RATIOS

(Industry Averages)	Year					Percent Change Year-to-Year			
	2005	2006	2007	2008	2009	05-06	06-07	07-08	08-09
Sales ($M)/Estab.	0.29	0.31	0.33	0.35	0.37	6.9%	6.7%	5.8%	5.5%
Sales ($) per Emp.	34,952	37,246	39,735	42,028	44,319	6.6%	6.7%	5.8%	5.5%
Emps. per Estab.	8.3	8.3	8.3	8.3	8.3	0.3%	0.0%	0.0%	0.0%

DRINKING PLACES & BARS INDUSTRY
(NAICS 72241)

SIZE OF FIRM INDUSTRY ESTIMATES

Year	Establishments by Size of Firm									Total
	1-4 Emps.	5-9 Emps.	10-19 Emps.	20-49 Emps.	50-99 Emps.	100-249 Emps.	250-499 Emps.	500+ Emps.	Unknown Emps.	
2006	26,877	10,350	4,925	3,057	691	148	10	2	162	46,221
2008	26,509	10,208	4,858	3,015	682	146	9	2	160	45,587
2009	26,145	10,068	4,791	2,974	672	144	9	2	158	44,963
	Sales ($Millions) by Size of Firm									Total
2006	2,745	2,349	2,794	4,163	1,725	1,090	142	2	217	15,227
2008	2,863	2,450	2,915	4,343	1,800	1,137	148	2	226	15,886
2009	2,978	2,549	3,032	4,517	1,872	1,183	154	2	237	16,525
	Employment by Size of Firm									Total
2006	80,631	62,097	68,953	97,832	41,467	19,069	2,860	124	10,176	383,211
2008	79,526	61,246	68,008	96,491	40,899	18,808	2,821	123	10,048	377,971
2009	78,436	60,407	67,076	95,169	40,339	18,550	2,783	121	9,984	372,864

SUB-INDUSTRIES — 2007 INDUSTRY ESTIMATES

Sub-Industries	Total Establishments	Total Employment	Total Sales ($M)
Drinking places	9,700	69,617	3,835
Bars and lounges	1,548	16,013	603
Bar (drinking places)	7,149	69,965	2,489
Beer garden (drinking places)	82	1,110	54
Cocktail lounge	5,423	45,514	1,661
Saloon	546	4,316	159
Tavern (drinking places)	17,342	117,100	4,339
Wine bar	93	629	28
Night clubs	4,143	54,835	1,929
Cabaret	124	3,229	102
Discotheque	70	883	29

Methodology

Barnes Reports' U.S. industry reports provide estimates of the size and characteristics of the largest industries in United States. These estimates are produced by a proprietary economic model that is based on a number of sources and factors:

-The size and characteristics of the largest U.S. industries (based on the U.S. Bureau of the Census publications, such as the U.S. Census 2000, U.S. Statistical Abstract, and County Business Patterns).
-The forecast estimates for establishments and employment (regression analysis on historical trends from Census statistics listed above).
-The forecast estimates for industry sales based on Census statistics (as well as a secondary research from sources such as Dunn & Bradstreet, Hoover's, the Economist, trade association research, and private research studies), historical industry sales trends and inflation rates.

NAICS codes (North American Classification System codes) are used in each industry definition in order to aid report users in clarifying and standardizing the definitions of each industry.

Number of Establishments

General Definition
An establishment is a single physical location at which business is conducted and/or services are provided. It is not necessarily identical with a company or enterprise, which may consist of one establishment or more. Economic census figures represent a summary of reports for individual establishments rather than companies. For cases where a census report was received, separate information was obtained for each location where business was conducted. When administrative records of other Federal agencies were used instead of a census report, no information was available on the number of locations operated. Each economic census establishment was tabulated according to the physical location at which the business was conducted.
When two activities or more were carried on at a single location under a single ownership, all activities generally were grouped together as a single establishment. The entire establishment was classified on the basis of its major activity and all data for it were included in that classification. However, when distinct and separate economic activities (for which different industry classification codes were appropriate) were conducted at a single location under a single ownership, separate establishment reports for each of the different activities were obtained in the census.
Sector-Specific Information
Construction sector. Establishments are defined as a relatively permanent office or other place of business where the usual business activities related to construction are conducted. Establishments do not represent each project or construction site. Includes all establishments that were in business at any time during the year. It covers all full-year and part-year operations. Construction establishments which were inactive or idle for the entire year were not included. Establishments are based on a survey which included all large employers and a sample of the smaller ones.
Information; Professional, Scientific, and Technical Services; Administrative and Support and Waste Management and Remediation Services; Educational Services; Health Care and Social Assistance; Arts, Entertainment, and Recreation; and Other Services (Except Public Administration) sectors. An establishment is included in the census if it is an employer, the establishment has $1,000 in payroll, and was in operation at any time during 1997. Leased service departments (separately owned businesses operated as departments or concessions of other service establishments or of retail businesses, such as a separately owned shoeshine parlor in a barber shop, or a beauty shop in a department store) are treated as separate service establishments for census purposes. Leased retail departments located in service

establishments (e.g., a gift shop located in a hotel) are considered separate retail establishments.

Manufacturing sector. Includes all manufacturing establishments (plants) with one employee or more and establishments in operation at any time during the year.

Mining sector. Includes all mineral establishments with one employee or more and establishments in operation at any time during the year. Establishments in the crude petroleum and natural gas and support activities for mining represent statewide operations rather than those at a single physical location.

Real Estate and Rental and Leasing sector. Data for individual properties leased or managed by property lessors or property managers are not normally considered separate establishments, but rather the permanent offices from which the properties are leased or managed are considered establishments. Data for separate automotive rental offices or concessions (e.g., airport locations) in the same metropolitan area for which a common fleet of cars is maintained are merged together and not considered as separate establishments.

Retail Trade sector. Leased departments are treated as separate establishments and are classified according to the kind of business they conduct. For example, a leased department selling shoes within a department store would be considered a separate retail establishment under the "shoe stores" classification.

Accommodation and Foodservices sector. Leased departments are treated as separate establishments and are classified according to the kind of business they conduct. For example, a leased department selling gifts/souvenirs within a hotel would be considered a separate retail establishment under the "gift, novelty, and souvenir stores" classification.

Auxiliaries sector. In the Standard Industrial Classification (SIC) system, auxiliary establishments (i.e., those establishments primarily serving other establishments of the same enterprise) were classified in the industry of the establishments served. In the North American Industry Classification System (NAICS), auxiliary establishments are classified according to the services performed rather than the industry served.

Sales, Shipments, Receipts, Revenue, or Business Done

General Definition

Includes the total sales, shipments, receipts, revenue, or business done by establishments within the scope of the economic census. The definition of each of these items is included in the information provided below.

Sector-Specific Information

Construction sector - Includes the value of construction work and other business receipts for work done by establishments during the year. Included is new construction, additions and alterations or reconstruction, and maintenance and repair construction work. Also included is the value of any construction work done by the reporting establishments for themselves.

Speculative builders were instructed to include the value of buildings and other structures built or being built for sale in the current year but not sold. They were to include the costs of such construction plus normal profit. Also included is the cost of construction work done on buildings for rent or lease.

Establishments engaged in the sale and installation of such construction components as plumbing, heating, and central air-conditioning supplies and equipment; lumber and building materials; paint, glass, and wallpaper; electrical and wiring supplies; and elevators or escalators were instructed to include both the value for the installation and the receipts covering the price of the items installed.

Excluded was the cost of industrial and other specialized machinery and equipment, which are not an integral part of a structure.

Finance and Insurance sector - Includes revenue from all business activities whether or not payment was received in the census year, including commissions and fees from all sources, rents, net investment income, interest, dividends, royalties, and net insurance premiums earned. Revenue from leasing property marketed under operating leases is included, as well as interest earned from property marketed in the census year under capital, finance, or full payout leases. Revenue also includes the total value of service contracts and amounts received for work subcontracted to others.

Revenue does not include sales and other taxes collected from customers and remitted directly by the firm to a local, state, or Federal tax agency.

Information sector - Includes receipts from customers or clients for services rendered, from the use of facilities, and from merchandise sold, whether or not payment was received. Receipts include royalties, license fees, and other payments from the marketing of intangible products (e.g., licensing the use of or granting reproduction rights for software, musical

compositions, and other intellectual property). Receipts also include the rental and leasing of vehicles, equipment, instruments, tools, etc.; total value of service contracts; market value of compensation received in lieu of cash; amounts received for work subcontracted to others; dues and assessments for members and affiliates; this establishment's share of receipts from departments, concessions, and vending and amusement machines operated by others. Receipts from services provided to foreign customers from U.S. locations, including services preformed for foreign parent firms, subsidiaries, and branches are included. For public broadcast stations and libraries, include receipts from contributions, gifts, grants, and income from interest, rental of real estate, and dividends.

Receipts DO NOT include sales and other taxes collected directly from customers or clients and paid directly to a local, state, or Federal tax agency. Also excluded are gross receipts collected on behalf of others; gross receipts or departments or concessions operated by others; sales of used equipment previously rented or leased to customers; proceeds from the sale of real estate (land and buildings), investments, or other assets (except inventory held for resale); contributions, gifts, grants, and income from interest, rental of real estate, and dividends EXCEPT for public broadcast stations and libraries; domestic intracompany transfers; receipts of foreign subsidiaries; and other nonoperating income.

Management of Companies and Enterprises sector- For holding companies, revenue includes revenue of only the holding company establishment, including net investment income, interest, and dividends.

Manufacturing sector - Covers the received or receivable net selling values, f.o.b. plant (exclusive of freight and taxes), of all products shipped, both primary and secondary, as well as all miscellaneous receipts, such as receipts for contract work performed for others, installation and repair, sales of scrap, and sales of products bought and resold without further processing. Included are all items made by or for the establishments from materials owned by it, whether sold, transferred to other plants of the same company, or shipped on consignment. The net selling value of products made in one plant on a contract basis from materials owned by another was reported by the plant providing the materials.

In the case of multiunit companies, the manufacturer was requested to report the value of products transferred to other establishments of the same company at full economic or commercial value, including not only the direct cost of production but also a reasonable proportion of "all other costs" (including company overhead) and profit.

Mining sector - Includes the net selling values, f.o.b. mine or plant after discounts and allowances, excluding freight charges and excise taxes. Shipments includes all products physically shipped from the establishment during the year, including material withdrawn from stockpiles and products shipped on consignment, whether or not sold in the current year. Prepared material or concentrates includes preparation from ores mined at the same establishment, purchased, received from other operations of the same company, or received for milling on a custom or toll basis. For products transferred to other establishments of the same company or prepared on a custom basis, companies were requested to report the estimated value, not merely the cost of producing the items. Multiestablishment companies were asked to report value information for each establishment as if it were a separate economic unit. They were instructed to report the value of all products transferred to other plants of the company at their full economic value; to include, in addition to direct cost of production, a reasonable proportion of company overhead and profits. For all establishments classified in an industry, value of shipments and receipts includes (1) the value of all primary products of the industry; (2) the value of secondary products which are primary to other industries; (3) the receipts for contract work done for others, except custom milling; and (4) the value of products purchased and resold without further processing. Receipts for custom milling are not included to avoid duplication with the value of custom milled ores included in an industry's primary and secondary products. Some duplication exists in industry and industry group totals because of the inclusion of materials transferred from one establishment to another for mineral preparation or resale.

Professional, Scientific, and Technical Services; Administrative and Support and Waste Management and Remediation Services; Educational Services; Health Care and Social Assistance; Arts, Entertainment, and Recreation; and Other Services (Except Public Administration) sectors - TAXABLE ESTABLISHMENTS: Includes receipts from customers or clients for services rendered, from the use of facilities, and from merchandise sold whether or not payment was received. For advertising agencies, travel industries, and other service establishments operating on a commission basis, receipts include commissions, fees, and other operating income, NOT gross billings and sales. Excise taxes on gasoline, liquor, tobacco, etc., which are paid by the manufacturer or wholesaler and passed on in the cost of goods purchased by the service establishment are also included. The establishments share of receipts from departments, concessions, and vending and amusement machines operated by others are included as part of receipts. Receipts also include the total value of service contracts, market value of compensation received in lieu of cash, amounts received for work subcontracted to others, and dues and assessments from members and affiliates. Receipts from services provided to foreign customers from U.S. locations, including services preformed for foreign parent firms, subsidiaries, and branches are included.

Receipts are net after deductions for refunds and allowances for merchandise returned by customers. Receipts DO NOT include sales, occupancy, admissions, or other taxes collected from customers and remitted directly by the firm to a local, state, or Federal tax agency, nor do they include income from such sources as contributions, gifts, and grants; dividends, interest, and investments; or sale or rental of real estate. Also excluded are receipts (gross) of departments and concessions which are operated by others; sales of used equipment rented or leased to customers; domestic intracompany transfers; receipts of foreign subsidiaries; and other nonoperating income, such as royalties, franchise fees, etc. Receipts DO NOT include service receipts of manufacturers, wholesalers, retail establishments, or other businesses whose primary activity is other than service. They do, however, include receipts other than from services rendered (e.g., sale of merchandise to individuals or other businesses) by establishments primarily engaged in performing services and classified in the service industries.

TAX EXEMPT ESTABLISHMENTS: Includes revenue from customers or clients for services rendered and merchandise, whether or not payment was received, and gross sales of merchandise, minus returns and allowances. Also included are income from interest, dividends, gross rents (including display space rentals and share of receipts from departments operated by other companies), gross contributions, gifts, grants (whether or not restricted for use in operations), royalties, dues and assessments from members and affiliates, commissions earned from the sale of merchandise owned by others (including commissions from vending machine operators), and gross receipts from fundraising activities. Receipts from taxable business activities of firms exempt from Federal income tax (unrelated business income) are also included in revenue. Revenue DOES NOT include sales, admissions, or other taxes collected by the organization from customers or clients and paid directly to a local, state, or Federal tax agency; income from the sale of real estate, investments, or other assets (except inventory held for resale); gross receipts of departments, concessions, etc., that are operated by others; and amounts transferred to operating funds from capital or reserve funds.

Real Estate and Rental and Leasing sector - Includes revenue from all business activities whether or not payment was received in the census year, including commissions and fees from all sources, rents, net investment income, interest, dividends, and royalties. Revenue from leasing property marketed under operating leases is included. Revenue also includes the total value of service contracts, amounts received for work subcontracted to others, and rents from real property sublet to others.

Revenue does not include sales and other taxes collected from customers and remitted directly by the firm to a local, state, or Federal tax agency.

Retail Trade sector - Includes merchandise sold for cash or credit at retail and wholesale by establishments primarily engaged in retail trade; amounts received from customers for layaway purchases; receipts from rental of vehicles, equipment, instruments, tools, etc.; receipts for delivery, installation, maintenance, repair, alteration, storage, and other services; the total value of service contracts; and gasoline, liquor, tobacco, and other excise taxes which are paid by the manufacturer or wholesaler and passed on to the retailer. Sales are net after deductions for refunds and allowances for merchandise returned by customers. Trade-in allowances are not deducted from sales. Sales do not include carrying or other credit charges; sales (or other) taxes collected from customers and forwarded to taxing authorities; gross sales and receipts of departments or concessions operated by other companies; and commissions or receipts from the sale of government lottery tickets.

Sales do not include retail sales made by manufacturers, wholesalers, service establishments, or other businesses whose primary activity is other than retail trade. They do include receipts other than from the sale of merchandise at retail, e.g., service receipts, sales to industrial users, and sales to other retailers, by establishments primarily engaged in retail trade.

Transportation and Warehousing sector - Includes revenue from all business activities whether or not payment was received in the census year, including commissions and fees for arranging the transportation of freight. Revenue does not include sales and other taxes collected from customers and remitted directly by the firm to a local, state, or Federal tax agency.

Utilities sector - Includes revenue from all business activities whether or not payment was received in the census year.

Revenue does not include sales and other taxes collected from customers and remitted directly by the firm to a local, state, or Federal tax agency.

Accommodation and Foodservices sector - Includes sales from customers for services rendered, from the use of facilities, and from merchandise sold. Also includes dues and assessments from members and affiliates.

Sales do not include carrying or other credit charges; sales (or other) taxes collected from customers and forwarded to taxing authorities; gross sales and receipts of departments or concessions operated by other companies; and commissions or receipts from the sale of government lottery tickets.

Excludes sales from civic and social organizations, amusement and recreation parks, theaters, and other recreation or entertainment facilities providing food and beverage services.

Number of Employees

General Definition

Paid employees consists of full-time and part-time employees, including salaried officers and executives of corporations. Included are employees on paid sick leave, paid holidays, and paid vacations; not included are proprietors and partners of unincorporated businesses. The definition of paid employees is the same as that used on IRS Form 941.

Sector-Specific Information

Construction and Manufacturing sectors. Comprises all full-time and part-time employees on the payrolls of establishments who worked or received pay for any part of the pay period including the 12th of March, May, August, and November, divided by 4.

Finance and Insurance sector. Includes all employees who were on the payroll during the pay period including March 12. Excludes independent (nonemployee) agents.

Information; Professional, Scientific, and Technical Services; Administrative and Support and Waste Management and Remediation Services; Educational Services; Health Care and Social Assistance; Arts, Entertainment, and Recreation; and Other Services (Except Public Administration) sectors - Includes all employees who were on the payroll during the pay period including March 12. Includes members of a professional service organization or association which operates under state professional corporation statutes and files a corporate Federal income tax return. Excludes employees of departments or concessions operated by other companies at the establishment.

Management of Companies and Enterprises sector. Includes all employees who were on the payroll during the pay period including March 12.

Mining sector. Also included are employees working for miners paid on a per ton, car, or yard basis. Excluded are employees at the mine but on the payroll of another employer (such as employees of contractors) and employees at company stores, boardinghouses, bunkhouses, and recreational centers. Also excluded are members of the Armed Forces and pensioners carried on the active rolls but not working during the period. Includes all employees who were on the payroll during the pay period including March 12.

Real Estate and Rental and Leasing sector. Includes all employees who were on the payroll during the pay period including March 12. Excludes independent (nonemployee) agents.

Retail Trade and Accommodation and Foodservices sectors. Includes all employees on the payroll during the pay period including March 12. Excludes employees of departments or concessions operated by other companies at the establishment.

Transportation and Warehousing sector. Includes all employees who were on the payroll during the pay period including March 12.

Utilities sector. Includes all employees who were on the payroll during the pay period including March 12.